W9-BZK-477

Gods, Men & Pharaohs

THE GLORY OF EGYPTIAN ART

GODS, MEN & PHARAOHS

The Glory of Egyptian Art

TEXT BY Irmgard Woldering

Harry N. Abrams, Inc., Publishers, New York

Translated by Ann E. Keep

Library of Congress Catalog Card Number 67-26468

Printed and bound in Switzerland

CONTENTS

LIST OF PLATES

COLOUR PLATES

BLACK-AND-WHITE PLATES

LINE DRAWINGS

Abbreviations:

Pl. I to XXIV: Colour Plates
Fig. 1 to 117: Black and white illustrations to the text
Cat. 1 to 102: Black and white illustrations to the catalogue
*: an asterisk before a number refers to a textual reference in the outer column of the page

INTRODUCTION

Whereas the civilizations of classical antiquity, of Greece and Rome, have exerted a varied influence upon the development of European life and art, those of the Near East had only a relatively slight effect upon the peoples with whom they came into contact. Even during the centuries when Egypt was ruled by Greek kings of the Ptolemaic dynasty and by Roman prefects little was done to transmit the cultural legacy of the ancient pharaonic kingdom to Greece or Rome.

If Egyptian art evoked reverence and admiration during late antiquity, it did so on account of its age, its monumentality and above all its indecipherable, mysterious content. Knowledge of Egyptian hieroglyphic writing had by then passed into oblivion, and scholars took it to be a symbolic script for the communication of magic secrets. As late as the seventeenth century traces of this idea survived, with the result that all attempts to decipher hieroglyphic writing led nowhere and whimsical interpretations were made. It was a fateful coincidence that gave the key to the ancient civilization on the Nile. During Napoleon's expedition to Egypt in 1798 a stone slab was found at Rosetta, on the Mediterranean coast, bearing an inscription in Greek and demotic script as well as in hieroglyphs. It stands today in the British Museum. It turned out to be a decree of 196 B.C. issued by the priests of Memphis in honour of Ptolemy V Epiphanes. In the Greek text, which could be read without difficulty, the names of Ptolemy and Cleopatra appear, and the French scholar Jean François Champollion, after many years of research, was enabled to decipher the system of hieroglyphic writing. The way was thus freed for the scientific study of Egyptian culture. The hieroglyphs which are to be found on almost all artistic monuments provided information about historical events, religious ideas and the everyday life of the ancient Egyptians. They were the most reliable and important source for the Egyptologists who, from the mid-nineteenth century onwards, began to study assiduously the land on the Nile. The antiquities of the Pharaonic age which are still to be seen throughout Egypt and the abundance of archaeological material that was soon obtained from the first excavations enabled the first steps to be taken towards a systematic, and eventually a chronological, classification and interpretation of the monuments and finds that have survived from Egyptian soil.

Today we have at our disposal a number of important sources for the chronology of Egyptian history. The sequence of pharaohs was divided into thirty dynasties already in the records of the Egyptian priest Manetho, dating from the middle of the third century B.C., of which fragments have been preserved in the writings of Josephus and of Julius Africanus. Egyptologists have accepted his classification according to dynasties and have also divided up the entire course of Egyptian history into several longer periods, known as the Old, Middle and New Kingdoms, and finally the Late Period.

Although there is no continuous enumeration of years in Egyptian sources, we nevertheless have some evidence that certain years were indicated. During Dynasty I, for example, the years were referred to on small ivory plaques by some special event which took place, and later dates were reckoned according to tax collections, which were undertaken every second year. From the Middle Kingdom onwards the reigns of the pharaohs were registered. The Palermo Stone, which takes its name from the town where it is preserved, contains an enumeration of the pharaohs from Dynasty I to Dynasty V. From the New Kingdom detailed king-lists have survived: the annals of Thutmosis III in the temple at Karnak, the king-lists of Sethos I at Abydos, and especially the 'Royal Papyrus' in

Turin, dating from the Ramesside period, in which the reigns of the rulers are recorded—all these sources give important information of a chronological nature.

These literary sources are supplemented by the royal names featured on monuments, by archaeological finds which can be classified by style and locality, and by comparisons with Near Eastern chronology. The travel accounts of ancient writers are also helpful in establishing a fairly firm framework for the sequence of events in Egyptian history.

When one says that a culture or a people enters history, this means that a stage of development has been reached in which such a culture appears for the first time as a distinct phenomenon, differentiated from the various other tendencies that exist. This is a moment the preparation of which takes thousands of years. The roots of an emergent polity, its civilization and culture, lie buried in prehistory, when there were many different possibilities of development. The first step into history is marked by a number of significant facts which indicate that man has become conscious of himself and his environment and that he is developing his creative powers. He sees his life within a temporal and spatial context and begins to comprehend and systematize the world about him.

It is in Egypt above all that the beginning of history is heralded by events and ideas of the utmost significance. At the turn of the fourth and third millennia B.C. the nomadic pastoralists and hunters who lived in the wild mountainous country of Upper Egypt and the peasant tribes settled in the Nile valley of Lower Egypt were united in a single state under Upper Egyptian hegemony.

The introduction of the calendar, which took place at approximately the same time, points to the fact that man was beginning to order his environment, and felt the need to comprehend and delimit the concept of time. It was natural that in calculating time the Egyptian peasants should have used the annual flooding of the Nile, which fertilizes the soil and determines the time of sowing. Thus mid-July, when the Nile usually began to rise, was regarded as the commencement of the year. Another sign was the heliacal rising of the fixed star Sothis (known to us by the name of Sirius), which, it was observed, almost coincided with the swelling of the Nile. As the waters started to rise irregularly each year, the heliacal rising of Sothis—on 17 July according to our calendar—was regarded as the first day of the new year. The year was divided into three seasons of four months with thirty days each, to which five intercalary days were added. Since this calendar of 365 days was shorter than the Nile year by a quarter of a day, the beginning of the Nile year did not coincide with the calendrical New Year's day, the difference amounting to one day every four years. Only after 1460 Sothic years would the flooding of the Nile and the heliacal rising of Sothis take place on the calendrical New Year's day. The Julian calendar introduced by Julius Caesar in 46 B.C. adjusted this discrepancy by incorporating an intercalary day every four years. As Egyptian texts occasionally mention the heliacal rising of Sothis, we are in a position to draw upon these Sothic dates in the schematic Egyptian calendar in order to establish the chronological sequence of events.

The development of writing is another characteristic sign of man's awakening consciousness at this stage, when he feels the need to record significant facts and events so that they may be endowed with permanence. The first written characters appear on cosmetic palettes from the period of the union of the two kingdoms, and are used to indicate the names of countries and cities, of titles and kings. The places and royal names referred to supplement the pictorial representations and relate them to particular locations or periods.

Toward the end of Dynasty II hieroglyphic writing had developed into a fully perfected system. The Egyptian script which the Greeks termed *hieroglyphoi*—'sacred carved signs'—sets out to render objects and ideas by a picture sign indicating the object itself. But also notions which are only indirectly connected with those represented can be expressed by a picture sign, which thus conveys their sense. For example, the image of the sun is used to denote, not only the sun itself, but also 'day' and 'hour.' In addition to these word signs, in which one can see the relation between picture and script, there are a large number of words for which the sign bears no relation to the meaning. The script probably developed in the following way: in this case the hieroglyph was borrowed from a word that was designated by an analogous picture and had the same sequence of sounds as the word to be written; as a result words with the same sound were written with the same hieroglyphs even though their meaning did not coincide with that of the hieroglyph. This method, whereby the sound value was taken as the basis of the script, made it possible to render abstract ideas as well as objects, and so to develop a genuine system of writing.

There are, however, also hieroglyphs which have no sound value and are used as determinatives or ideograms to explain the content of a word. Thus, for example, a proper name is accompanied by a picture of a seated man or woman. In Egyptian script only the consonants are rendered; vowels and endings are not written. The reason for this is that consonants denote the unvarying stem of a word, whereas vowels express inflected forms such as participles, infinitive etc. Thus we have only an incomplete notion of what the spoken language sounded like.

Subsequently the system of writing was developed further. Words consisting of a single consonant and a single vowel were employed as symbols or characters for a single consonant. Although in this way 24 alphabetic signs were in existence, these were not used as an alphabet, but the multi-consonantal signs and determinatives continued to be employed.

Hieroglyphic script was used above all for inscriptions on stone monuments, the walls of tombs and temples, plinths, supporting back-pillars of statues and stelae. In the New Kingdom a simplified cursive script, hieratic, was developed for everyday use, and this was employed mainly for writing on papyrus. During the Late Period this hieratic script was simplified and reduced even further, so that the pictorial origin of the script, still perceptible in the hieratic script, could no longer be recognized. This abbreviated script, demotic, was used almost exclusively in official documents.

During the third century A.D. the script underwent further modification. The Egyptian language was rendered in Greek letters, with the vowels represented as well. From this script of the Coptic Christians, called 'Coptic script' for short, many inferences can be drawn with regard to vowels not given in hieroglyphic writing.

In addition to inscriptions on monuments a writing surface was provided by layers of wafers of pith from the papyrus plant, which were laid on top of one another at right angles, pressed, cut and pasted together to form a roll. In writing a reed was used with a tip frayed like a brush. Black ink was made of carbon soot and red ink of ground red ochre, which were mixed with a gum solution. Writing was in lines from right to left or in vertical columns from top to bottom.

By creating a state and by introducing a calendar and script, the early Egyptians established the framework for one of the most impressive civilizations of antiquity. It is not surprising that the finds of the early historical period which have survived reveal a clearly-defined artistic style and that all spheres of life give expression to the organizing, creative spirit of the people on the Nile. It was this spirit which carried them into the light of history at the end of the fourth and the beginning of the third millennium B.C.

In order to comprehend the immense achievement which this spiritual awakening represented, it is as well to cast a glimpse into prehistoric times—into the abundance of phenomena from which Egyptian culture arose in all its splendour.

THE PREHISTORIC ERA

The distribution of settlement, the mode of life adopted, and the pattern of cultural development depend upon the physical environment, upon such factors as territory and climate. Well into the Neolithic Egypt had a predominantly tropical climate, rainy and hot. The regions that today are nothing but desert were at that time covered by dense primeval forest, steppe areas and oases with abundant fauna. A change in the climate led to a gradual process of desiccation; the water-level of the Nile began to sink, leaving behind on its banks barren mountain terraces. Prehistoric man followed the receding waters into the Nile valley, which afforded better conditions of life than the desert waste. He settled on the banks of the Nile, which each year in July inundates the surrounding countryside and makes it fertile. From nomads who had obtained their livelihood by hunting they became settled farmers who tilled the soil, raised cattle and united to form communities where they worked and lived together.

Whereas the Upper Egyptian valley, with its narrow strips of fertile land sometimes only a few miles wide and its steep barren mountains, was inhabited mainly by nomadic hunters and herdsmen, the fertile plain of Lower Egypt, bounded by the endless sandy wastes, was well suited to a farming people. Thus both parts of the country evolved very different patterns of life. The sharp contrast between Lower and Upper Egypt can be observed even in later periods.

The Egyptian state was referred to as 'the Two Lands', and the pharaoh wore the Double Crown, comprising the crowns of Lower and Upper Egypt. Both parts of the country had their own plant symbols (Lower Egypt the papyrus and Upper Egypt the sedge) and their own tutelary deities (Horus and Seth).

This sharp distinction between the two areas also derives from ethnic differences in the population. The Upper Egyptian nomads of the fifth and fourth millennia, who were probably the descendants of the original indigenous population, belong to the Hamitic group of African peoples, whereas the agricultural population of Lower Egypt has affinities with the Semitic tribes of Palestine and Syria. The existence of these differences in racial origin has been corroborated by anthropological and philological studies.

During the Prehistoric era the two groups, which were originally very distinct, intermingled.

The life of a nomadic hunter and herdsman is both freer and harsher than that of a settled agriculturalist. In the seclusion and solitude of the barren mountains he retains his vitality and his desire for conquest, which in historical times enable him to advance northwards and to take control of the emergent Egyptian state. On the other hand, in Lower Egypt the settled farming population forms the first communities based on common interests and so acquires a sense of political order which later constitutes a sound foundation for the state.

Among the external factors upon which cultural development depends are the existence of mineral resources, stone, timber and other basic materials employed in making implements, utensils and works of art. Egypt has little in the way of timber and minerals, so that already in prehistoric times these vital raw materials had to be procured from elsewhere. Expeditions were mounted to the Lebanon to bring back timber; the Sinai Peninsula yielded copper and turquoise; and Nubia's ample supplies of gold supplemented the scanty resources of what is today the area of Wadi Hammamat. On the other hand, large quantities of the most varied kinds of stone were available, and this proved to be an excellent material for temples and statues. The fine-grained white limestone quarried around

Pl. I Vessel with loops through which straps were passed, featuring flamingo and ibex. Buff-coloured clay with painting in red. Nagada II, latter half of 4th millennium B.C. Height 21.5 cm. Roemer-Pelizaeus Museum, Hildesheim.

Memphis, near Tura, was used frequently, above all in the Old Kingdom. In Upper Egypt in the district of Edfu and Gebel Silsila a fine-grained sandstone was obtained which enjoyed particular popularity in the New Kingdom. Near Aswan on the First Nile Cataract red and black granite were quarried, and were often transported for hundreds of miles to the building-sites where they were to be used. In Middle Egypt there were stone quarries which yielded gleaming yellowish-white alabaster; from the Wadi Hammamat came porphyry, speckled breccia, green and black grey-wacke slate, as well as semi-precious stones.

Our knowledge of the life of prehistoric man in Egypt is drawn exclusively from archaeological evidence. The many varied finds obtained from the excavation of prehistoric burial-places and settlements show that we are dealing not with the gradual and regular development of a single culture, but that there was a range of formal elements which coexisted, overlapped or replaced each other; it is therefore difficult to place these finds in chronological sequence. Our picture of Prehistoric times must therefore leave a good deal unaccounted for. Further excavations in years to come may close some of the gaps and either substantiate or modify current hypotheses.

On the barren mountain peaks near Thebes on the edge of the Nile valley in Upper Egypt a large number of Palaeolithic flint implements were discovered which provide the first clues to the settlement of Egypt. The sites are located in various levels, so that one can follow the gradual descent of the settlers from the mountain tops into the valley. These flint implements are light brown, or in the case of surface finds brown; they can be dated from geological evidence and by comparison with Lower Palaeolithic finds in Europe, and are ascribed to approximately 13,000 B.C. In Lower Egypt finds have been authenticated from the Lower Palaeolithic, especially in the flooded area of the present-day Nile valley. At Abbasiya,

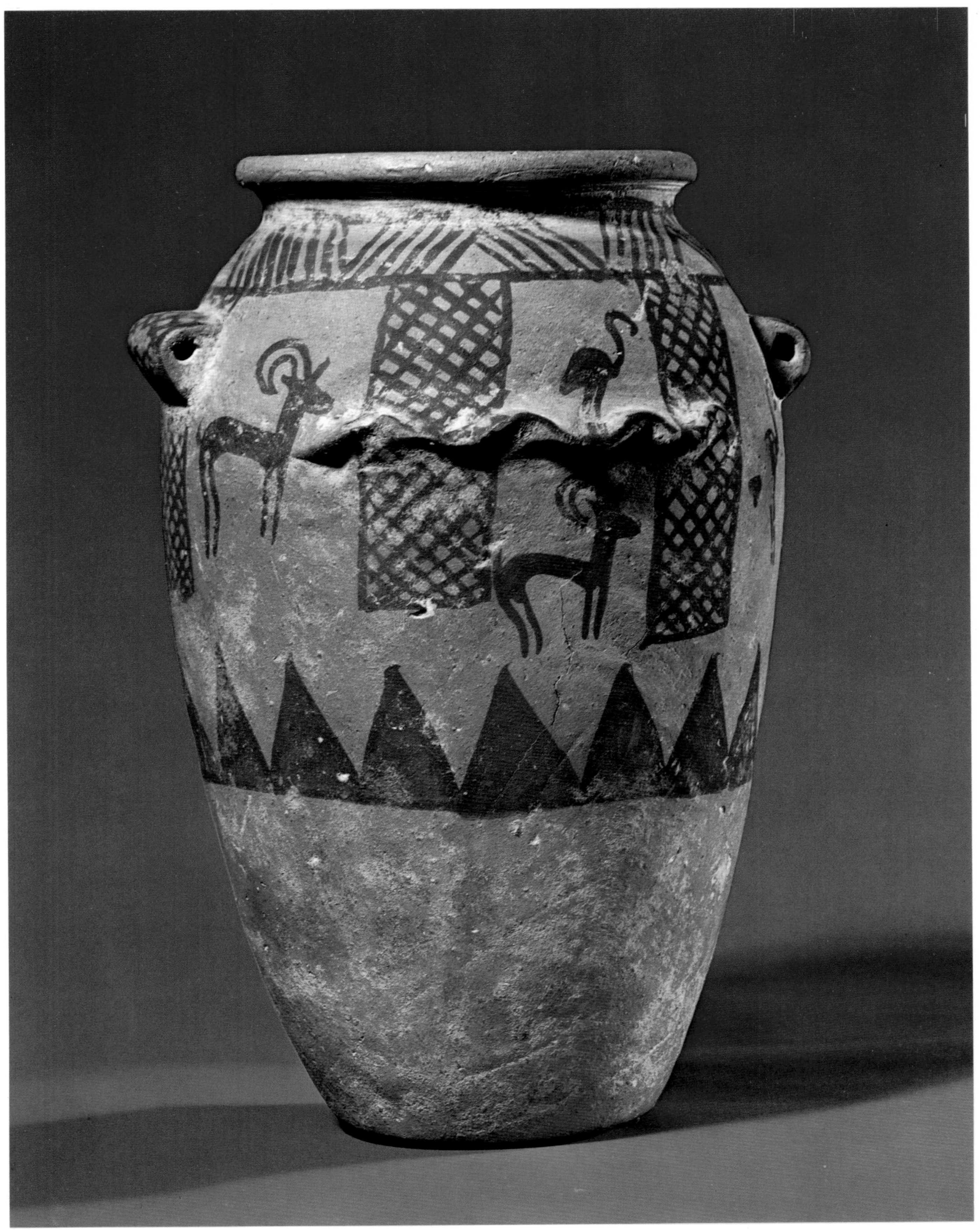

Pl. 1 Female figure. Ivory. From Badari. Badarian culture. Beginning of 4th millennium B.C. Height 14 cm. British Museum, London.

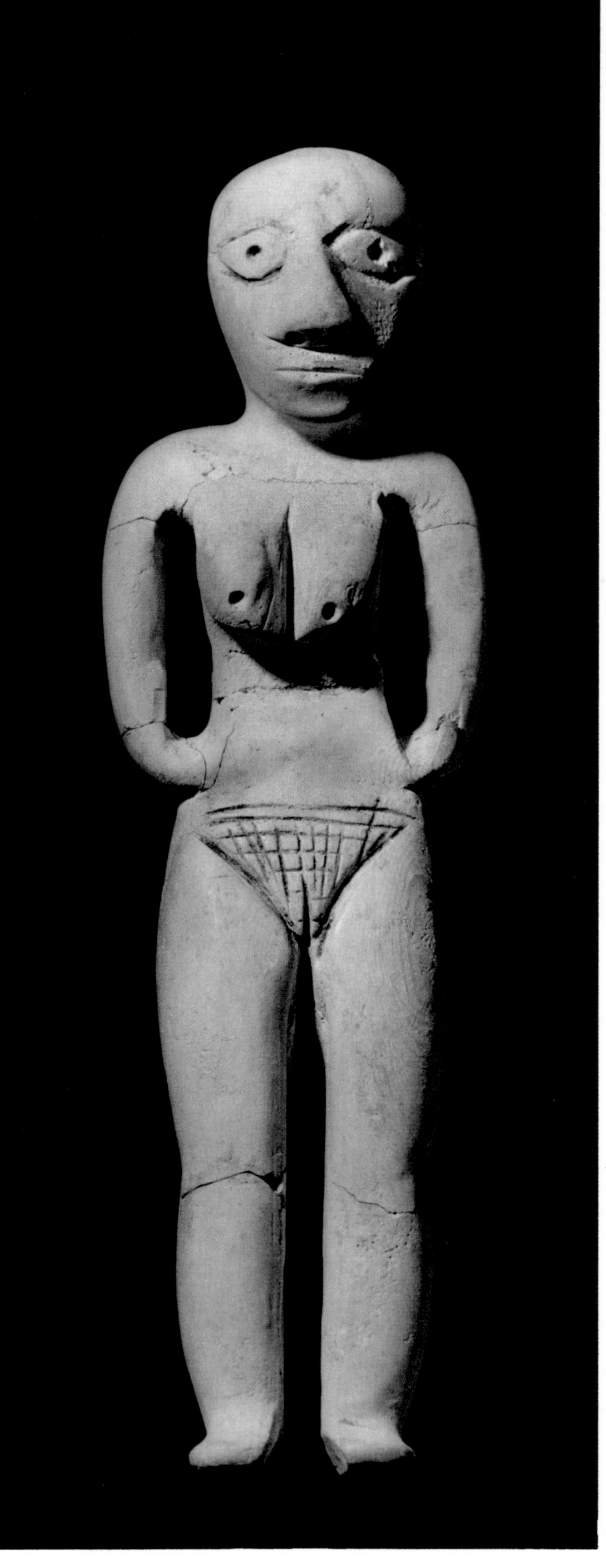

not far from Cairo, flint implements were found in various levels corresponding to the Palaeolithic cultural sequence known in France.

During the Early and Middle Palaeolithic the finds made in north Africa and western Europe bear a great resemblance to one another (at that time Europe and Africa were still linked by a land bridge between Tunisia and southern Italy); on the other hand, during the Late Palaeolithic the implements in north Africa, southern Spain and Palestine differ markedly from the western European finds. During the Early Palaeolithic in particular we encounter crudely made hand axes and scrapers, whereas the Middle and Upper Palaeolithic yielded quantities of small knife-blades with indented edges and arrow-heads, which during the Chalcolithic (Stone and Copper Age) are executed in a particularly fine technique.

The few flint implements of the Archaic Period are of cruder workmanship. They illustrate the final phase of a development which ceased when flint was replaced by other materials.

At a few sites in Lower Egypt—Merimde, on the western edge of the Delta, El-Omari near Helwan, and in the Faiyum—traces of settlements have been brought to light which may be assigned to the Neolithic or New Stone Age. It could be ascertained that in these places the people lived in oval huts made of Nile mud and reeds. In addition to a large number of the most varied kind of flint implements, finds were made of bone needles and awls, clay vessels, spindle whorls and weaving weights, and coiled basketry. The dead were not buried in separate necropolises but in the settlement itself. In this way they remained linked with the living, and therefore did not need any special funerary gifts. In Upper Egypt we have evidence of the Neolithic in the settlement at Tara, which yielded few finds apart from beaker-shaped vessels, burnished black and bearing incised designs filled in with white paste.

At the beginning of the fourth millennium the use of copper for tool-making led to significant technical progress. The settlements discovered mainly in Upper Egypt are by no means so large as the Neolithic ones in Lower Egypt. The dead were buried in a crouched posture, with the face oriented towards the settlement, in a cemetery situated some distance from the village. To provide for their needs flint and bone implements, cosmetic palettes, jewellery and clay vessels were placed in the grave. This complex of finds is assigned to the Badarian culture, named after the chief site, El Badari, south of Asyut. Characteristic of this culture are the red burnished, black-topped, clay vessels, which are akin to the contemporary Nubian ware in form and technique.

The funerary goods also include renderings of animals and human beings. They were intended to help the deceased in the world beyond on account of the magic power with which it was thought they were imbued. Female figurines were added to keep the deceased company. Male figurines, sometimes mutilated, are thought to be servants who in the world beyond were to relieve the dead of the need to work. Animal figures are either designed to be used in sacrifice or, where they were of species venerated in cults, as tutelary amulets or votive gifts. These funerary sculptures, which were mostly small, were made of bone and especially of clay.

These early attempts to render animals and men plastically testify to a vigorous sense of observation, capable of capturing the characteristic features in broad outline. The types are very varied, and the possibilities fully exploited—especially during the latter half of the fourth millennium.

Badarian is superseded by the Nagada culture, named after a site in Upper Egypt. It is divided into two phases, Nagada I and Nagada II. Of the settlements only a few remains have survived, but on the other hand the abundant finds made in the extensive cemeteries have enabled prehistorians to establish the chronological sequence of development on the basis of the styles of the pottery vessels. In Nagada I the dead were buried in oval or round pits, in a crouched position and covered with mats or animal skins. Grave goods comprised stone or clay vessels, cosmetic palettes, maces and mace-heads, combs, jewellery, weapons and small sculpted figurines of animals and human beings. In Nagada II the dead were buried in larger almost rectangular pits, at times lined with bricks made of Nile mud, which occasionally had a separate chamber for funerary gifts. The radical transformation that took place at the beginning of Nagada II is shown most clearly in the highly diversified types of the pottery.

During Nagada I we encounter initially red pottery vessels burnished on the outside or covered with a coat of red paint. The pot was turned upside down and placed over the fire, so that the brim and the inside were frequently black. Especially characteristic of this period are the red burnished pots bearing painted ornaments and figured representations in a yellowish-white colour. The designs are executed with simple strokes and have lattice-like filled-in decoration. In most cases these are hunting scenes. The animals most commonly featured are the hippopotamus and the crocodile. Whereas in Neolithic ceramic finds only little importance is attached to the decoration, which is subordinate to the shape of the vessel, here the picture assumes an importance in its own right and frequently represents a scene in a systematic way. During Nagada II the red burnished ware is superseded by pottery of yellowish-grey and light red clay. A particular group comprises vessels with wavy handles, usually made of buff-coloured clay and covered with a yellowish-grey slip. The earliest examples of this group are pot-bellied vessels with two bulging handles set horizontally, in which three or four depressions were made with the finger. Towards the end of the Prehistoric era the vessels take on

* Pl. 1, 2; Pl. 3, Cat. 85

a more slender shape, the most frequent being cylindrical. The bulging handles are placed on the shoulder of the vessel and gradually come to assume the shape of a wavy ornamental band running around the vessel. At the beginning of the Archaic Period this is superseded by a row of perforated dots.

Another group comprises vessels painted in reddish-brown, mainly featuring figures. The principal motif, which recurs with many modifications, is that of a boat with several oars, cabins and standards, and bearing dancers, both male and female; frequently antelopes, ibexes
Pl. 1 and flamingoes were added, although these have no logical connection with the main motif. During Nagada I it was the custom for the body to be depicted stylistically, reduced to lattice-like designs; now it is represented in a compact reddish-brown mass and is thus accentuated rather more than the ornament, which is usually geometric. It does not appear to represent a scene.

Toward the end of the Prehistoric era figured renderings recede more and more into the background and are superseded by simple ornaments such as spirals and wavy lines. Like flint implements, painted pots reached their apogee during the Prehistoric era, about the middle of the fourth millennium. Subsequently pottery forms were ousted by stone or metal ones, which were left without any decoration if they were used purely for storage or other everyday purposes. The transition from clay to stone vessels is already fairly distinct during the Prehistoric era. From the Badarian culture we have only isolated specimens of vessels in black basalt. During Nagada I other kinds of stone were also employed, but preference continued to be given to black basalt. The vessels are larger and in most
Cat. 86 cases cylindrical or beaker-like in shape. From Nagada II we have an abundance of vessels in coloured hard stone of outstanding workmanship. The most common types are
Cat. 87 large pot-bellied vessels and smaller barrel-shaped ones with loops on the sides, through which leather straps were passed so that the vessels could be suspended. In the case of large and heavy vessels the cord loop acted as a handle.

In any assessment of Egyptian prehistory much must remain obscure; nevertheless some essential features can be distinguished which set the scene for the later development of the historical Egyptian state. It is in a nomadic group of African peoples in Upper Egypt that man is authenticated for the first time on Egyptian soil. In Lower Egypt anthropological, philological and archaeological evidence suggests that agricultural settlements were established in the Neolithic, during the fifth millennium, by a people of oriental, Semitic origin. During the first half of the fourth millennium there developed in Upper Egypt the Badarian culture, which was closely linked with Nubia. This was superseded by Nagada I, which consisted mainly of nomadic and African elements. Nagada II, during the latter half of the fourth millennium, was centred upon the Nile valley, the area that was to become the core of the Egyptian state. It was this culture in which, at the beginning of the third millennium, a united high civilization developed out of the multifarious prehistoric cultures that had gone before.

In so far as one can infer anything from prehistoric finds about people's ideas, their concepts of life and death, it may be said that the prevalent view of life was a magical one such as is found in the early stage of all primitive cultures. At this level man is unable to perceive any separation between his own ego and the surrounding world, nor can he distinguish between earthly phenomena and the incomprehensible powers of nature. Death seems to him inexplicable; time and space are unfamiliar concepts. He believes that magic forces are latent in nature and in the objects by which he is surrounded; he is afraid of their incomprehensible effects and worships them as fetishes, as a reflection of eternal forces, trying to influence them by invocations.

Pl. 2 Female figure. Painted clay. From Mamarija. Early half of 4th millennium B.C. Height 29 cm. Brooklyn Museum, New York.

As Neolithic man began to emerge from the undifferentiated world about him and to seek to exercise control over nature as farmer or hunter, so he developed a consciousness of his individuality, intellect and will. He came to perceive the world not as a unit but as comprising distinct phenomena, with which he had to establish some relationship. The unidentifiable mysterious forces to which his life had hitherto been subject became definite phenomena and beings which he worshipped and invoked by means of symbols and images. Thus the various nomadic tribes may have carried with them standards featuring objects and animals which they worshipped or whose protection they sought. Such poles bearing symbols or animals survived into the historical period in the form of the signs of nomes or districts.

As settlement progressed and communities were established, the venerated numen acquired a fixed place of worship. Among the phenomena imbued with magic power the most important were the animals with which these hunters and farmers were closely connected in their everyday lives, and whose particular qualities they knew well. They may have felt themselves threatened by crocodiles, snakes and lions; birds may have been admired for their ability to raise themselves above the earth in flight. It was also during the Late Prehistoric era that figures first appeared of Min, the god of generative power, carved in human form and larger than life.

The effects of the cosmic forces of nature could be seen in the succession of day and night, in the flooding of the Nile which brought fertility after drought, and in the rhythmic sequence of the seasons. In the play of cosmic forces early man no doubt soon came to recognize divine forces which he worshipped.

This outlook, based on a view of the world as imbued with forces, which one sought to influence by magic means, is not characteristic of the Prehistoric period alone.

Pl. 3 Red polished clay vessel with white decoration. Nagada I, c. 3500 B.C. Height 29 cm. Musées Royaux d'Art et d'Histoire, Brussels. ▷

The popular beliefs and also the great religions which evolved in Egypt over the millennia never completely shook off this magic outlook on life.

THE ARCHAIC PERIOD

In all the literary sources of later periods the establishment of a united Egyptian state is ascribed to the pharaoh Menes, with whose reign Dynasty I begins. But his name has not been preserved on any of the monuments of the Archaic Period, such as cosmetic palettes, mace-heads and small ivory plaques, which do however bear the names of three other persons, Scorpion, Narmer and Aha, who are said to have ruled over the Two Lands. This confusion can be explained by the fact that the official titles of the Egyptian king included several names. Contemporary monuments feature the so-called 'Horus name,' which shows the king as the incarnation of the sky-god Horus in his guise as a falcon. Identification with the magic qualities of this great deity serves as a means of legitimizing and emphasizing the royal claim to supremacy. During the Archaic Period two other titles appear, one of which, 'King of Upper and Lower Egypt,' designates the pharaoh in his function as ruler, while the other relates to the heraldic animals of Lower and Upper Egypt, called *nebty*, the two mistresses. During the subsequent period two more names were added, one referring to the king as a 'strong bull' and the other as 'son of the sun-god Rē.' It can now be taken that Aha was the Horus name of the pharaoh Menes recorded in the king-lists of a later period.

The unification of the kingdom was undoubtedly a lengthy process. All the three kings mentioned on the monuments—Scorpion, Narmer and Aha—are known to have held sway over Upper Egypt and parts of Lower Egypt. A number of cosmetic palettes decorated in relief give a graphic rendering of the events that led to the founding of the state. These so-called cosmetic palettes continue the tradition of the slate ceremonial palettes discovered in almost all prehistoric tombs. They were used for grinding eye-paint. The early prehistoric cosmetic palettes, which were fairly thick and in most cases lozenge-shaped, were superseded in the Late Prehistoric era either by thin spear-shaped palettes with stylized birds' heads or by animal- Pl. 11
shaped ones which in turn gave way, toward the end of the Prehistoric era, to simple geometric slate palettes.

In the case of the archaic ceremonial palettes almost the entire surface is covered with reliefs on either side. The hollowed-out depression for grinding the paint suggests that they were not only votive offerings for temples but that they may have been used to 'make up' the divine images. On the so-called 'battlefield palette' of the Late Pl. 4
Prehistoric period a lion is seen tearing a man to pieces: the beast may be regarded as a symbol of the triumphant pharaoh, for such symbolism is found later as well; vultures are depicted swooping upon the corpses. A palette ascribed to King Scorpion depicts the royal symbols of power—lion, falcon and scorpion—destroying fortresses; on the reverse, as well as a listing of booty, are some hieroglyphs which have been interpreted as referring to Libya. Whereas on ceremonial palettes almost the only theme one finds is that of royal battles and victories, on the mace-head of King Scorpion, discovered at Hierakonpolis, we find a representation of the people of Lower Egypt paying homage. The papyrus plants and peewits featured on the tutelary standards indicate the Delta and Lower Egypt. The king is portrayed wearing the conical Upper Egyptian crown and performing a ceremonial act with a hoe, which is thought to symbolize the peaceful prosperous life of the country—the tilling and irrigation of the fields.

Of the utmost significance—both as an historical source as well as an example of stylistic development during the Archaic Period—is the ceremonial palette of King Narmer, Pl. 5, 6, Cat. 67
which also originates from the temple at Hierakonpolis.
The obverse is divided into three registers. In the topmost Pl. 6, Cat. 67
register, as the inscription records, the triumphant king,

Pl. 4 Battlefield Palette. Part of a cosmetic palette. Slate. Nagada II, late 4th millennium B.C. British Museum, London.

wearing the Lower Egyptian crown, is escorted to Buto, the national temple in Lower Egypt, in a ceremonial procession headed by standard-bearers. On the right-hand side of this register are heaped the enemy dead, their heads severed from their bodies. In the middle register the hollowed-out depression is enclosed within the long
★ Pl. 5 serpent-like necks of two mythical animals. On the right and left is the figure of a man, distinguishable from his costume as an enemy, who tries to separate the necks of the two animals with a rope or an implement of some kind. In the lower register the king, standing over a prostrate enemy, is depicted as a 'strong bull' forcing the walls of a fortress. On the top of the palette, on both sides, is the name Narmer, framed by two heads of Hathor, the sky-goddess, with cow's ears and horns. The reverse features a design which was to symbolize the triumphant pharaoh

Pl. 5 Narmer Palette. Reverse of Pl. 6.

right up to the last period of Egyptian civilization. The king, here wearing the Upper Egyptian crown, is depicted holding the stricken enemy by a tuft of his hair, about to deal him a mortal blow with his mace. The inscription refers to him as a representative of the 'harpoon district' in the Delta. At the top on the right the king, in the guise of the Horus falcon, leads up as his captive the conquered Land of the Papyrus. The lower register depicts the representatives of two other defeated nomes, one of which, according to the inscription, may be identified as Memphis. While the content of the scenes on these ceremonial palettes provides information about the battles that ultimately led to the unification of the kingdom, the style of these reliefs affords evidence of the great intellectual transformation which took place at the beginning of the historical period: a sense of system, structure and order which was to influence decisively the style of Egyptian reliefs. In the case of the Late Prehistoric 'battlefield palette' the representations are distributed over the entire surface without any apparent articulation of the scene as a whole. Care was taken to avoid overlappings which could indicate perspective. The way in which the individual pictures are combined does not permit the scenes to be read in chronological sequence. With the Narmer palette, on the other hand, the abundant and varied pictures are linked together by the tectonic arrangement of the plane as a whole. The register is subdivided by horizontal lines which serve both to unite and to separate the individual scenes, and at the same time form the base line for the figures. The composition of the individual figures is rigid and clearly defined. In the case of the king, the principal figure, who as befits his importance is rendered on a larger scale than the others, the details are executed with particular care. Here for the first time a human figure comes to play a central part and by his costume, attributes and gesture is shown to have special significance.

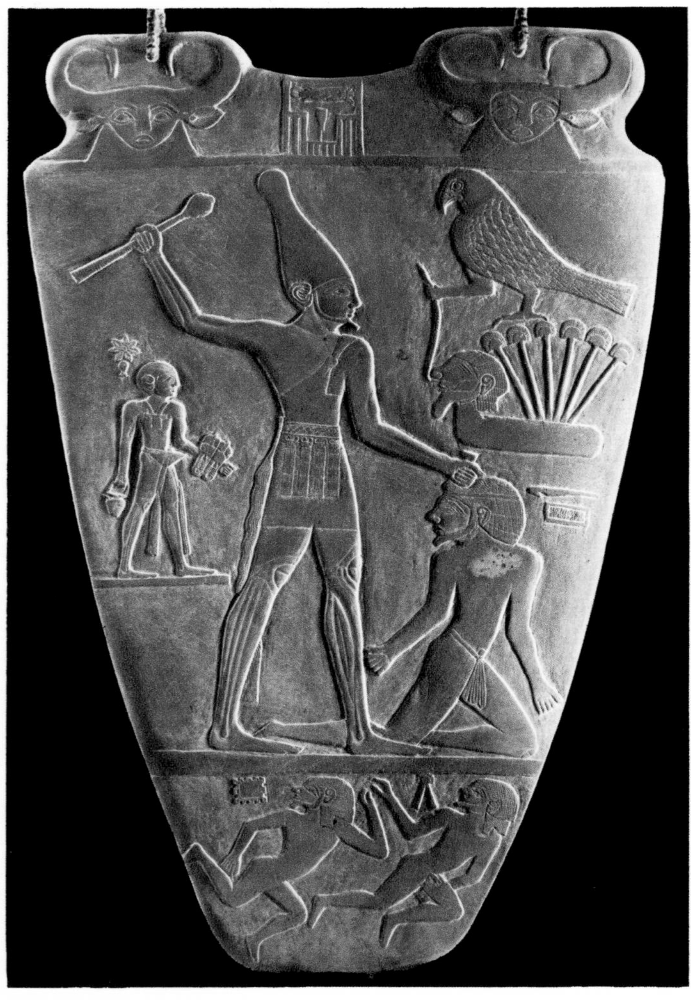

Pl. II Cosmetic palette in the shape of a hippopotamus with inlaid eye. Slate. C. mid-4th millennium B.C. Height 7.9 cm., length 15.4 cm. Museum für Kunst und Gewerbe, Hamburg.

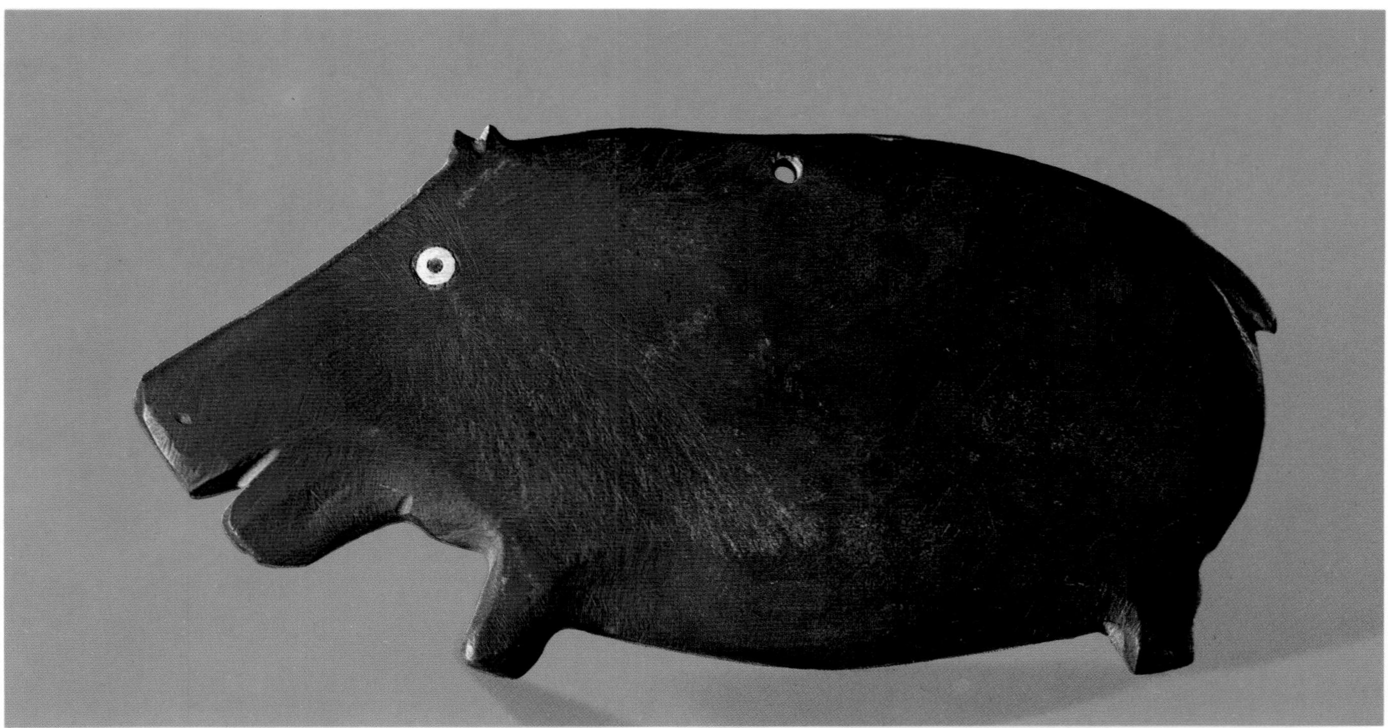

It is wholly in accordance with the course of historical development—that is to say, the formation of a united Egyptian state—that from among the various tribal chiefs *one* single person should come into prominence as the representative of the new order, of the emergent state. His position is reinforced by the belief in his special magic powers, whereby he controls the menacing forces that surround mankind. This interpretation of the royal authority springs from the magic outlook of prehistoric times when, as with all primitive peoples, the tribal chieftain was thought to have the ability to exert an influence upon the forces of nature and so to determine the fortunes of the community for good or ill. The costume and attributes of the king as well as his various titles point to his magic powers and to his relationship with divine forces. The essential principles governing the representation of the pharaoh were evolved as early as the Archaic Period and, characteristically enough, survived right into the Late Period. The official costume of the king consists of the kilt, which appears in various forms, the animal tail and the ceremonial beard, tied on by a band. Alternatively he may wear the conical white crown of Upper Egypt or the red crown of Lower Egypt. On his forehead is the erect uraeus snake; his sceptre has the shape of a crooked staff. All these objects derive from the beliefs and customs of various groups of people and are linked in a variety of ways with the magic outlook of prehistoric man. In the course of time belief in the magic efficacy of these symbols of royal power declined, and they came to be valued merely as the traditional costume of the ruler.

Little information has been preserved about the functions which the king had to fulfil during the Archaic Period.

Pl. 6 Narmer Palette. Detail of obverse side with jar for make-up. Slate. From Hierakonpolis. Archaic Period, c. 3000 B.C. Overall height 64 cm. Cairo Museum (cf. Cat. 67 and Pl. 5).

Pl. 7 Stele of King Serpent. Limestone relief. From Abydos. Dynasty I, c. *2800 B.C. Height* c. *250 cm., width 64 cm. Musée du Louvre, Paris.*

Pl. 8 Baboon. Blue and green glazed faience. From the earliest temple area at Abydos. Dynasty I, c. *2900 B.C. Height 5.7 cm. E. and M. Kofler-Truniger Collection, Lucerne.*

As the embodiment of the sky-god Horus in his guise as a falcon, he holds sway over the world on his behalf. His divine nature and magic powers single him out from the community of men. He alone can perform ritual acts; he alone has a link with the gods; it is to him alone that all historically recorded deeds are ascribed.

The area over which the kings of Dynasty I exercised power extended from the Delta to Aswan at the First Cataract. There is a tradition that during Narmer's reign expeditions were launched to the stone quarries between the Nile and the Red Sea, and evidence that there were trade links with Palestine. It can be proved that during King Aha's reign there were indeed such connections with the Lebanon, whence precious timber was obtained, as it had been already in the Prehistoric era. The successor of Menes—Aha, King Djer(Zer), extended his power into Nubia and engaged in battles against the Libyans on the north-western border.

During the reign of King Serpent expeditions were mounted into the eastern desert, the purpose of which was to secure mineral resources. In the area of Edfu a graffito has been found bearing his name. Of his successor King Udimu, the first to bear the title of King of Lower and Upper Egypt, information is recorded in small anniversary tablets stating that he fought battles against the Beduin of the Sinai Peninsula.

The activities of the archaic rulers, as we see, served to protect the frontiers of the state and to expand its influence over territories that were of economic importance. Among the most vital political preoccupations of later sovereigns, too, were wars against Libyans and Beduin, expeditions to Sinai, and the maintenance of trade links with Lebanon. The advance into Nubia and expansion eastward were also sustained later, with minor ups and downs. The foreign and commercial policy of the Egyptian kingdom was determined by its geographical location and physical

Pl. 9 Cloaked figure of a city-god. From the earliest temple area at Abydos. Dynasty I, c. 2900 B.C. Height 29.8 cm. E. and M. Kofler-Truniger Collection, Lucerne.

conditions; the main lines of this policy were laid down already in the Archaic Period.

During the reigns of the three last kings of Dynasty I it seems that political troubles began. Possibly Lower Egyptian forces tried to oppose the Upper Egyptian dynasty, which originated from This near Abydos. It is now that we first come across a case where a ruler's name is erased from monuments—a sign that he was losing political power and simultaneously that his magic efficacy was waning. Little is known about the internal administration of the kingdom. One of the ritual acts of the kings was to inaugurate the sowing season symbolically each year by hoeing the soil, and during the harvest season they would cut the first sheaf of corn. Also when hippopotamuses or big game were hunted the god-king took part in order to ensure the success of the expedition. He led the sacred bull, Apis, the archetypal symbol of power and fertility, and performed other priestly functions: these are recorded already from the period of Dynasty I. Just as these ritual acts presupposed belief in his magic powers, so these ideas also played a major role in determining his administrative duties. This explains why at first no real bureaucracy could develop. Only those who had close blood-ties with the ruler, in particular his sons, were able to have contact with him, to pass on his commands, and to occupy the highest offices in the land.

According to Herodotus the foundation of the city and royal residence of Memphis, near present-day Cairo, dates from King Menes, to whom is also ascribed the foundation of a temple dedicated to Ptah—a god in human guise worshipped in the nome of Memphis. Menes' tomb has been discovered not far from Memphis, near the modern village of Saqqara. His predecessors, 'Scorpion' and Narmer, still had their residence on Upper Egyptian soil, in the region of This, and were also buried there, near Abydos.

Pl. III Frog. Dark green glazed faience. From the earliest temple area at Abydos. Period of the unification of the Two Lands, c. 2900 B.C. Height 3.1 cm. E. and M. Kofler-Truniger Collection, Lucerne.

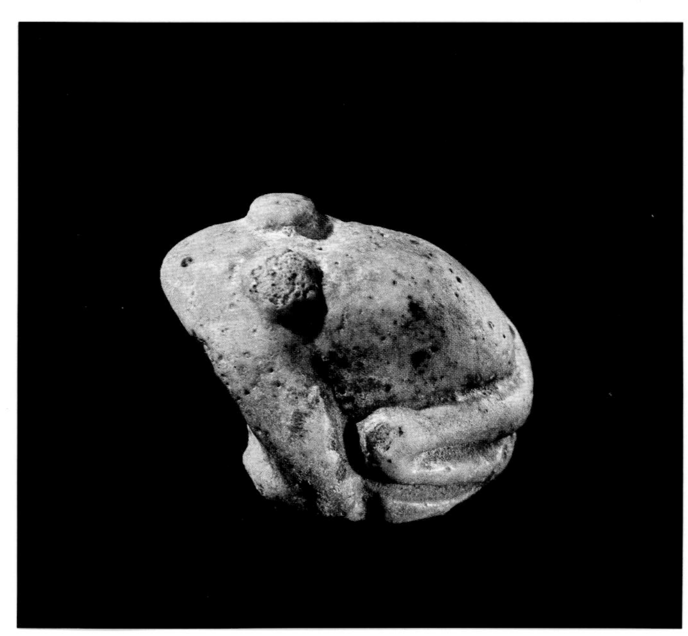

The town of Abydos played an outstanding role throughout Egyptian history as the city of the dead and the centre of religious life. This had its origin in the fact that it was the burial-place of the first kings, and also the main cult centre of the god Osiris. Already in Prehistoric times this area served as a necropolis. Archaeological excavations have revealed, beneath a Nagada II stratum, burials from the Nagada I period. Today the tombs of the first Egyptian kings are badly damaged—and this was probably the case already in antiquity; from the fragments that have been preserved it can be ascertained that the subterranean part consisted of mud-brick-lined pits, rectangular in plan, and that the burial-chamber proper was a wooden structure shaped like a tent. On top of the tomb a mound of sand was heaped up, and on the eastern side of this was the place of sacrifice, between two stelae. Individual tombs may be ascribed to certain kings on the basis of seals bearing royal names, small anniversary tablets and grave goods.

From the reign of King Djer onward the tombs become larger, with articulated façades. The posts of the burial-chamber proper are connected with the external brick wall by inserted cross-walls. The floor has a wooden covering which rests upon a layer of bricks. Around the tombs, which are now no longer orientated toward the east but toward the south-west, there were discovered smaller ancillary burials, used for the interment of members of the royal court and as storage-places for funerary gifts. Apparently these ancillary burials were completed at the same time as the royal tomb, so that one cannot rule out the notion that in this early period, when a ruler died, he was accompanied into the beyond by his closest companions.

The tombs of the kings and their retinue are located in barren desert country, but on the edge of the fertile land were small huts, built of wood and matting, used as places

of worship for the dead. Not far away was the temple of the tutelary god of this sacred district, Khentamentiu, 'First of the Westerners,' who during the Old Kingdom merged with the god Osiris.

In interpreting the significance of the cemetery at Abydos, scholars faced a new problem when in the 1930s a Dynasty I necropolis was excavated at Saqqara, near the royal residence of Memphis. These royal tombs possess an architecturally articulated enclosing wall or temenos with false ceremonial doors and are far larger than those at Abydos. At Saqqara, too, the discovery was made of ancillary burials, which suggests that members of the royal court were buried together with the king upon his death. With the exception of Semerkhet, all the rulers of the Archaic Period have tombs at Saqqara; from this it can be inferred that at Saqqara we have the actual burial-places, whereas the tombs at Abydos were not in fact used for burial at all. They may probably be regarded as symbolic magic monuments, which took account of Abydos' religious and historical significance in the Upper Egyptian homeland of the Thinite dynasty. With the beginning of Dynasty II the tradition of erecting a second tomb at Abydos comes to an end. This fact may reflect the break which the new dynasty made with Upper Egyptian tradition.

Little is known about Dynasty II. From the almost fifty-year-long reign of Ninutjer the celebration of several Sed festivals has been recorded. These were jubilees commemorating the ruler's accession to the throne by a ritual which served to renew his magic and divine powers. The Sed festival is closely linked with the idea of divine * Pl. 7 kingship and with the belief in the magic efficacy of ritual acts. It enabled the pharaoh to consolidate his divine power in a spectacular way during times of crisis, and so helped to strengthen the kingdom. The unification of Upper and Lower Egypt into a single state did not entirely put an end to the development of separate centres of power in the two parts of the country. The union had been effected by Upper Egyptian forces and the Thinite dynasty could maintain its power for over two hundred years. The political troubles that began during the reigns of the last kings of Dynasty I culminated in the seizure of power by a new dynasty, under which the political and religious centre of gravity shifted to Lower Egypt. After a few generations, during the reign of King Peribsen, Upper Egypt once again came to the fore. Whereas all previous rulers had regarded themselves as the embodiment of the falcon-god Horus, Peribsen ostentatiously reverted to the name of Seth, the Upper Egyptian god of the desert, and thus stressed the fact that he regarded himself as the embodiment of this powerful ancient god of Upper Egypt. He had his tomb built at Abydos, and this decision too served to emphasize the connection with the glorious tradition of the first kings of Upper Egypt.

It was not until the reign of Khasekhemui that the tension and wars between the Two Lands could be concluded, and peace and unity restored. Above his royal name there appear together the Horus falcon and the Seth animal, symbolizing the peaceful coexistence of the Two Lands. Trade links flourish once again and in Upper Egypt there is a modest beginning of building activity, stone being employed as a material for the first time. Khasekhemui's reign laid the foundation for a peaceful period in which Egyptian civilization underwent its first efflorescence.

Most of the archaeological finds from the Archaic Period originate from the necropolis at Abydos. An impressive example of the stylistic development of Egyptian reliefs is a stele, some 7 ½ feet high, originally erected over the burial of King Serpent. The clear tectonic structure of the representation and the concentration of the motif, intensified to the point of symbolism, are far in advance of the Narmer palette, produced at the beginning of Dynasty I,

Pl. 10 King wearing Upper Egyptian crown, in profile. Ivory. From the temple at Abydos. Dynasty I, c. 2900 B.C. Height 8.5 cm. British Museum, London.

Pl. 11 Detail of Pl. 10.

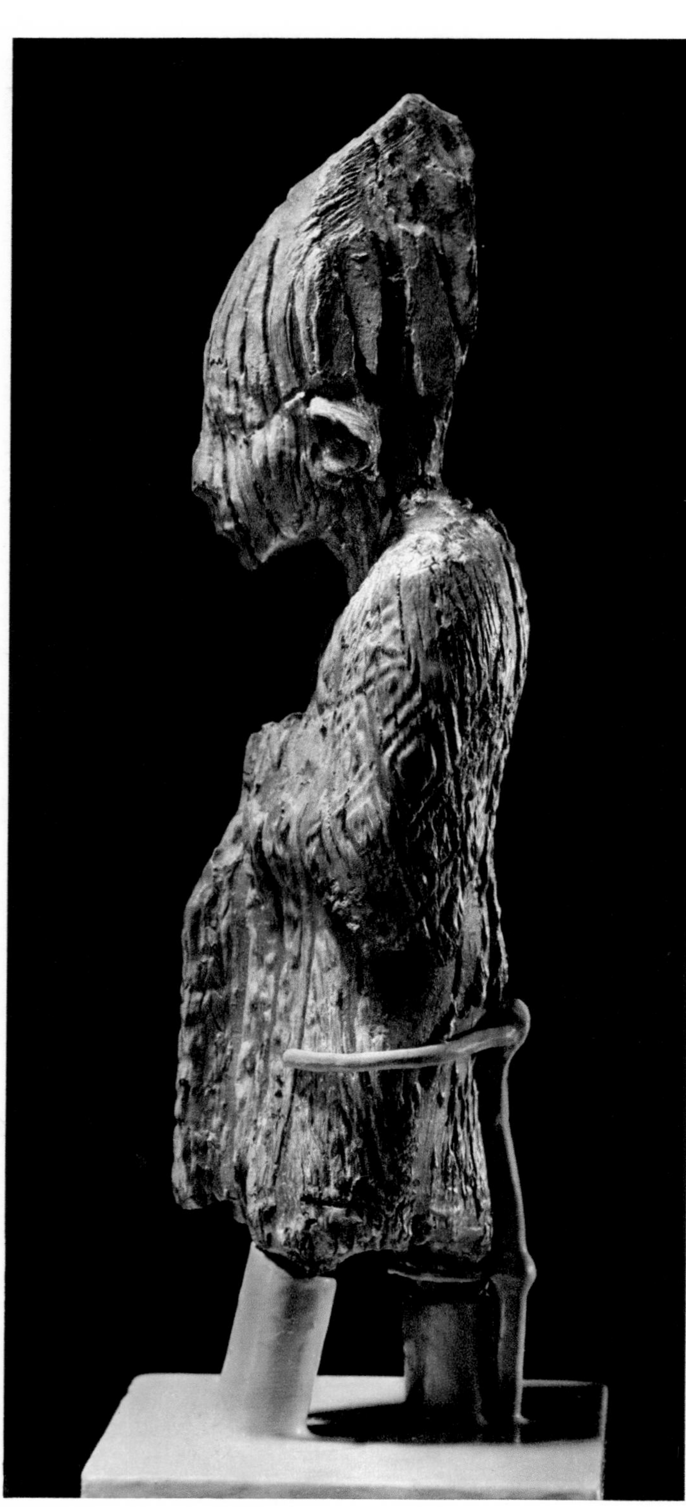

and other related works of art. The raised projection at the edge accentuates the spatial limitations and gives the stele a monumental character. At the very top on the right, in a design, and above the 'palace façade,' is the name of the king, 'Serpent.' But the impression of monumentality comes from the erect Horus falcon, whose height is no less than two-thirds that of the palace façade, including the royal name. The natural model upon which it is based is clearly seen, but at the same time there radiates from it the dignity and power of the sky-god whom he embodies—he has become a symbol of belief and a monument to divine kingship.

For members of the royal court smaller stelae were erected, bearing in addition to the title and name a representation of the deceased in simple outline, which acts as a determinative, illustrating the wording pictorially. Cat. 73

Already among finds from tombs of the Prehistoric era we have animal and human figures in clay and bone. During prehistoric times the use of clay as a material declined, and when it was used at all it was usually glazed; in bone carving, on the other hand, the old tradition continued. In animal sculpture one can sense the pleasure which man now took in observing his environment. The faience and bone sculptures in the round, most of them small, depict baboons, frogs or hippopotamuses, and render the subject in a telling way. Generally the figure rests upon a base. At the same time the composition of the sculpture becomes more rigid and there is greater balance and proportion between the individual parts. Most of these minor sculptures are grave goods; a smaller number can be identified as votive gifts. A limestone figure of a city-god in human guise, now in the Kofler-Truniger Collection, was discovered in the oldest temple area at Abydos. Compact and columnar, it is an early example of the way plastic forms were contained rigidly in an imagined inorganic space. The long cloak envelops

(Pl. III, Pl. 8, Cat. 79; Pl. 9)

Fig. 1 The sun-god Rē in his barque.

Fig. 2 Corn growing out of the dead body of Osiris, the god of fertility and of growth and decay in nature. Below: the character for 'life,' repeated and framed by the character for 'good fortune and well being.' (Philae, Ptolemaic Period.)

the entire figure, leaving only the feet uncovered. Formerly the eyes were worked in a different material and inlaid into the eye sockets. The figure stands upon a circular plinth bearing the hieroglyph for 'city.'

Besides standing figures there are also seated ones, especially from Dynasty II. The person portrayed is usually seated upon a block-shaped stool, from which projects a foot-rest upon which his feet rest, placed close together; usually the right arm is pressed tightly against the body and the right hand lies upon the knee, whereas the left arm is bent at the elbow and projects forward. The cubic shape of the stool gives the effect of a border on each side and at the back, while the foot-rest defines the space toward the front.

In Dynasty I bone carvings one can observe rapid progress in the development of characteristic stylistic elements, which in the late classical era were to take on the character of formal laws. This is true both of carvings in relief and of many ivory statuettes, such as a figurine of a king wearing the Upper Egyptian crown and a tight-fitting cloak, which shows an astonishing balance and maturity both in the shape of the body and in the treatment of the face.

Under the impression of this amazingly rapid development of artistic talent at the beginning of Dynasty I, the question has been raised whether some external influence may not have been responsible. In the case of certain motifs influence from Mesopotamia need not be ruled out, but one must exclude beyond all doubt the possibility that Mesopotamian culture exerted any far-reaching impact upon Egypt. * Pl. 12, 13 In regard to religious concepts, too, the Archaic Period witnesses a very profound transformation which points the way to future developments. Once man has become conscious of his identity and has begun to order his environment, he is no longer content to worship the power of divine forces in their reflected form as a fetish. Nor could he accept as sufficient a belief in the supernatural force of animals. As a result of his growing self-awareness man begins to make gods in his own image and to ascribe to them experiences similar to his own. Thus the pantheon acquires a humanized character, and the gods are represented as hybrid beings with human * Pl. 10, 11 body and animal head, or even in human guise with their earlier animal form occasionally added as an attribute. Thus the ancient belief in the magic power of animals is

Pl. IV Man kneeling and resting on his arms. Light green glazed faience. From the earliest temple area at Abydos. Archaic Period, c. 3000 B.C. Height 7.8 cm., length 9.8 cm. E. and M. Kofler-Truniger Collection, Lucerne.

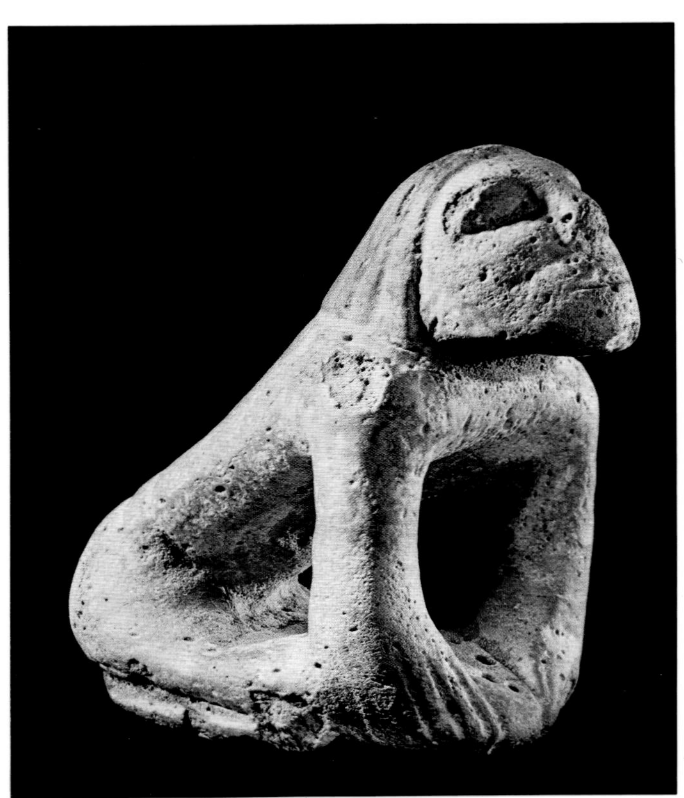

combined with a view of the gods as beings who live and act as men. From incomprehensible divine forces they have become individuals, whose nature and conduct can be explained in human terms.

The character of each animal concerned—falcon, snake or crocodile—continues to give these hybrid deities an individual note and determines the functions they fulfil. They acquire a place of worship of their own, becoming local gods or nome-gods. Some of them, to whom special powers were ascribed, and whose functions exceeded those of a local deity, are venerated throughout the country. Thus the jackal-headed Anubis becomes the god of embalming and burial, and the ibis-headed Thoth is worshipped as the god of writing and wisdom.

As the importance of the deity worshipped in a particular nome grew, so did the political significance of the area concerned. Thus attempts were made to enhance the esteem of the local god beyond his immediate sphere of activity, by ascribing to him the qualities of other gods and occasionally also adding to his name that of another powerful deity. Apart from its political aspect, this syncretism shows that, the more powerful his tutelary deity, the safer man feels amidst the uncertainties of life.

The prehistoric magic concept of the world is superseded by a mythical interpretation. The gods are viewed imaginatively: like human beings, they are friendly or hostile to one another, form families or groups, and have clearly marked individual characters and functions.

Now that man's intellectual capacities have been awakened, he inquires into the laws of nature and the universe. His exuberant imagination leads him to invent the most varied interpretations, which coexist with or overlap one another. Modern man, who thinks in a logical way, finds it hard to comprehend an outlook in which the same phenomena may be viewed in terms of several images which differ widely yet do not exclude one another.

Fig. 3 The sky-goddess Hathor in the guise of a cow, supported by Shu, god of the air, and his retainers. On the body of the sky-goddess are the sun barque and stars.

Fig. 4 The sky-goddess Nut in human guise, supported by the god of the air, Shu, with the earth-god Geb at her feet.

The observation of growth and decay in nature, of spring and autumn, leads man to see in these events, which play such an important part in his life, the workings of a god, whom he worships in Osiris, the god of vegetation and fertility. This growth and decay suggests parallels to his own fate. Just as Osiris gives the soil new life after death, so he can also grant man resurrection in the life beyond.

The concepts of the after-life correspond to those of life on this earth. In the 'Goodly West', where the sun never sets, lies the land of the dead, in which the deceased have the same tasks and duties to fulfil as in their terrestrial existence. The mummification of the dead and their provisioning with grave goods—food, implements, weapons and servant figurines—will, as they believe, ensure that they are well equipped to enter upon their new life.

Similarly, man took note of the alternation of day and night, and of the movement of the stars. During the Prehistoric era he saw in the vaulted heavens the falcon-god Horus, whose outspread wings afforded protection to the world. As his outlook changed, and the gods appeared in more human guise, these concepts recede into the background: the sky takes on the shape of a woman, the goddess Nut, who encompasses the earth, personified in the god Geb. The earth-god and sky-goddess beget the sun, which is reborn each morning. A little later this concept was broadened by interpolating Shu, god of the air, who supports the sky-goddess and bridges the void between earth and heaven. In a different version the cow-goddess Hathor takes the place of Nut, the goddess in human guise. Across the horizon, which is envisaged as an ocean, move the stars, touching the body of the sky-goddess as they go.

As this survey shows, the great transformation that took place in all spheres of human activity during the Archaic Period was the result of the development of man himself: his capacity to think and perceive attained a stage at which his creative powers were released; he was able to emerge

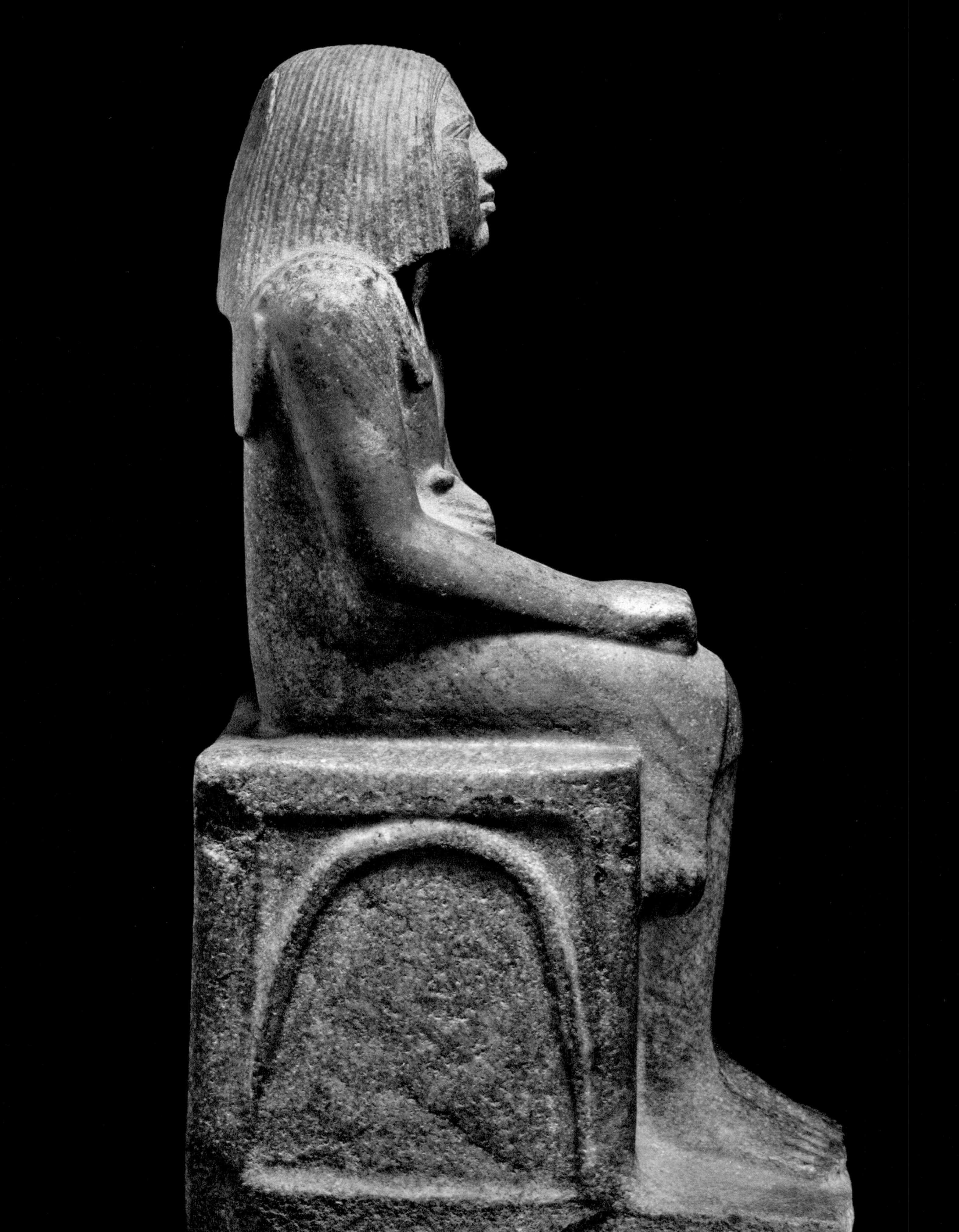

Pl. 12 Statuette of Ankh-tekh, in profile. Granite. Dynasties II/III, c. 2600 B.C. Height 62 cm. Rijksmuseum van Oudheden, Leyden.

Pl. 13 Frontal view of the statuette in Pl. 12.

from the disorderly chaos of prehistory and to systematize the world about him.

The introduction of a written script and the calendar are the expression of this desire to mark out and delimit the realm that has been conquered. The formation of a centralized state ruled by a god-king is the decisive step, which not only makes possible the ordering of all spheres of life but also establishes a relationship between man and supernatural forces. The humanization of the gods and the mythical interpretation of their qualities and of cosmic forces constitutes the beginning of religion. Man expresses his knowledge of his environment and his concepts of the nature of things in his art, demonstrating the new principles of order in rigid forms.

PHARAOH - GOD AND MAN

THE OLD KINGDOM

★ Pl. 15

The accession to the throne in about 2660 B.C. of King Zoser, the first king of Dynasty III, marks the beginning of the Old Kingdom. The divine and human legitimation of the new dynasty rested upon Queen Nimaathapi, who was probably a daughter of King Khasekhemui and the mother of Zoser. Her name contains the designation of Hapi, the Apis bull worshipped at Memphis, and thus points to Lower Egypt, which takes over the leading role during the Old Kingdom. Manetho refers to Dynasty III expressly as 'of Memphis.' Whereas there is no noticeable upheaval in political life at the beginning of the Old Kingdom, in cultural and spiritual life such a tremendous development sets in that we are justified in considering this a new epoch in Egyptian history.

Upon the scanty foundations laid in the Archaic Period there developed within a single life-span monumental stone buildings at which contemporaries and later generations marvelled. Nothing expresses better the timelessness of Egyptian art than the geometric austerity of the Pyramids, which even today arouse our admiration among the world's most splendid technical and artistic achievements. On the desert plateau at Saqqara King Zoser built
Pl. 14 his tomb, a step pyramid 180 feet high, and surrounded it with all the buildings necessary for a royal residence. The capital at Memphis, built of perishable material, was translated into durable stone in the form of dummy buildings,
★ Cat. 19 which would enable the ruler to exercise his royal functions throughout eternity.

This splendid architectural complex, which for the first time in Egyptian history may be designated as architecture, is evidence of the kingdom's growing aspirations, and also of the belief in a life after death which subsumes all man's obligations and rights in this world.

In a chamber on the northern side of the Pyramid was discovered a seated statue of King Zoser, wearing the costume used during the Sed festivals—the ceremonies in which the power of the god-king was renewed. The austere block-like statue, still very archaic in appearance, is today in the Egyptian Museum in Cairo. The prominent cheek-bones and thick lips give the face a look of sombre imperiousness. Although one cannot help noticing in this first work of monumental sculpture some forcefulness in the way forms are made to comply with a single principle of treatment, the Zoser statue affords a convincing example of the consistency with which the laws of composition, heralded already in the Archaic Period, developed later in Egyptian art. The making of a sculpture in the round begins with the block of stone, its faces hewn at right angles, the vertical planes forming the framework of the sculpture. A preliminary drawing is executed on the surface of the block, following a system of lines that enables the proportions to be calculated. Thereupon the stone-mason sets to work. The figure is carved around a central axis, working inwards from the external planes, and is thus orientated solely toward a profile or frontal view. The surface at the rear is at first untouched, and forms a back support or pillar, or else the cube-shaped stool upon which the figure is seated. The posture of the body is determined by the relationship to the outer planes of the cube and to the central axis. This ensures an austere approach to sculptural composition which excludes any kind of transitoriness. The representation follows the natural human figure, but divests it of all that is incidental or transient, in order to give shape to that which is timeless and everlasting. Only in this way can it possess magic qualities and 'supra-temporal' significance, and so fulfil its function in the cult of the dead. The sculptures erected in the statue-chambers of private tombs and inside royal tombs are the seat of the *ka*, the immortal

Fig. 5 The ram-headed god Khnum gives shape to Amenophis III on the potter's wheel as well as to his 'ka,' his immortal alter ego, which has the same shape. The goddess Hathor presents the symbol of life. (Temple at Luxor. Dynasty XVIII.)

vital power, of the deceased occupant, and thus embody his hope of eternal life. In any great work of art there must be a correlation between technique, style and content; this was most certainly the case in Egyptian art, which within a short time was able to develop a style that conformed to the Egyptian outlook, and which at the beginning of the Old Kingdom took on an unmistakable character of its own.

About King Zoser as a person little has been recorded, although his memory lived on for thousands of years. Even in the Late Ptolemaic Period the so-called 'Famine Stele' records a seven-year famine during his reign, which the king was able to bring to an end by giving to Khnum of Elephantine, the god of the Cataracts, the Nubian territory between the First and Second Cataract, which must therefore have formed part of his possessions at that time. It is also known that during his reign the copper mines of Sinai were worked and that the trade links with Byblos were maintained. For centuries Zoser was venerated by his descendants for having utilized stone as a durable material in architecture and sculpture, as may be seen from an inscription left by a visitor during the New Kingdom, which refers to him as 'he who opened the stone.'

Closely linked with the technical and artistic miracle of Zoser's burial district is the name of Imhotep, the principal royal architect and priest. During the Late Period he was deified as an architect, seer and healer. The Greeks saw in him an equivalent of their god of healing, Asklepios. Since in more recent times his name has been discovered
on the base of a statue of Zoser, we know that Imhotep Pl. 16
was indeed a historical figure. The eminent titles he bore suggest that he was related to the royal family; for also at the beginning of the Old Kingdom officials related to the reigning dynasty carried out the chief administrative functions in the state.

Not far from the Zoser pyramid are the tombs of court officials, which in their layout follow the archaic pattern. On the eastern side is a niche for offerings; set into the rear wall is a limestone plaque depicting the deceased
seated at the dining-table and indicating his title and name. Pl. 17
The purpose of this is to ensure that the deceased is materially provided for in the after-life; mention of his name serves to guarantee that the offerings cannot be exchanged for those of others; for the Egyptians believed that an image and an inscribed name were imbued with magic efficacy. The 'dining-table scene' is therefore one of the most important representations found in tombs, and was indispensable even in later times. It not only indicates the place where offerings for the dead should be placed but by its very existence guarantees fulfilment of his desire to be provided with material goods.

The laws of composition for reliefs and sculpture in officials' tombs were evolved at the beginning of Dynasty III. In a wooden plaque from the tomb of Hesy-ra Pl. 18
one can sense a fresh clarity and compactness: on the body of the figure the muscles, collar-bone and joints are elaborately modelled, following nature, so that the figure has a buoyant vitality. At the same time the figure is not simply conceived as a copy of nature, but is supposed to express

Pl. 14 Funerary complex of King Zoser at Saqqara. Dynasty III c. 2650 B.C.

the essence of the man or object concerned. The Egyptian artist abstracts what he sees in the here and now, and elevates it to represent a higher and more valid truth. He is not concerned to render what meets the eye but what is typical; he seeks to create a symbol which acquires expressive force only through its magic efficacy.

These requirements are met in the style adopted for reliefs. The picture is divided in the plane into individual parts, which are held together by the outline to form a compact whole. Each single part is formed in a manner appropriate to its meaning, but the entire figure represents the ideal of human perfection. Thus the head is shown in

Pl. 15 Life-size statue of King Zoser. Limestone with traces of painting. From the serdab *of the Step Pyramid at Saqqara. Dynasty III,* c. *2650 B.C. Cairo Museum.*

profile but the eye is viewed frontally; the body is in frontal view from the shoulders to the pelvis while the legs are rendered in profile. The deceased is depicted in a motionless posture, either seated or standing; there is nothing that could be interpreted as the expression of a momentary, transient event. The belief in the magic properties of images, which were made to last for ever, precludes any movement, foreshortening of perspective or overlap. The background of the relief plaques is smooth, without any indication of the surrounding space, without shadow, without any kind of attribute which could relate the figure to a point in time or space. Similarly, the artist avoids any indication of personal characteristics, even the subject's age. Only the title and name relate this timeless ideal human image to a particular deceased person. Cat. 43

Also in painting a relief the Egyptian artist at first proceeds from life but develops a colour scheme which does not correspond to the colours found in the real world. His pigments, which are derived from mineral substances, are red, yellow, white, blue, green and black; they are used singly and not blended. The rigid scheme which was evolved for reliefs is in complete harmony, spiritually and stylistically, with the Egyptian genius. In a clear and compelling way it illustrates the austere linear treatment which alone was suited to express absolute form, in which reality becomes a symbol.

In fashioning reliefs and sculpture significance is mainly attached not to artistic inventiveness but to technical achievement. One must imagine that various systems and rules were worked out by a community of artisans in a workshop and were then handed down to later generations in books of patterns. Some incomplete reliefs have survived which provide information about working methods, and the technique of these corresponds to that employed in sculpture. To begin with, for purposes of measurement, the plane was divided by lines into a number of units, in

Pl. 16 Statuette of Imhotep. Bronze. Dynasty XXVI, 6th cent. B.C. Height 18.5 cm. Hermitage, Leningrad.

which the preliminary drawing was made; then the sculptor cut the contour lines with a copper chisel and hollowed out the space around the figure. The next stages were the modelling of the figure and the polishing of the surface, which was subsequently plastered and painted. Artisans were available who specialized in executing various phases of the work, which was thus the product, not of a single talented individual artist, but of various skilled artisans. Nevertheless their work is the fruit of a creative process —the establishment of spiritual, stylistic and technical prerequisites—which remain as anonymous as the practical execution.

The development of such a basic scheme, which met so perfectly the requirements of the Egyptian outlook on life, did indeed make it harder for individual artists to emerge, but on the other hand it did ensure that even in periods of decline art maintained a certain standard of achievement.

The principles of composition that attained a classical equilibrium during the Old Kingdom constitute the criterion whereby we may assess stylistic development in later Egyptian history. As in other cultures, the original timeless ideal image gives way, to a greater or lesser degree, to a realistic likeness. But even when differentiation reached its utmost extent in later times, the formal concepts of the age of the Pyramids, and the spiritual background which gave rise to them, retain their vitality and exert the most decisive influence upon art.

Little is known about the last two rulers of Dynasty III, Sekhemkhet and Huni. Sekhemkhet, whose name is not mentioned in the king-lists, ordered work to commence on the building of his tomb near the Zoser pyramid, which served him as a model. It was not completed before his death, and when it was explored the alabaster sarcophagus in the burial-chamber was found to be empty. A similar fate awaited his successor Huni, whose pyramid near

Pl. 17 Dje-fai-ni-tut seated before the dining-table. Limestone relief. Dynasty III, c. 2650 B.C. Height 33.8 cm., width 47.5 cm. Kestner Museum, Hanover.

Pl. V Bird-trapping and domestic animals. Coloured sunk limestone relief. From the mastaba *of Nefermaat (chamber of Atet) at Saqqara. Dynasty III,* c. *2600 B. C. Height 100 cm., width 117 cm. Ny Carlsberg Glyptotek, Copenhagen.*

Meidum was continued by Snefru, his son-in-law and successor, but was never completed.

With King Snefru, whose claim to the throne was legitimized by his marriage with Hetep-heres, one of Huni's daughters, a new dynasty acceded to power, under whose rule the great spiritual and cultural upsurge continued and, as it attained further refinement, generated the first flourishing period of Egyptian civilization. In later literary sources Snefru is described as a kind-hearted sovereign. During the Middle Kingdom he was worshipped as a god in his mortuary temple at Dahshur and even during the Late Period his name was kept in reverent memory. From the inscription on the Palermo Stone we learn that during his twenty-four-year reign Snefru returned with ample booty from his wars against the Libyans and Nubians. Expeditions to Sinai and Byblos yielded minerals and timber. The annals tell of the building of ships to facilitate maritime traffic between Egypt and the Lebanon. These extensive and ever-growing political functions necessitated changes in the internal administration of the kingdom. Hitherto the pharaoh had entrusted various tasks and offices to members of his royal court on an *ad hoc* basis, but it now became necessary to introduce a regular bureaucratic system. From Dynasty III onwards a vizier took

* Pl. 19

charge of administrative affairs, including the administration of justice, supply and revenue-collection.

As the highest position in the land the office of vizier, which attains real importance from Dynasty IV onwards, continues to be the preserve of princes of royal blood, whereas the lower administrative posts are filled by men who come to form a distinct official class in their own right. This development opens the way to a gradual decentralization of power and the formation of professional groups whose status and privileges were enhanced as time went on.

One of the great achievements of Snefru's reign was that the idea of building a royal tomb now came to maturity. In his plans for the pyramid at Meidum his predecessor had already made provision for a true pyramid, with a square base, in which the step-like core was to have been enclosed within a limestone casing, the outer surface of which would have a uniform gradient. Snefru continued work on his predecessor's design only for a short while and then instead had two pyramids erected at Dahshur : the 'Bent Pyramid', which looks bent when seen in outline because the angle of the slope differs at the top and bottom, and the so-called 'Red Pyramid,' in which the abstract geometric form is kept to consistently and the angle of the slope is less acute. On the eastern side of the pyramid is the mortuary temple, used in the cult of the dead; it is connected by an open causeway (which in later complexes was covered over) with a temple in the valley, located on the edge of the fertile land and the desert. In which of these pyramids Snefru was buried is to this day a matter of doubt.

The tombs of the king's senior officials and relatives are built in close proximity to the pyramids at Meidum and Dahshur. Instead of the hitherto customary place for ceremonial functions on the outer face of the eastern wall of the tomb, the private tombs at Meidum have a ritual chamber inside the tomb complex, which is enclosed on the western side by a door niche—the so-called false door. Above the door-lintel is a representation of the deceased at the dining-table. As the Egyptians saw it, he would step out through this door to receive the funerary offerings upon invocation by the priest. Behind the false door is the statue-chamber or *serdab*, in which the deceased, in the form of a statue, lived on for eternity. The ritual chamber was decorated with reliefs and paintings. Representations of the occupant of the tomb receiving the funerary offerings of his relatives and servants, as well as pictures depicting the slaughter of sacrificial cattle, were intended to supplement the actual funerary bequest for the deceased. But in addition there occur hunting scenes showing birds and desert animals, fishing and husbandry, which are supposed, by the magic properties of the image, to keep alive for the deceased in the beyond the memory of his earthly existence.

Action is expressed by an attitude characteristic of the type of activity concerned. Such an attitude does not therefore represent a specific action carried out by a certain person at a certain time and place, but is a symbolic, absolute portrayal of the *concept* of this specific activity. A group of persons is indicated by placing them in a row, side by side, or stacked up in such a way that the outlines run parallel. Certain groups of people or professional classes are characterized by some typical posture, by their costume, or by the addition of distinguishing attributes.

In addition to such noble works in high relief, the artists of the tombs at Meidum tried their hand at new techniques, as for example sunk reliefs, in which the representation was carved out of the stone slab. The depressions thus produced were filled with coloured paste. But it was soon evident that this new technique was not very durable, for the coloured paste shrivelled up and dropped out; for this reason the practice was soon discontinued.

Pl. 18 Hesy-ra seated before the dining-table. Wooden relief from Hesy-ra's tomb at Saqqara. Dynasty III, c. *2650 B.C. Height 114 cm. Cairo Museum.*

In the tomb of Princess Atet at Meidum the walls are coated with stucco and painted. Unfortunately only little has been preserved of these funerary paintings. The famous 'geese of Meidum' bear witness to the naive delight which the Egyptian artist took in rendering, in a lifelike manner, the animals that were so familiar to him. The range of colours is extensive and now also comprises different nuances of shading. Pl. VI

The creative initiative manifest in Snefru's reign is exemplified in spiritual ideas and in artistic experimentation : the first attempts at formal artistic treatment are succeeded by an intensification of the means used and a more austere approach; this leads in turn to the balanced, mature classical style of the next generation. This development stems in large part from a change in the religious outlook; for at the beginning of the Old Kingdom the ancient ideas were reinterpreted and new criteria were established for architecture and art.

According to the myths of the Archaic Period Osiris was the personification of fertility, the god of growth and decay in nature. In a more recent version Osiris is identified as a king of primeval times who is murdered by his adversary, Seth, the Upper Egyptian god of the desert and of drought, but is resurrected to new life. In the original myth Osiris has for his consort Isis and Seth is espoused to the goddess Nephthys. The resurrected Osiris becomes ruler of the land of the dead. In this version the death of Osiris is reinterpreted as a unique historical event such as can easily be comprehended by the human imagination.

During the Old Kingdom man's growing need to systematize the world about him extended also to religious concepts. An important step in this direction was the inclusion of the god Horus in the Osiris sphere. The god Seth, who was formerly venerated as the tutelary deity of Upper Egypt, now takes on the role of an evil murderer, whereas Horus becomes the son of Osiris, who avenges

Pl. 19 False door from Ateti's tomb at Saqqara. Painted limestone Dynasty VI, c. 2200 B.C. Cairo Museum.

the death of his father and succeeds him as ruler of the world of the living. When the pharaoh on his accession to the throne adopted the Horus name, which identified him with this god, he became at the same time the son of Osiris. This idea soon became linked with the hope and belief that the king would be resurrected after his death and that his reign would continue in the world beyond. At his burial a special ritual was performed which made him an Osiris, i.e. one who is being resurrected.

During Archaic times the mythological interpretation of cosmic and earthly phenomena had enabled man to comprehend the world in which he lived; during the Old Kingdom he began to ask the question how the world had come into being. According to the doctrine of Heliopolis it had been created by Atum, a primordial deity who was the source of his own existence; he was depicted in human guise wearing the Egyptian Double Crown. He begat of himself Shu, god of the air, and his sister Tefnut, goddess of moisture, whom he is said to have spewed forth. Their children are Geb, the earth-god, and Nut, the sky-goddess; they in turn have four children: Osiris, Isis, Seth and Nephthys. The holy family of Heliopolis constitutes the sacred Ennead. The place of Atum is occasionally taken by Nun, the god of the chaotic primordial ocean. According to another doctrine, which originated from Hermopolis in Middle Egypt, the creation of the world began with the rise of a mound of earth from this ocean. Closely linked to the Ennead of Heliopolis is the sun-god Rē, who sails in his barque across the horizon, which is formed by the body of the goddess Nut. The sun-god is venerated in three guises: in the morning he appears as a scarab, called *kheper*, 'one which is coming into existence'; at noon he takes the shape of the falcon-headed god Rē; and in the evening he sets as Atum, a god in human guise. Whereas the early interpretation of heaven and earth endeavoured only to explain their nature, the new doctrine of Heliopolis

is the first instance of theological speculation. The act of creation, performed by the god Atum, whose name may be construed as 'the universe,' is not interpreted in a mythical sense but is seen as a miracle.

In the doctrine of Hermopolis theological inquiry is even more in evidence. The origin of the world is explained in terms of eight primordial forces (*ogdoad*): the primordial ocean, Nun, and his counterpart, Naunet; Heh, infinite space, and Hehet; Kek, darkness, and Keket; Amun, 'the hidden (god),' and Amaunet. These represent the original state of the world before order was established in the cosmos and the laws of nature were created. These pairs of concepts are represented as primeval beings which emerged from the mud: the males are depicted as frogs and the females as snakes. From the waters there rises a mound; on it is an egg, from which the sun-god ascends; his birth signifies the birth of the cosmic order.

Thanks to a later record from the time of the Ethiopian king Shabaka, who reigned in about 700 B.C., a document has survived which is of the utmost significance for the history of religion: it has come to be known as the 'monument of Menphite theology' and is now in the British Museum. The inscription of this stone slab refers to a much earlier tradition which probably originates from the time of Snefru. The inscription gives in mythological form a historical account of the unification of the kingdom, according to which the earth-god Geb assigns Lower Egypt to Horus and Upper Egypt to Seth 'in order to make up the quarrel over the land.' In this text the god Horus is given preference and is equated with the god Ptah, who was worshipped at Menphis, the royal residence during the Old Kingdom, and whose character is explained in the second part of the inscription. His special significance is justified firstly by the statement that all the great gods who play a role in popular cosmogony are united in the nature of the god Ptah. The eight primordial gods of Hermopolis have taken shape in him, and the gods of the sacred Enneal of Heliopolis are seen only as manifestations and properties of Ptah, the great creator of the world. He is accorded pride of place as god of the royal residence, the seat of political power. Second place is given to the god Atum, who according to the Heliopolis doctrine is supposed to have begotten the pantheon. He and his Ennead are referred to as 'teeth and lips in the mouth of Ptah,' by whom they were created. Ptah alone knows the nature and name of things, and by speaking their names gives them life:

'In this way all gods were created / and each word of the god (Ptah) arose / from what the heart knew and the tongue commanded.'

After having created the gods Ptah ensured the fertility of the soil, so that life might be preserved, and introduced law and justice, so guaranteeing order in the world. At the end of his work of creation 'Ptah rested, having made all the divine words.'

There is a digression about the significance of heart and tongue, which ends with an exposition of the creative forces that created the world. 'It is he (the heart) who brings forth all knowledge, and it is the tongue which repeats the thought of the heart.'

In contrast to all religious concepts that had hitherto held sway, the god Ptah stands above all natural phenomena; he is the product of philosophical and theological cerebration; he is the primordial spiritual force whose field of operation lies in the transcendental world. The act of creation is not primarily one of procreation; it is a spiritual act which proceeds from the growth of the intellect, of perception and reason, and which becomes effective through the creative word.

The philosophy underlying this interpretation might have pointed the way to monotheism; but it was doubtless

Pl. VI Geese. Detail from a bird-trapping scene. Painting on plaster. From Atet's tomb near Meidum. Early Dynasty IV, c. 2600 B.C. Cairo Museum.

restricted to a small group of the social élite with intellectual interests, whereas the broad masses felt themselves more readily drawn to the concrete ideas of the Heliopolis doctrine.

Surprising as it may seem that the Egyptian freed himself from the entanglements of mythology to arrive at an abstract spiritual cast of thought, one should not underestimate the fact that there is common ground between abstract thinking, such as one finds in Memphite theology, and the magic outlook fundamental to man: both share a belief in supernatural forces. Already in early times knowledge of esoteric maxims and mystic names was taken as signifying superiority and possession of magic power.

At the time when Cheops, Chephren and Mycerinus built the Pyramids at Giza, man's religious life was also subordinated to the king, who was designated 'the great living god.' He alone vouchsafes in his person *maat*, the 'rightness' or lawfulness of cosmic forces, of the state order, and also of the link between it and the realm of the gods. His divine nature affords the guarantee that he may mingle with the gods on the same terms, as a mighty being.

The Pyramid texts even claim for the deceased king the highest place in the assembly of the gods, to which he is entitled as the son of Osiris, who like his father has risen from the dead. His power and occult knowledge qualify him personally to hold this highest office.

'The Ennead of Horus is dazzled, the Lords of Forms are in terror of him. The entire Double Ennead (of Atum) serveth him and he sitteth on the throne of the Lord of All. He seizeth the sky, cleaveth its metal. He is led along the road to Khepre (Kheper), he setteth alive in the west, (and) the dwellers in the nether world follow him, and riseth renewed in the east. He that adjudged the quarrel (Thoth, the god of wisdom) cometh to him, making obeisance. The gods are afraid of him, for he is

Pl. 20 Valley-temple of Chefren with Sphinx and Cheops Pyramid in Giza. C. 2550 B.C.

older than the Great One. He it is that hath power over his seat. He layeth hold on command (power to rule), Eternity is brought to him. Discernment is placed for him at his feet. Cry aloud to him in joy, he hath captured the horizon.'[1]

'His glory is in the sky, his power in the horizon, like Atum his father that begat him—he begat him but he is stronger than he.'[2]

This mighty god-king confers honour upon his courtiers and officials by assigning to them tombs not far from his own pyramid and granting them offerings for their funerary rite. The subjects of the pharaoh are dependent on his mercy for their prospect of an after-life.

Little has been handed down about King Cheops, who succeeded his father Snefru on the throne. The Palermo Stone contains no information about him or his successors.

Pl. 21 King Chephren. Detail. Diorite. From his valley-temple at Giza. Dynasty IV, c. 2500 B.C. Overall height 168 cm Cairo Museum (cf. Cat. 1).

Pl. 22 King Mycerinus and his wife Khamerernebty II. Grey stone. From the valley-temple of Mycerinus at Giza. Dynasty IV, c. 2490 B.C. Height 140 cm. Museum of Fine Arts, Boston.

Later sources, Herodotus in particular, depict Cheops and his son Chephren as despotic rulers who suppressed and exploited the people in order to finance and build their enormous city of the dead. For this purpose they are said to have taken the offerings even from the temples of the gods. From these descriptions it becomes clear that in later times the ideological prerequisites for pyramid-building no longer existed or were no longer understood, and that the image of the god-king had become distorted into that of a tyrant.

Pl. 20 To this very day the Pyramids of Cheops, Chephren and Mycerinus on the desert plateau at Giza testify to the magnificent power and consistency of the idea of divine kingship. Its strength and immortality found expression in the geometric, mathematical regularity of pyramid architecture.

The Cheops Pyramid is 475 feet high. It was formerly faced with white limestone slabs, each weighing about 2 ½ tons. The temples around the pyramids are best preserved in the Chephren complex. As was the case in Snefru's burial district at Dahshur, a temple was located in the valley, on the edge of the fertile land. In its first hall, sited at an oblique angle, the embalming of the royal body took place. In the adjoining pillared hall, in which statues of the king were erected, the rite of becoming Osiris was carried out, as well as the ceremony of 'opening the mouth,' which served to allow the soul of the deceased, the *ka*, to enter the statue where it would henceforward live on for all eternity. Afterwards the funeral procession mounted a covered causeway to the mortuary temple below the pyramid, in which further ritual acts were performed. In an open court statues of the king were erected in twelve shrines; five adjoining chapels each contained a statue of a deity. Behind the mortuary temple, separated by an enclosure wall, was the pyramid. In its core was the burial-chamber, where the deceased was interred.

Pl. 23 King Userkaf. Slate. From the royal mortuary temple at Abu Sir. Dynasty V, c. 2460 B.C. Life-size. Cairo Museum.

The entire architectonic layout is determined by the burial rite and the cult of the dead. Every detail of the building follows strict mathematical rules, which give the whole complex an abstract timeless quality, clarity and balance.

None of the architectural elements show any trace of derivation from natural forms, as was still the case with the architecture of the Zoser tomb complex. The geometric form of the pyramid and the square pillars convey perfectly the impression of timeless existence, detached from the reality of life. The treatment of the burial-chamber of the god-king clearly derives from the abstract thought and religious-philosophical speculation of Dynasty IV.

The image of the mighty god-king of the Pyramid Period is encountered in its most compelling form in the well-known diorite statue of Chephren from the valley-temple of his tomb complex at Giza. The cube-shaped throne, with its back support reaching up as far as the king's shoulders and its foot support, indicate the external frame of an imaginary cube into which the image of the seated ruler has been set, austere and motionless. His right hand, with fist clenched, rests upon his right thigh, and his left hand is stretched out on his left knee. The arms are held close to the body and are taut; the legs, placed close together and side by side, are connected by a fillet to the front edge of the throne. The king is portrayed in ceremonial costume: a short kilt, the royal head-dress featuring the uraeus snake, and the beard upon the chin. Perched on the back support is the Horus falcon, encompassing the divine pharaoh's head with its outstretched wings. The body, well-proportioned and elaborately modelled down to the last detail, gives an impression of rigidity and strength; the face suggests a tense vitality. The claim to an eternal existence has displaced all personal temporal features. The strict compact form conveys a message of enduring validity. The external naturalness

* Pl. 21, Cat. 1

Pl. VII Funerary stele of Princess Nefertiabet. Painted limestone. From her tomb at Giza. Dynasty IV, c. 2550 B.C. Height 37.5 cm., width 52.5 cm. Musée du Louvre, Paris.

and vitality of the figure—which portrays a young man
★ Pl. 22 in the prime of life—is linked with the idea of eternal, immutable divine kingship. It heralds a classical balance of content and form, such as occurs in art history only during short periods of splendour, when man briefly attains an integrated view of the world about him.

In the statuary of Mycerinus, who succeeded Chephren on the throne, a slight transformation may be noted in the concept of divine kingship. In his mortuary temple at Giza a group of figures was found portraying the king and his consort on the same plinth. Mycerinus is depicted striding along, with his left leg in front; his wife is shown with her arm around him and her left hand resting upon the upper part of his left arm. She is slightly smaller than he is, has a shorter stride, and by the act of embracing him seems to be a little way behind the king. The conjunction

Pl. 24 King Shepseskaf (?). Alabaster. From Giza. Dynasty IV, c. 2480 B.C. Height 25.4 cm. Museum of Fine Arts, Boston.

of the two figures, which are juxtaposed to one another as independent entities, has a somewhat stereotyped character: it is as though the artist were expressing the concept 'to embrace.' Neither in the form nor in any expression of emotion is there a hint that the two figures form a single whole.

This sculptural group demonstrates with particular clarity the extent to which Egyptian sculpture in the round is limited strictly by the planes of the cube in which the figures are conceived as standing. Such a motif would have normally suggested that the figures should incline towards one another and step out from the spatial framework; instead the principle whereby the theme is treated requires that the forms should be firmly contained in the imaginary spatial framework; every figure has to be represented either *en face* or in profile, and a three-quarter view is entirely ruled out. Thus the juxtaposition of the two statues gives an impression of mutual unconcern, of the indiscriminate addition of individual values whose relationship is suggested merely by a stereotyped gestures. The fact that the king is portrayed in close conjunction with his consort does, however, indicate a weakening of the concept of the pharaoh as an unapproachable being possessed of divine power. In the portrait of Mycerinus the expression of imperturbability and calm strength associated with the god-king is no longer given prominence; instead we can detect a physical and spiritual tension, the slight hint of a connection with the transient human world, of a diminution of the king's claim to divinity.

The uniform layout of the tombs of the court officials at Giza was obviously in accordance with King Cheops' instructions. The tombs are in the form of rectangular tumuli with sloping walls. Today they are called *mastaba*, from the Arabic term for 'bank.' They are placed on access roads that intersect at right angles, so that a mathe-

Pl. 25 Prince Hemon. Limestone. From Giza. Dynasty IV, c. 2500 B.C. Height 156 cm. Roemer-Pelizaeus Museum, Hildesheim.

Pl. 26 Portrait head of a princess. Limestone. From Giza. Dynasty IV, c. 2550 B.C. Museum of Fine Arts, Boston.

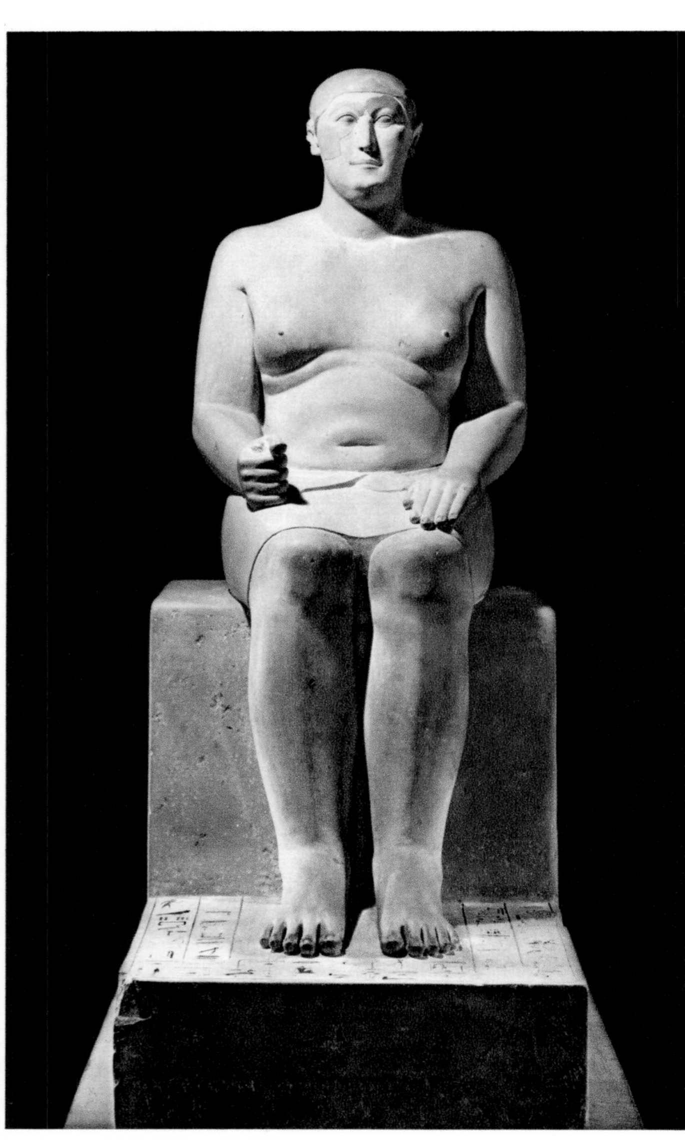

matical plan for the whole area is apparent. Instead of an offering-room in the core of the tomb, a limestone plaque bearing a dining-table scene is set into the outer face of the eastern wall. Access into the burial-chamber was gained by a vertical shaft, which was closed by stone slabs after interment had taken place. There was also no room in the interior of the tomb for the statue-chamber or *serdab*, so that instead of a funerary statue a so-called 'reserve head' was placed in a niche in the shaft.

Toward the close of Dynasty IV the strict building regulations of the Cheops period were abandoned. These rules had dispensed with two vital elements in tomb architecture, the offering-room and the *serdab*. Before long a great variety of buildings developed, both at Giza and at Saqqara.

An outstanding example of private sculpture during
Dynasty IV has survived in the life-size statue of Prince Pl. 25
Hemon, a nephew of Cheops. Of Cheops himself only a small ivory figurine is known. The fine limestone statue of Hemon is instructive from two points of view. The balanced and clearly-marked monumentality is in complete conformity with the Dynasty IV style. Particular points of conception and detail, however, definitely go beyond the formal laws which were strictly followed in royal sculpture. The cube-shaped seat has a foot-rest but no back support. The prince is portrayed in a severe but less constrained pose. His arms are detached from his body, his right hand with fist clenched and thumb turned upwards rests upon his right thigh, and his left hand is stretched out flat on his knee. The massive figure, with plump legs separated from each other, shows that we have here not an impersonal ideal human image but the physical person of Prince Hemon. Nevertheless this statue must not be taken as a realistic likeness of the person portrayed, but as the translation of his natural appearance into the characteristic features of the man Hemon, rendered in a

Pl. 27 Portrait bust of Prince Ankh-haf. Limestone. From Giza. Dynasty IV, c. 2500 B.C. Height 50.6 cm. Museum of Fine Arts, Boston.

stylized form. The modelling of the surface, the muscles, bones and joints are executed with such subtlety that the heavy cubic form is invigorated by fresh vitality. The forceful, dignified facial expression suggests a person imbued with self-control and unapproachable reserve, aware of the importance and responsibility of the position he holds.

To the Cheops period also belong the 'reserve heads' which took over the function of the *ka* statue in private tombs at Giza. It was natural that in these the facial expression should convey even more compellingly the characteristic features of the deceased; for it was not possible here, by rendering the body and especially by inscribing the subject's name and title, to turn their magic properties to the benefit of the deceased person for whom the heads were made. The elaborately modelled head and the expressive treatment of the nose, chin and mouth give each face an individual expression. Despite this fact we cannot say of these reserve heads, of which approximately twenty are known, that they bear any resemblance to portraits. From the facial features it is, for example, never possible to deduce the age of the person represented. The image has been stylized and compressed in an attempt to render the intrinsic value, in much the same way as Rilke, in his book on Rodin, describes the function of the artist as 'to seek eternity in a given face, to separate the ageless from all that is transitory.' Unlike all other sculpture —statues in the round and reliefs—the reserve heads were left unpainted, from which it may be inferred that they were indeed only regarded as substitutes. Pl. 26

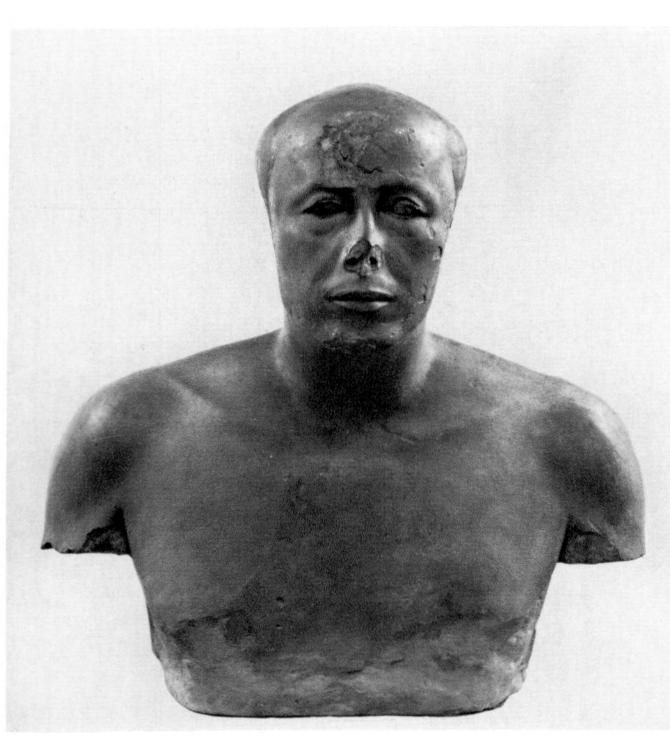

A special case among funerary sculptures is the bust of Prince Ankh-haf, now in Boston. It is polished on the lower edge and at the stubs of the arms, i.e. it is consciously worked as a bust, which hardly occurs elsewhere in Egyptian art. Ankh-haf was the husband of one of Cheops' daughters and thus belongs to the generation of Pl. 27

Pl. VIII Donkeys threshing. Limestone relief. Dynasty V, c. 2400 B.C. Width 44 cm. Rijksmuseum van Oudheden, Leyden.

King Chephren. This bust was discovered in an offering-room, built of brick, which adjoined his stone *mastaba* at Giza, and presumably once stood on a stone base. The limestone surface is covered with a layer of plaster and was painted reddish-brown. The ears and beard were added in plaster. The fact that plaster, which lent itself to modelling, was preferred to durable stone is in accordance with the trend towards a realistic style, which was achieved so impressively in the image of Ankh-haf. The bone structure of the skull and of the shoulders and chest is anatomically true. The folds of the eyelids, the pronounced lachrymal bags below the eyes, the lines between the nostrils and the corners of the mouth—all these features testify to keen observation of the subject's external appearance and to outstanding craftsmanship. To the viewer the Ankh-haf bust presents a person of character imbued with self-confidence and expressive vitality; it seems to be impregnated as much by spiritual potency as by the maturity of age.

In spite of these splendid attempts at naturalistic treatment, which characteristically enough occur less commonly with complete sculptures in the round than with busts and heads, which the Egyptians regarded as incomplete, future artists were to continue to represent the human image as timeless and impersonal. But there is no mistaking the fact that soon after the establishment of classical formal laws in Egyptian art, which were related to an ideal human image, progress was made towards the creation of a realistic likeness. In future artists were to move to and fro between these two poles, although the

commitment to the formal laws of the classical style always remains the criterion of artistic form.

By comparison with architecture and sculpture in the round, we have only relatively few examples of works in relief from the Pyramid Period. Of representations in the royal mortuary temples not much has survived. The blocks carved in relief from the royal mortuary temple at Dahshur are in a very poor state of preservation, so that they give a most imperfect impression of the subtle artistry with which they were executed. Another reason why so few reliefs are to be found, apart from the fortuitousness of survival and discovery, is the fact that the private tombs at Giza had no offering-rooms in which
Pl. vii, Cat. 44 representations could be erected. The dining-table scenes which were set into the outer face of the tombs' eastern wall show that the versatile artistic and technical achievements of Snefru's reign had led during that of Cheops to a well-established and austere style of relief work. With its clearly-marked division of the plane and the immobile austerity of its linear style, it conforms to the spirit of the Pyramid Period. Painting, too, follows a colour scheme which sets out from the natural model but does not keep to it unconditionally.

The great transformation which began with the transition from Dynasty IV to Dynasty V is indicated in a tale of the Papyrus Westcar.

The sons of Cheops entertain their father with tales of the magic deeds which took place in the times of Zoser and Snefru, as well as during his own reign. Prince Hardedef, who is the last to speak, relates the prophecy of the centenarian, the magician Dedi, who predicted the birth of a new dynasty. Cheops has this soothsayer brought to him and consults him about his magic deeds and the great hidden truth of the future, known only to Thoth, god of wisdom. The magician Dedi replies: 'O king, my lord, lo, it is not I that bring it thee... It is the eldest of the three children who are in the womb of Red-dedet. It is the wife of a priest of the sun-god Rē, that hath conceived three children of Rē... The eldest of them will be high priest in Heliopolis.' Then the text runs: 'Then his majesty's heart grew sad thereat. And Dedi said: "Pray, what is this mood, O king, my lord ? Is it because of the three children ? Then I say unto thee: thy son, his son, and then one of them..." '[3] This is followed by a description of the miraculous birth of the three children of the sun-god: Userkaf, Sahura and Kakai.

The historical core of this tale consists in the prophecy of a change of dynasty and the close link between the new dynasty and the sun-god Rē of Heliopolis, which was to bring about a significant change both in religion and in art. The royal names of Dynasty IV, which include that of the sun-god Rē, point to the fact that gradually the sun cult of Heliopolis came to hold a pre-eminent position. Chephren had already designated himself son of Rē, thus assuming a title which in the subsequent period was adopted firmly into the royal titulary.

The ancient concept, according to which the king was identified as a personification of the sky-god Horus, comes to be replaced by a new doctrine. According to the new interpretation the sun-god, in the guise of the king, begets with the queen the successor to the throne, who is thus regarded as the son of Rē. The king is now no longer the 'great god' on earth; as the son of a deity he may be superior to all other men but he is responsible to his divine father; his absolute autocratic power has been diminished. The divine authority proof against all criticism has had to give way to a sovereign with personal dignity and an ethical approach. The designation 'the kind god,' frequently employed on inscriptions, expresses this yearning for a human quality on the ruler's part.

The identification of the deceased king with the god Osiris gains in lucidity and consistency from this new

Pl. 28 The goddess of Diospolis Parva (7th Upper Egyptian nome). Detail of a limestone relief from the southern gallery of the mortuary temple of King Sahura at Abu Sir. Dynasty V, c. 2450 B.C. Height 53 cm., width 56 cm. Kestner Museum, Hanover.

Pl. 29 Presentation of gifts. Limestone relief with remains of paint. Dynasty V, c. 2450 B.C. Height 42 cm., width 86 cm. Kestner Museum, Hanover.

interpretation. As a god the king did not actually need any glorification; now as a human being he is exposed to death like all other mortals, and his resurrection becomes an event of great religious significance. The Osiris myth was thus in no way supplanted by the sun cult, but came to occupy a firm place in popular religious life. Now as before the most important desire of mortal men is for life after death, which is guaranteed to those who are granted a tomb by the king, with the funerary offerings that go with it.

This change in the concept of the divine nature of the pharaoh entailed sweeping alterations in all spheres of life, in government as well as in religious ideas. The relation between man and the gods had hitherto been one of fear and magic invocation. Man needed the mediation of the deified king in order to communicate with them. But the solar doctrine of Heliopolis is based upon great cosmic affinities. It is due to the sun-god Rē that nature is constantly renewed in the alternation of day and night and in the sequence of the seasons. The conditions which prevail on earth had to seem good and perfect, since Rē himself had created the world order, the *maat*, and preserved it by his generative power. The world beyond can only be similar to this world. This knowledge removed much of

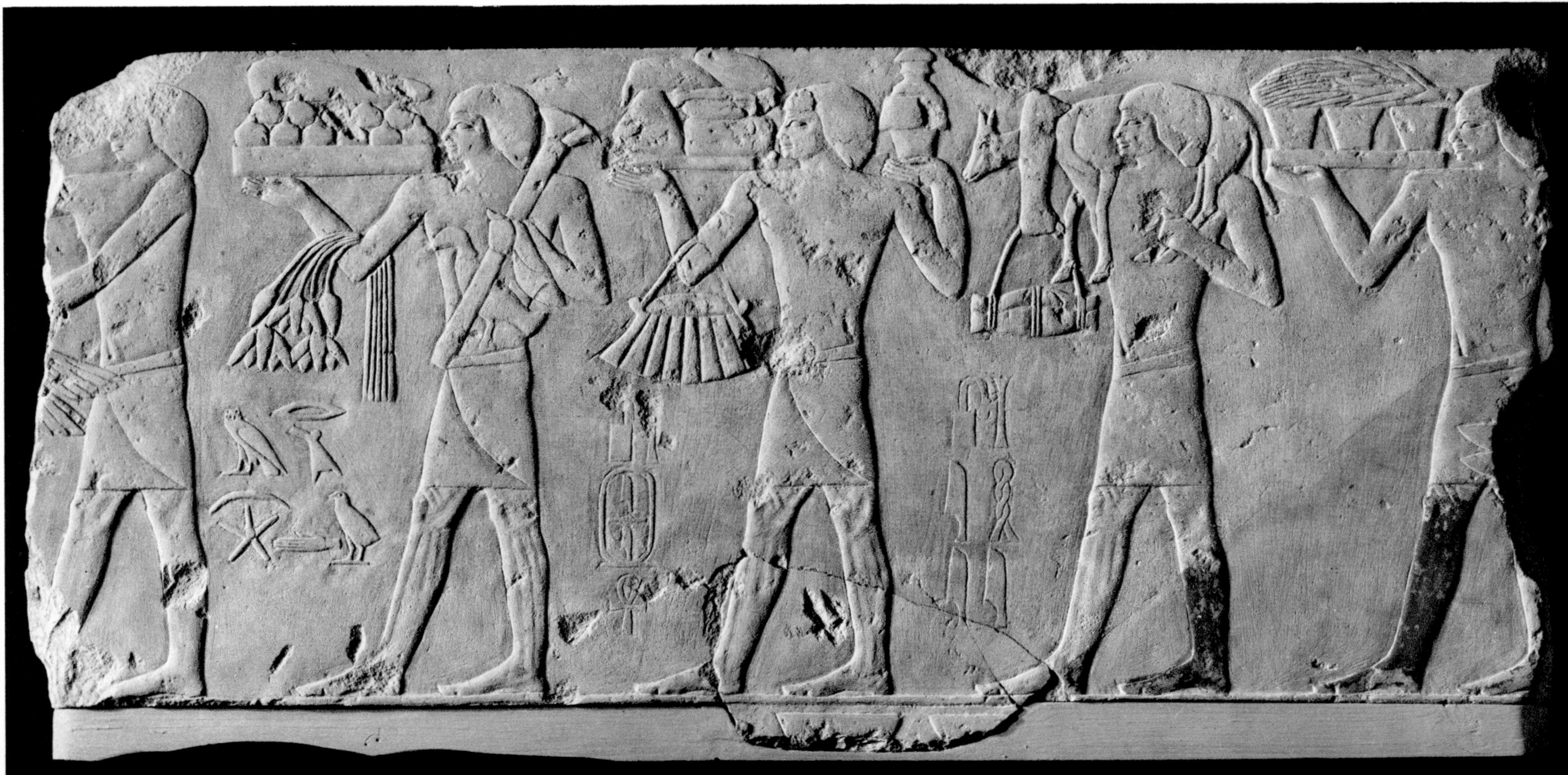

Pl. IX Unknown scribe. Painted limestone. From Saqqara. Dynasty V, c. 2420 B.C. Height 50 cm. Cairo Museum.

the fear of an uncertain life after death and brought a serene this-worldly character to the Egyptian outlook.

Linked with the worship of the sun-god, Rē, and the god of the dead, Osiris, are very varied concepts of the after-life which in many cases coexist and overlap. In both gods man finds analogies with his own individual destiny, with death and the hope of resurrection. The world beyond he seeks both in the sky, the realm of Rē, and below the earth, in the 'nether world,' with the god Osiris. He hopes to live in the 'Field of Rushes' in the east, where the sun-god Re appears in the morning, where the fields are so fertile and rich that no man knows want or suffering. Alternatively he hopes to traverse the sky in the sun-barque of Rē and to render him support in his battle against the demons as he passes across the nocturnal sky.

According to a different concept the realm of the dead is thought to be among the 'stars which never set' (circumpolar stars). The old belief in a land of the dead in the 'Goodly West' survives along with these ideas, which were introduced by the cosmological sun cult, just as man continued to believe that the dead lived on in the *ka* statues erected in tombs. The abstract and impersonal cast of thought gives way to a positive approach to life, rooted in an acceptance of the natural world, in which there is a place for the individual. Not only the king is expected to possess personal dignity and an ethical attitude to life; it is recognized that conduct based on ethical maxims is essential for the preservation of the divinely established order in state and society.

Biographical inscriptions and the so-called 'books of wisdom' contain instructions as to the conduct to be adopted in various situations by one who wishes to be held in esteem in this world and the beyond. The advice given in these books of wisdom is naturally not related to the development of a spiritual ethic, but mainly consists of

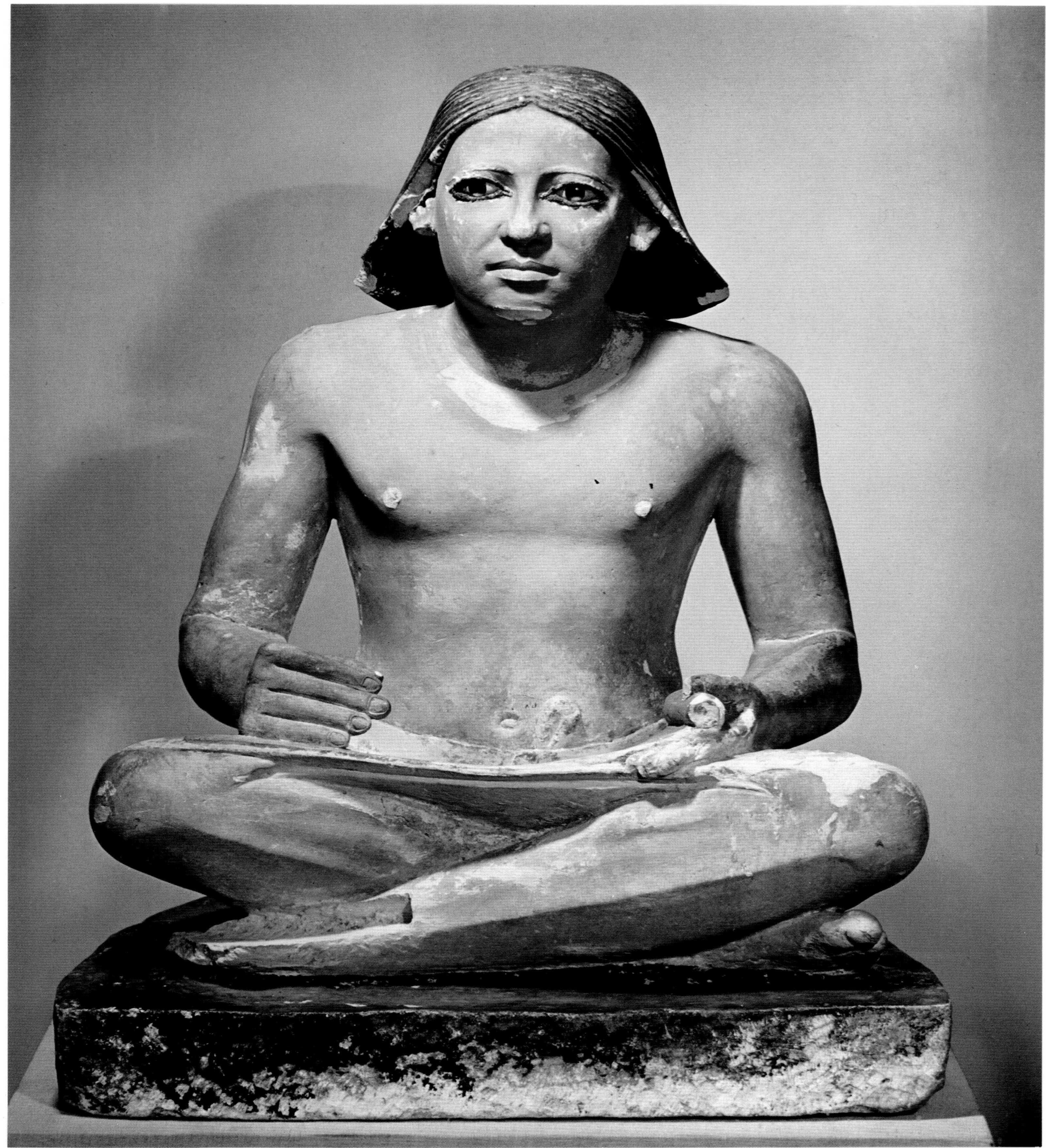

Pl. 30 Hunting hippopotamus in a thicket of papyrus. Detail from a limestone relief on the north wall of the offering-room in the tomb of Ti at Saqqara. Dynasty V, c. *2400 B.C.*

useful precepts for practical life. Ptah-hotep, vizier of King Isosi, enjoins his son as follows:

'If thou art a man in a leading position, be patient when thou hearkenest to the speech of a petitioner... Even if thou canst not fulfil his petition, a favourable audience gladdeneth the heart... If thou attainest greatness after thou wast small ... in a city that thou knowest, among men who know how thou once fared, then be not thrifty with thy riches, for they were given to thee as a gift of God.' In the fifth section of the book of wisdom we read the following: 'Great is *maat* and ever effective. It has remained undisturbed since the days of Osiris.' This concept of *maat*, of order, is the basis of wisdom: whoever shows understanding and adheres to these teachings is assured of esteem and success.

The transformation of the idea of sacrosanct kingship

Pl. 31 Craftsmen working at a wharf. Detail from a limestone relief in the tomb of Ti at Saqqara. Dynasty V, c. 2400 B.C.

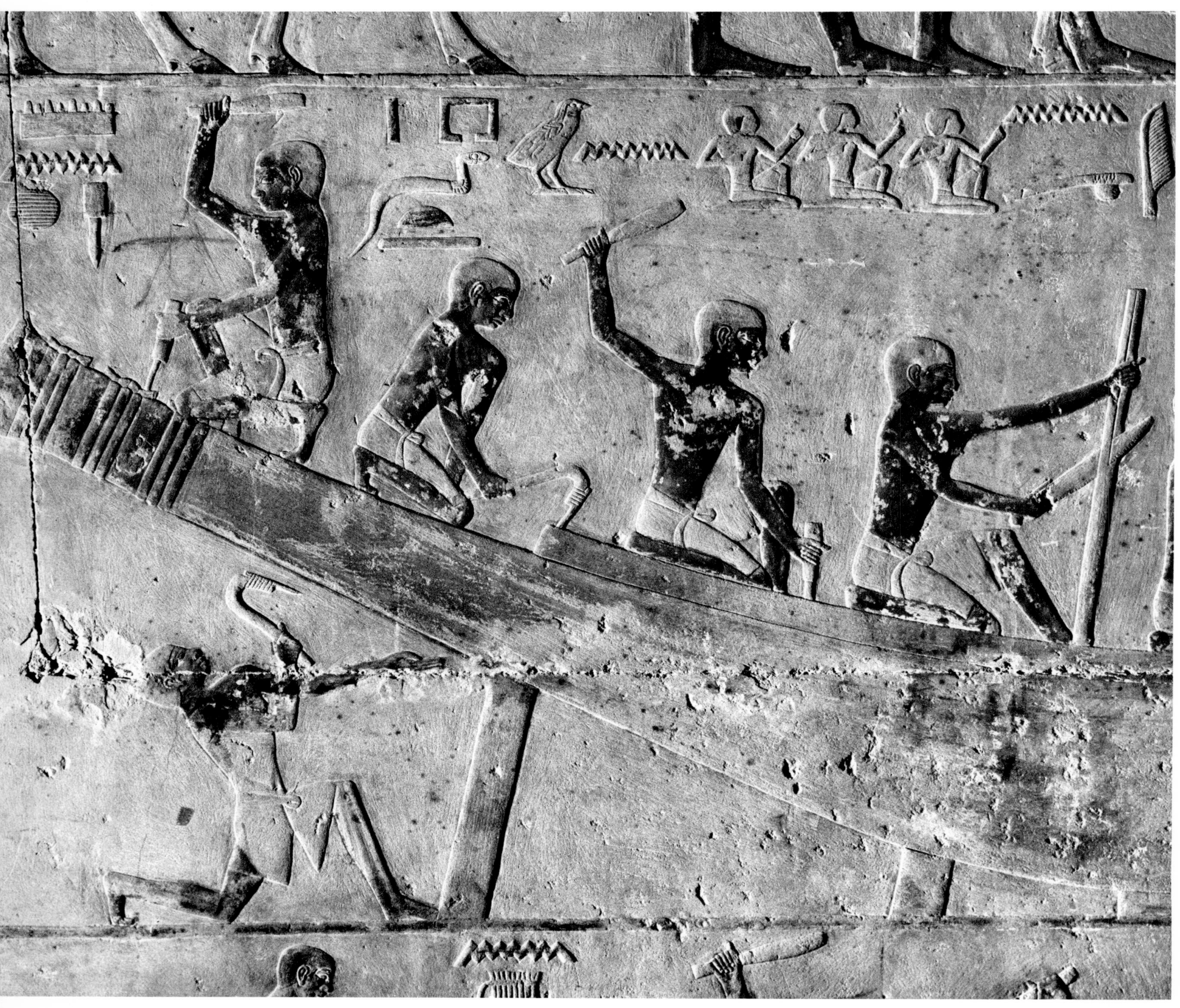

Pl. 32 Statue of Ranofer, high priest of Memphis. Painted limestone. From Saqqara. Dynasty V, c. 2460 B.C. Height 180 cm. Cairo Museum.

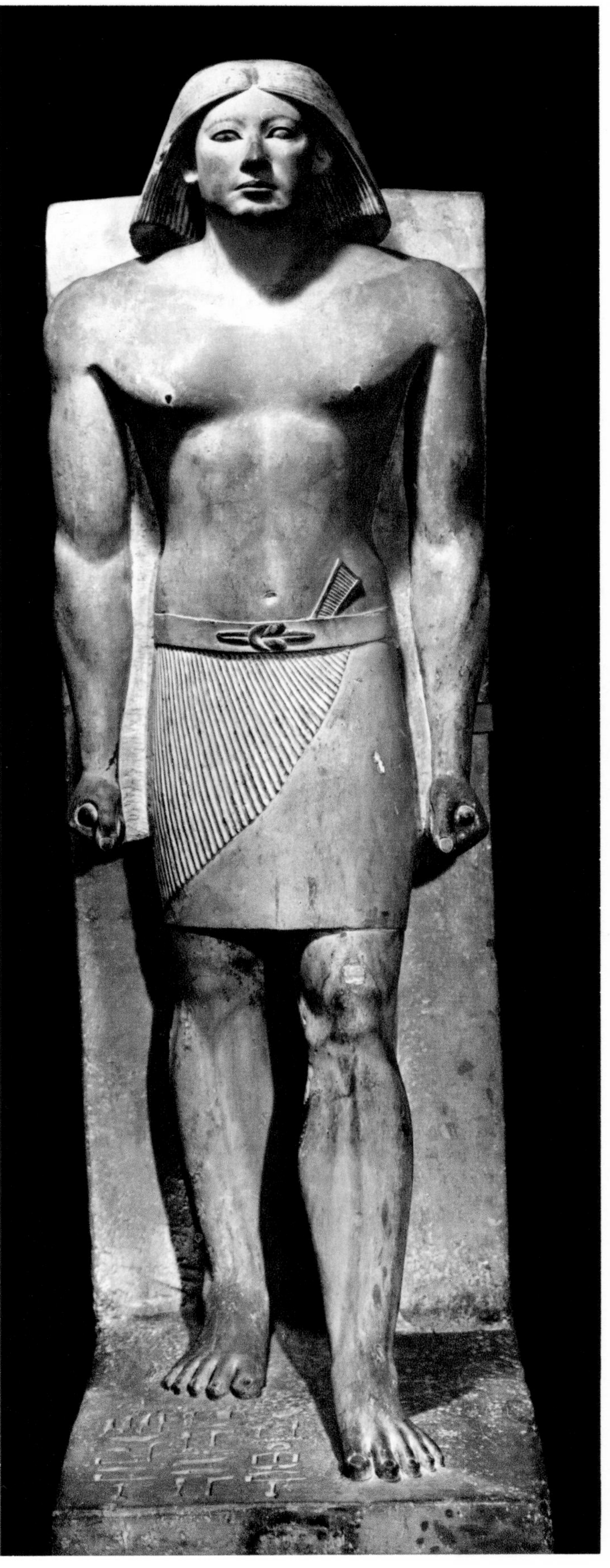

and the rise of the cosmological sun cult have an impact upon all spheres of activity. They also set new problems in art and architecture.

The tomb complexes of the sun kings are far more modest and human in their proportions than were those of the great pyramid-builders. Although they comprise the traditional valley-temple, causeway, mortuary temple and burial-chamber, in the architectural details the movement toward naturalistic forms makes itself plainly felt. Pillars are superseded by columns which imitate in stylized form and vivid colours papyrus plants, lotus-blossoms or palm-fronds. In the court of the mortuary temple of Sahura, for example, palmiform columns in red granite rise up from the black basalt floor. On the walls are gaily-coloured reliefs giving a cheerful picture of the terrestrial world: they portray the king in the company of the gods, performing ritual acts, or triumphing over traditional enemies, Nubians, Libyans and Asiatics, who are tellingly identified by their costume and facial features. These are not pictures of some unique battle, but a demonstration of the king's power to conquer the foes of Egypt.

In the hunting scenes the game is distributed here and there over the surface. The terrain is depicted as an undulating landscape, in which grow various plants. The natural setting in which the scene takes place is incorporated into the picture. A delight in the variety and multiformity of natural phenomena inspires the artists of this generation, who succeed in merging this world and the world beyond into a single unity, in a free and unconstrained manner.

The temple of the god Rē at Heliopolis has not been preserved, but the sun temples of Sahura and Niuserra at Abu Sir, which were no doubt modelled upon it, convey an idea of the temples that were erected to Rē. The tripartite layout conforms to that of the royal tomb complexes. From the valley-temple a causeway leads up to

Pl. 33 Head of a statue of Ranofer, high priest at Memphis. Painted limestone. From Saqqara. Dynasty V, c. 2460 B.C. Overall height 185 cm. Cairo Museum.

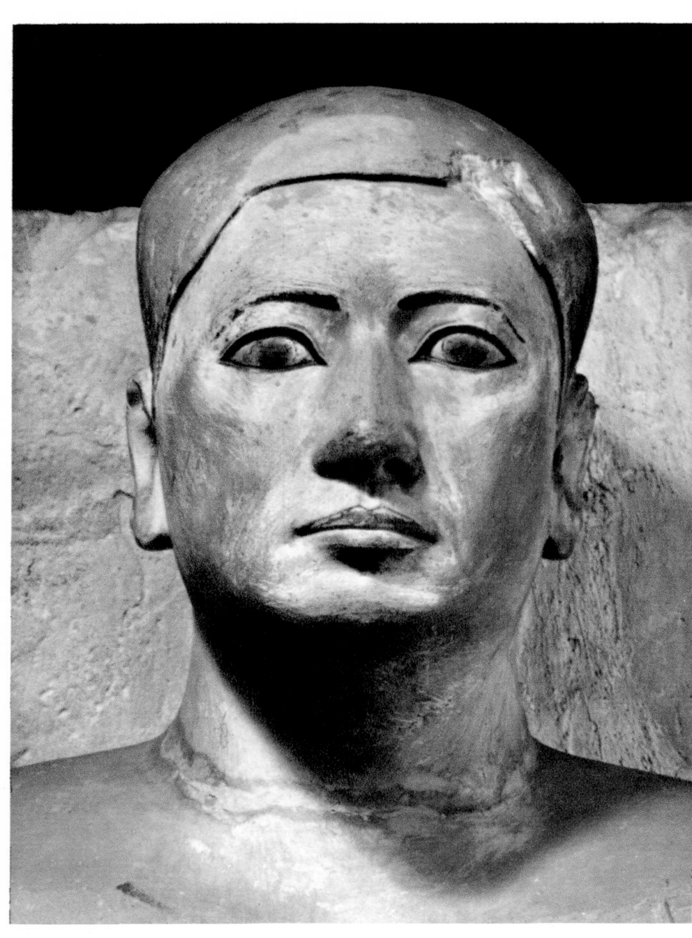

the ritual temple, which has the shape of an open court, where a huge obelisk stood on a plinth. Its tip was gilded and gleamed in the sun, visible to all from afar off, telling of the life and light that come from the sun-god. In front of it stood an altar of alabaster. On the walls lively Pl. 28
reliefs painted in delicate colours depicted the world of nature in the different seasons, which according to the Heliopolis doctrine was kept eternally young and fresh by the sun-god Rē, in conformity with the rhythm of cosmic forces. Outside the temple complex of Niuserra was a huge boat, built of brick, a rendering of the barque in which the sun-god Rē traverses the horizon.

The changed outlook of Egyptians in Dynasty V is reflected, just as clearly as in the royal monuments, in the numerous lavishly-furnished tombs of officials at Saqqara. The offering-room, which from the end of Dynasty IV onward had been transferred back into the interior of the tomb, is decorated with reliefs depicting man's earthly existence in an exuberant sequence of scenes. The life-sized statues of the occupant of the tomb give an indication of the growing esteem and importance enjoyed by the courtiers and aristocratic officials. In addition to the traditional renderings of funerary offerings there occur Pl. 29, Cat. 45
scenes which depict agriculture, hunting or various stages in the work of craftsmen.

It is no longer a matter of representing a situation, the terrestrial world as it is, but of rendering the human actions which shape it. Unique events, however, are depicted, if only extremely seldom; they occur for the first time toward the end of Dynasty V. Generally speaking, the motifs are taken from the everyday world and with their Cat. 46
rich variety afford an insight into the Egyptian life of the period. The occupant of the tomb is only an observer of these stirring scenes and does not take part in them. The concept of an eternal life for the deceased is linked with that of the fullness of life on earth to give the effect of an

Pl. X Statue of Methethy. Wood coated with painted plaster. From Saqqara. Dynasty V, c. 2420 B.C. Height 61.5 cm. Brooklyn Museum, New York.

actuality that is timeless and everlasting. Hitherto in reliefs the individual figures had been arranged in a row, without any correlation to each other; now, with the rendering of action, it is necessary to relax the strict laws governing style. The persons who are shown partici-
Cat. 55, 57 pating in some common activity are combined to form a group. Occasionally foreshortening or overlapping are required in order to render the typical posture adopted when performing some task. The figures are sometimes set in front of or behind one another. In the well-known
Pl. 30, 31, Cat. 58 tombs of Ti and Ptah-hotep at Saqqara we have reliefs of subtlety and delicacy. The animated realm of nature, of
Pl. VIII animals and of men engaged in some kind of activity, embodies what is characteristic in each case, and can thus fulfil its function in the tomb as a representation of timeless existence. In spite of the varied repertoire of motifs and the differentiated renderings of detail, the pictures have an ageless quality.

Although only a few specimens of royal sculpture have
Pl. 23 survived from Dynasty V, a number of fine sculptures in the round from private tombs convey an impression of the way the human image was viewed during this period. With the decentralization of the administration the court officials had gained in importance. The personal responsibility which they assumed in public life gave them a self-
Pl. 32, 33 confident air such as we encounter in Fifth-Dynasty private sculpture. The two standing figures of the high priest of Memphis, Ranofer, follow in regard to motif and structure the classical stylistic laws governing Egyptian free-standing sculpture. The alert, intelligent eyes and the noble seriousness of the features express his lofty and self-confident attitude, which accords with the seniority of the office he holds but also gives an insight into the subject's personality.

Already during the Zoser period the scribe had been one of the most highly respected officials at court. To

Pl. 34 Cattle on their way to slaughter. Detail from a limestone relief in the tomb of Mereruka. Dynasty VI, c. *2300 B.C.*

Pl. 35 Registration of taxes. Detail from a limestone relief in the tomb of Mereruka at Saqqara. Dynasty VI, c. *2300 B.C.*

portray him a particular scheme was evolved. He is shown seated cross-legged on a plinth, holding the papyrus scroll upon his knees. In the feudal society of Dynasty V the scribe was more than at any other time a member of the intellectual élite, and high-ranking courtiers and princes took a delight in having themselves portrayed as scribes. Thus this motif now attains its final form, one which survived until the Late Period with minor modifications that reflected subsequent stylistic development. * Pl. IX Although in their general outline the scribe statuettes appear more animated than the standing and seated figures, their structure is nevertheless basically geometric. The crossed legs resting upon the plinth constitute the base of the equilateral triangle in which the sculpture is conceived as resting. The squared-off arms, detached from the body, continue to be contained within the pyramid form, the

Pl. 36 Last Judgment. Detail from the 'Book of the Dead' compiled for the woman Nehemes-ra-taui. Papyrus. 6th cent. B.C. Kestner Museum, Hanover.

top of which is formed by the scribe's head. His erect torso is elaborately modelled; in his left hand he holds the papyrus scroll and in his right the reed-pen. The facial expression suggests spiritual tension and a power of critical observation. The animated piercing look of the eyes, which were indicated by inlaid paste or paint of a strongly
* Cat. 20, 21 contrasting colour, conveys the impression of a shrewd and worldly-wise individual. The head is, for example, not inclined over the scroll, as would have accorded with the activity in which scribes engaged, as it would have been if a realistic likeness had been sought after. In spite of the characteristic features and the attributes, in the last analysis the motif of the scribe is a scheme, a formula designating the professional class of scribes in general.

Statue groups are also now found more frequently in private tombs. Quite often not only are husband and wife

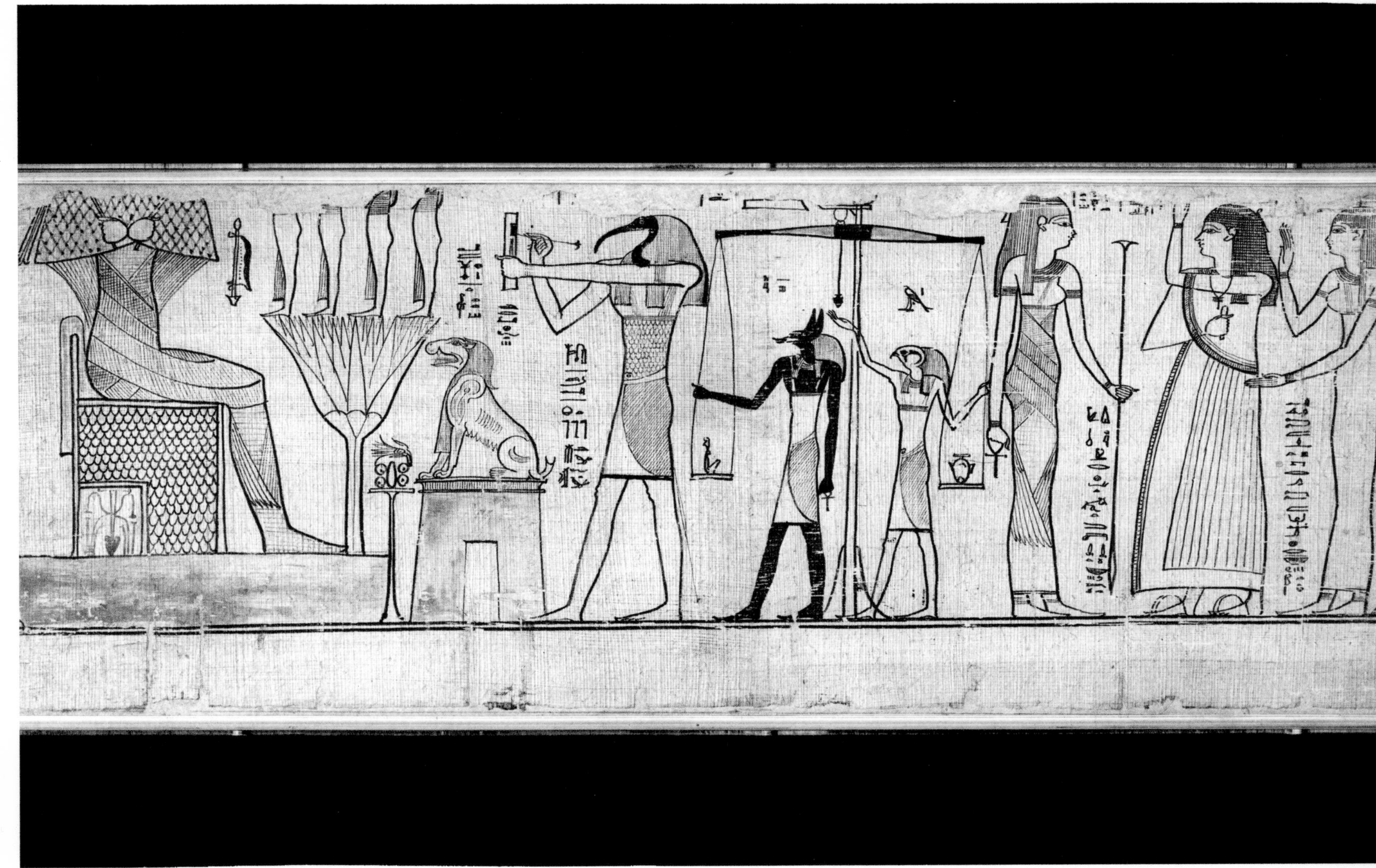

Pl. 37 Statuette of Meryra-hashtef. Wood. From Sedment. Dynasty VI, c. 2200 B.C. Height 51 cm. British Museum, London.

portrayed side by side, either standing or seated, but children as well are incorporated into the composition, which thus acquires a more exuberant and animated character, both in outline and in the details.

In conformity with the rich repertoire of motifs and lively style of relief art, we have a variety of types in sculpture. In both fields, however, artists were endeavouring to develop a style which would do justice to the requirements both of outer appearance and of inner content.

Toward the end of Dynasty V noticeable changes take place in political and religious life which indicate that the Old Kingdom is entering its final phase. The last two kings, Unas and Isosi, did not erect any temples to the sun-god Rē. Their tombs are in the ancient city of Saqqara, where their successors, the rulers of Dynasty VI, also erected their pyramids.

On the walls of their burial-chambers they had carved the formulae used in the funerary rites. These so-called 'Pyramid texts' are the most important and also the most ancient collection of religious spells. Perhaps the turbulent times made the king doubt whether the burial rites and cult ceremonies would be carried out in a proper and orderly manner. Thus the formulae which were necessary for his glorification were to surround his last resting-place, to ensure that he would live for ever, whatever priests and succeeding generations might do.

At this time the central power of the monarchy recedes more and more into the background. Political and social disorders gradually bring about a collapse. In the provinces the nomarchs develop political ambitions, attain more power, and make themselves independent of the royal residence. Characteristically enough, Pepi I married two daughters of the powerful nomarch of Abydos in order to strengthen his dynasty. His sons, Merenra and Pepi II, were the offspring of these alliances. The weakening of the formerly rigid centralized administration had an effect upon economic life and trade; there were famines which led to unrest; authority and law were called in question; the royal pyramids and the burial-chambers of the wealthy were plundered and destroyed. Literary texts describe the * Pl. 36 chaos which ensued when the old order collapsed, and convey a shattering impression of the despair and uncertainty which men felt. They began to doubt the divine nature of the king and the divine order of the world, and so brought into question faith in the gods and in life after death.

A dialogue between a man tired of life and his soul contains the following passage:

'Buildings were put up of granite stone / and halls erected as pyramids, / executed with fine workmanship, / and the builders became gods. / Their offering-tables are empty, as are those of the tired; / who passed away on the dykes without descendants /—the flood takes its share, the heat another—/with whom the fish of the shore hold converse.'[4]

In coming to grips with these profoundly moving problems man was led to express in words his innermost ideas. A lyric poetry develops which stands in contrast to the formalism of biographical inscriptions and funerary texts, * Pl. 34, 35, Cat. 48 and gives voice to the spiritual and emotional response which this period of decline evokes:

'Bodies pass away and others remain / since the time of them that were before, / the gods that were aforetime rest in their pyramids. / What are their habitations ? / Their walls are destroyed. / Their habitations are no more, / as if they had never been.'[5]

The joyful belief in an order created by the sun-god himself, in a world that is continually renewed, gives way to ideas of a world beyond in which many dangers lie hidden, and which man must overcome. The decline of royal power also undermines belief in the divinity of the pharaoh, who had hitherto been the mediator between man and the gods. Now it is seen as the task of the individual to establish a relationship with the gods. The individual assumes political as well as religious responsibilities. Under the impact of the transitoriness of worldly things an ethic develops which views human life as governed by fate and the god Osiris as a righteous judge, who adjudicates men not according to their wealth or success but according to their deeds. Like Osiris, who withstands the accusations of Seth in the court of the gods and is vindicated as 'true of speech', he hopes to be judged impartially at the end of his days on earth. When face to face with this judge of the dead, his ethical attitude will make him an Osiris, one who is vindicated and enters into eternal life. The claim to be magically transmuted into an Osiris finds expression in inscriptions, where the name of Osiris is placed before that of the deceased.

During Dynasty V and during the period of transition to the new dynasty the tombs of officials at Saqqara become ramified complexes with a large number of rooms and courts. They no longer comprise merely chambers necessary for burial and the ritual acts associated with this, but afford space for all members of the family, like a house for the living. The Sixth-Dynasty tomb of the vizier Mereruka, for example, has thirty-two rooms, lavishly decorated with relief panels which, however, cannot match in subtlety and perfection those of the Fifth-Dynasty style.

The uncertainty of the times, which made an orderly performance of the funerary rite appear doubtful, led to an instructive modification in the layout of private tombs. The offering-room disappears completely and its function is taken over by reliefs on the walls of the sarcophagus-chamber, which feature the deceased provided with the gifts he needs in the after-life. In addition to these servant figures and models are placed in the tomb. It may be that the offering-room was abandoned, not only on account of the general uncertainty of the times, but also because

Pl. 38 Queen Ankhnes-Meryra with her son Pepi II. Alabaster. Dynasty VI, c. 2300 B.C. Height 39 cm. Brooklyn Museum, New York.

doubts arose as to the actual effectiveness of the funerary offering.

The age of the palatial tombs of officials is now past and the nobles have gone over to the practice of erecting their burial-places in their own native nomes, far from the royal residence. The necropolises built during the flourishing period of the Old Kingdom in the area of Qaw-el-Kebir and Naga-ed-Deir are unpretentious in appearance. The Sixth-Dynasty tombs near Dendera, for example, are built mainly of brick. The physical setting in Upper and Middle Egypt required a completely different architectonic treatment of the tomb than the *mastaba*, for which there was ample space in the endless desert plateau of Lower Egypt. Gradually the tombs came to be sited in rocky cliff-faces. The chamber hewn out of the rock serves as an offering-room, and a shaft leads from it into the sarcophagus-chamber. The development of the rock-cut tomb was to be a pointer to the later period, when the nomarchs had consolidated their independent power.

In the tombs of the nomarchs of Elephantine at Meir, El Bersha and Asyut the evolution of the rock-cut tomb can be followed from the end of the Old Kingdom into the Middle Kingdom.

We can assess the changes in the style of free-standing sculpture during this troubled period from a number of informative specimens which have survived. In some of these the rigid rules of classical form continue to be applied—as in the seated statuette of King Pepi I, ★ Cat. 13 a modification of the motif of the Chephren statue—whereas others show clear traces of the disintegration of the spiritual world from which they sprang. A statuette now in Brooklyn depicts Pepi I in a kneeling posture, ★ Cat. 14 so illustrating the subjection of the ruler to the gods. The smoothness of the green stone accentuates the rigid facial features, which no longer express the noble dignity of the pharaoh or have any spiritual content. One alabaster statuette

Pl. 38 portrays Pepi II as a child in the lap of his mother, a
Pl. 37 daughter of the nomarch of Abydos. Wooden statuettes
from tombs in the residential necropolis or from nomarchs'
tombs in the provinces suggest that works of sculpture
varied greatly in quality at this time. Alongside figures of
excellent workmanship, which combined a vigorous
conception with the balanced formal language of ancient
tradition, there were mannered works which retained the
external form but had lost their spiritual content. The
Cat. 37, 38 large number of servant figurines are of no particular
significance. They are depicted as engaged in variety of
actions, as bakers, brewers of beer, or potters.

They reflect a tentative groping after new solutions as
well as a fresh and vigorous inventiveness. Toward the
Cat. 39 end of the Old Kingdom they are superseded by wooden
models which represent entire cattle-yards or groups of
soldiers, and resemble doll's houses.

Looked at as a whole, it becomes clear that at the close of the Old Kingdom, as the spiritual content disappears from funerary art, so also artistic power begins to flag. In the subsequent period, which we refer to as the First Intermediate Period, the names of numerous kings have survived who are accounted as belonging to Dynasties VII and VIII. The dissolution of the state gave rise to revolutionary conditions, especially in Lower Egypt. In Upper Egypt the nomarchs of Abydos and Coptos were able to unite parts of the country under their hegemony. The nomarchs of Herakleopolis are mentioned in the king-lists as the rulers of Dynasties IX and X. The area over which they held sway comprised Lower and Middle Egypt, while Upper Egypt retained its independence under the leadership of the princely house of Thebes. The conflicts between these two mighty dynasties were resolved by a victory of the Thebans. Under Mentuhotep I the entire country was once again united under a single sovereign. With his reign a new epoch begins in Egyptian history.

PHARAOH - MAN AND GOD

THE MIDDLE KINGDOM

The claim of the Theban nomarchs to the throne of the pharaohs had to be asserted in a bitter struggle against the ruling dynasty of Herakleopolis which ruled over Lower and Middle Egypt. Like his antagonist, the Theban prince Antef I bore a royal title as early as about 2130 B.C., although his power hardly extended beyond the Theban nome. He appears in the later king-lists as the founder of Dynasty XI. During the reign of his brother, Antef II, and the latter's son, Antef III, it gradually became possible to extend the area under Theban sway, but it was not until about 2040 B.C. that Mentuhotep I could conquer Herakleopolis and exercise dominion over the entire country. During the Old Kingdom the pharaohs had won legitimation and exercised absolute power by virtue of their divine nature. The political and spiritual atmosphere at he beginning of the Middle Kingdom was, however, very different. The pharaoh could plead neither divine nor royal origin. He owed his position as ruler exclusively to his military superiority and his personal talent for diplomacy, which had enabled him to check the power of the nomarchs, who had enjoyed virtual independence for over two hundred years, or to enrol them into his service. On the other hand the social revolution that had taken place at the close of the Old Kingdom and during the First Intermediate Period had produced a self-confident middle class which took an active part in political life. If it could be won over for the interests of the crown, it could become a more reliable support for the dynasty than the provincial aristocracy, who clung to their ancient inherited rights.

During the Middle Kingdom the new state could for the first time rely for protection upon a small regular army as a special royal guard for the king. In the course of establishing a powerful centralized administration there came into being at the royal residence a new aristocracy of officials who gradually gained in esteem and importance.

Years of disruption and lack of political leadership made it urgent, not only to solve these internal political tasks, but also to consolidate the state externally. From the Archaic Period onward foreign policy had been determined to a greater or lesser extent by the need to supply the country with essential raw materials. The frontiers did not have to be defended against large-scale attack by neighbours, nor did the Egyptians have any aspirations to world-wide power which might have led them into major wars. The superiority of the Egyptian political system and of its culture *vis-à-vis* those of adjacent states, sustained by religious notions, led to the view that Egypt was, as it were, 'God's own country,' possessed of absolute power and incontestable rights. Egypt's political and philosophical self-sufficiency meant that external influences could have only limited effect.

The foreign policy objectives of the Middle Kingdom were at first, just as in earlier times, the strategic protection of its borders by building fortifications and the maintenance of access to vital sources of raw materials in Sinai; only in the south did it become necessary to undertake active intervention. In Nubia the balance of power had shifted during the First Intermediate Period. A tribal group settled on the Third Nile Cataract, near Kerma, had driven the Nubians northwards to the Egyptian border. A counter-attack was mounted which drove the troublesome invaders back from the southern frontier and subjugated the area as far as the Third Nile Cataract.

Commercial and economic life was limited in the main to the import of timber from the Lebanon and expeditions to Punt, the land of fragrant incense on the east coast of Africa, and to the quarries at Wadi Hammamat. The relationship with neighbouring states in the east under-

Pl. 39 King Mentuhotep II. Detail. Painted sandstone. From Thebes, Deir el-Bahari. Dynasty XI, c. 2000 B.C. Overall height 183 cm. Cairo Museum (cf. Cat. 2).

went a radical change during the Middle Kingdom. As we know from Egyptian finds in the area of Minoan culture, commercial relations were carried on with Crete, which proceeded as peacefully as those between Egypt and Palestine. Finds have been made in Egypt of objects from Crete and also of precious vessels from Mesopotamia. In the temple of Mont near Tod, not far from Thebes, cylinder seals from Dynasty III at Ur have been unearthed. These far-reaching ties with neighbouring countries in the Near East and Mediterranean brought the Egyptians into contact with other highly developed civilizations. Their autochthonous systems of government, religion and art were bound to widen the Egyptians' own intellectual horizons and to influence their outlook on the world. The delight which they took in exploring this variegated new world is evident from the accounts they have left of journeys and expeditions, which convey the element of adventure inseparable from the conquest of foreign parts. Thus a shipwrecked person relates the following:

'I had set out for the mines of the Sovereign and gone to sea in a ship one hundred and twenty cubits in length and forty cubits in breadth; and therein were one hundred and twenty sailors, of the pick of Egypt... A storm burst while we were yet at sea, before we could reach the land. The force of the wind caused a whirlpool. One wave was eight cubits high... The ship perished, and of those that were in it not one survived. I was cast on to an island by a wave of the sea, and I spent three days alone with my heart as my (only) companion. I slept under the shelter of a tree and embraced the shade. Then I lifted up my feet in order to find out what I could put into my mouth. I found figs and vines there and all manner of fine vegetables, kau-fruit together with nekut-fruit and cucumbers... There were fish there and fowl, and there was nothing that was not upon (that island). I satisfied myself and put the rest aside, for it was too much for my

Pl. XI Cow and calf. Wall-painting from the tomb of Itimisure at Gebelein. Dynasty XI, c. 2000 B.C. Height 54 cm., width 80 cm. Museo Egizio, Turin.

hands. When I had made myself a fire-drill, I kindled a fire and made a burnt offering for the gods.' [6]

During the First Intermediate Period religious dogma receded into the background in favour of a direct relationship between man and the gods, based upon ethical principles of conduct. With the decline of belief in divine kingship and the emergence of a middle class which enjoyed status and esteem, there naturally arose an equalization of the chances for men to maintain a relationship with the gods and to achieve an after-life. It was no longer

sufficient to furnish one's tomb; one secured from the king the right to erect a statue of oneself in the temple so that one might be near the god, and partake in the ritual ceremonies in the temple.

Hitherto it had been reserved to the king to share in death the fate of Osiris and to rise from the dead as the god had done; now everyone endeavoured by magic practices to become an Osiris. People sought to be buried at Abydos, where the tomb of the god Osiris was believed to be, or at least to journey once in a lifetime to this sacred place and to erect a stele there. According to ancient magic belief the image of the deceased and the mention of his name ensured for him the privilege of proximity to and blessing by the great god of the dead; so, too, did participation in mystery plays at his tomb. In the inscription on his stele the deceased introduces himself as a man of noble sentiments who has performed good deeds during his life. He asks the passer-by to say a prayer and at the end of the inscription refers to himself as an Osiris, one who has been vindicated and blessed. As is so often the case in Egyptian religious history, genuine piety and
* Pl. 43 spiritual or philosophical thought, including the ethical code that this implied, are superseded by magic beliefs.

The concept of a 'last judgment' also underwent a characteristic transformation during the Middle Kingdom. In the presence of the judge of the dead a catalogue of bad and shameful deeds is drawn up and the deceased confirms that he has not committed them. With such 'negative confessions' of guilt the sense of personal responsibility once again recedes into the background. The judgment of eternity becomes a ceremony. The confession takes its course according to fixed rules of the game and exoneration follows, as it had done earlier, from recognition of the deceased's magic powers. During Dynasty V the god Rē had held sway over heaven and earth, and had also fulfilled the office of judge of the dead; now it is the ancient god Osiris who takes over this function and exercises power over the realm of the dead.

The Egyptian's relationship to supernatural forces is perhaps reflected most distinctly in the coexistence of two great religions which derived their origin from very different spiritual ideas. In the last analysis worship of the sun-god Rē shows that the concept of a great god of the cosmos is alive. His image encourages abstract thinking. But Rē is a god of the living; the god Osiris, in his mythological interpretation, had a much stronger attraction for those who sought a belief in the beyond. Right up to the Late Period the realm of the beyond remained linked with the Osiris myth—even at times when people's outlook on life was predominantly intellectual.

The new dynasty which had tackled its political tasks so energetically at home and abroad also soon developed an intense activity in the building of temples. Unfortunately only little of this has survived. Later generations replaced the edifices of the Middle Kingdom by larger and more spectacular complexes, in which blocks of stone from demolished temples were often used again as building material. Remains of royal tombs are likewise sparse, but this loss is offset by the mortuary temple complex of Mentuhotep II, which provides information about the new architectonic style. His tomb, erected in the cleft of Deir el-Bahari, on the western bank of the river at Thebes, combines the idea of the pyramid tomb with that of the rock-cut tomb, such as was developed by the Upper Egyptian nomarchs from the close of the Old Kingdom, and makes allowances for the physical setting in this southern mountainous region. This return to the Old Kingdom form of royal tomb expresses the rulers' claim to be the successors of the god-kings of the Pyramid Period.

By means of a broad causeway one enters the forecourt of the tomb, which is closed off at the western end by two

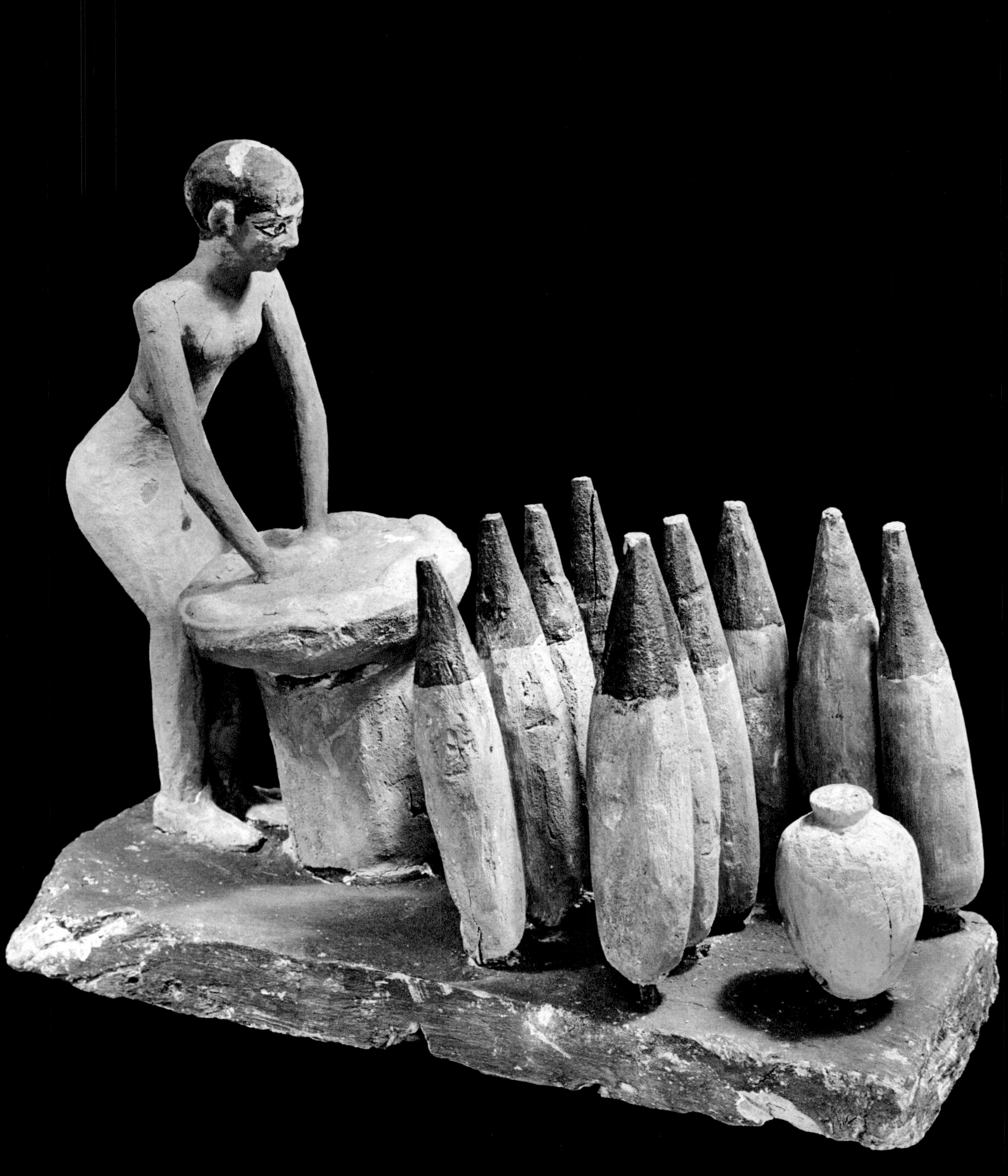

Pl. 40 Brewer. Wooden model. From Asyut. Dynasty XI, c. 2000 B.C. Length 35.5 cm. British Museum, London.

Pl. 41 King Mentuhotep III and the goddess Uto. Detail. Limestone relief from Armant. Dynasty XI, c. 1995 B.C. Height 81 cm., overall width 130 cm. Brooklyn Museum, New York (cf. Cat. 40).

colonnades, from the middle of which a ramp leads to a terrace and the mortuary temple proper. The pyramid rose above this main room of the temple, a great hall containing one hundred and forty octagonal pillars and surrounded on three sides by pillared porticoes. To the west is an adjoining small court with access to the burial-chamber, located in the rocky cliff. In a chamber exactly beneath the centre of the pyramid was discovered a seated statue of King Mentuhotep wearing the crown of Lower Egypt. This points to the fact that the ancient tradition was resumed whereby, in addition to the royal tomb proper, a second one was erected which was not used. Another pillared hall and the funerary chapel are built into the cliff-face.

In spite of numerous echoes of ancient traditions, the architectonic form of the mortuary temple evidences a fundamental transformation of spiritual concepts, which is reflected in a new style of architecture. The proportions of the tomb complex are modest by comparison with those of the Pyramid Period. In lieu of the abstract monumentality of compact rooms and forms we have bold and precise articulation by arrangements of pillars, which serve both to let the sunlight into the sacred temple halls and to provide access for visitors so that they may observe the rites performed there. The steeply rising mountains which provide a backcloth to the mortuary temple enhance the impression one gains that the scale of the architecture does not exceed limits that man can live with, so to speak. Thus the Mentuhotep temple is the expression of a period in which man shaped his own life on his own responsibility as an individual. The splendid monumentality and abstract austerity of the Pyramid Period, which sprang from the notion of divine kingship, is superseded by an architectural style which makes allowances for the changed political and religious atmosphere. Simple clarity of style and elaborately balanced propor-

Pl. XII Woman bringing gifts. Painted wood. From Drukan near Asyut. Dynasty XI, c. 2000 B.C. Height 52.8 cm. Kestner Museum, Hanover.

tions are the characteristic features of Middle Kingdom architecture.

The tombs of the new court aristocracy of Dynasty XI were built in the cliffs surrounding the mortuary temple of Mentuhotep II. Access to them is gained by a causeway leading up to the entrance, sometimes accentuated by a pillared portico. The tomb proper consists of a corridor, decorated with reliefs, terminating in a chapel which contains the funerary statue of the deceased. A shaft leads to the burial-chamber below.

The nomarchs, who were able to retain a certain amount of independence until the middle of Dynasty XII, from the close of the Old Kingdom onward had themselves buried in their native nomes. Their tombs are an informative contribution to the art history of the Middle Kingdom. They correspond to the spirit of the age both in the rhythmic proportion of the sequence of rooms and in the sense of harmony evident in the arrangement of the architectural members. The astonishing variety between the individual tombs is explained by the isolation of these provincial areas, where there was little interest in the creation of a new style, and where people were content either to continue the traditions of the end of the Old Kingdom or else gradually to develop singular local features.

In pictorial art the change in artistic style is manifest most strikingly in works of sculpture. Apart from the fact that a relatively large number of statues and statuettes have survived from the Middle Kingdom, sculpture in the round is the artistic form which expresses most compellingly the spirit of the age.

The sculpture of the Pyramid Period, in the seclusion of royal mortuary temples and the statue-chambers of private tombs, had embodied the deceased's claim to eternal life. As timeless ideal images they had offered an abode for the *ka*, the immortal second ego of the subject. Likewise royal temple sculpture, which served to represent

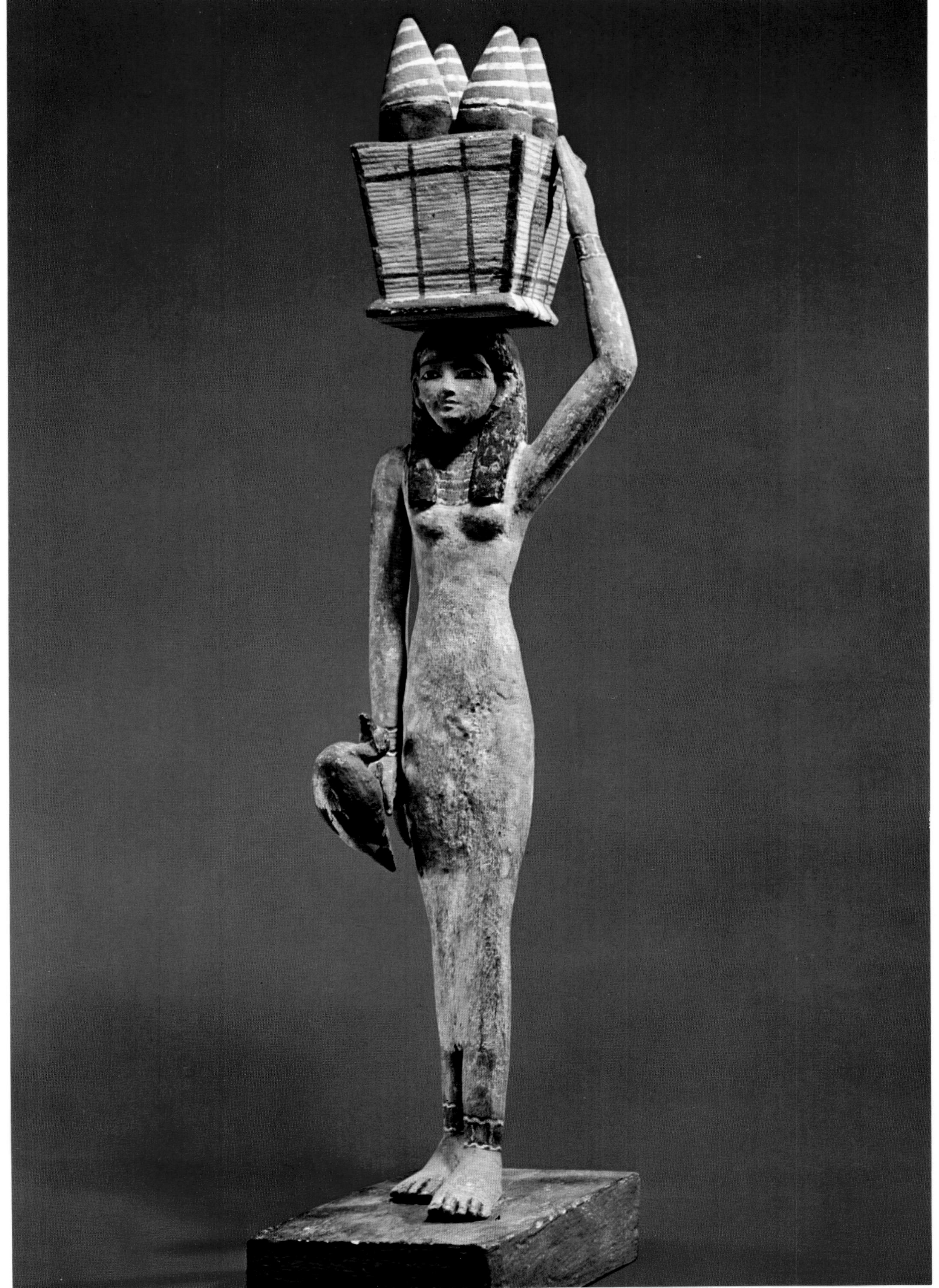

the sovereign at festivals, had an exclusively ritual purpose. Neither in making it nor in erecting it was any consideration given to the effect it would produce upon a viewer.

Toward the close of the Old Kingdom the approximation of the artistic form to natural appearance with all its * Pl. 39, Cat. 2 fortuitous features had made for a gradual relaxation of the strict formal canon and had thus opened the way to the rendering of specific qualities of individual groups of people. This showed that free-standing statues were becoming to an ever greater extent personal monuments to the deceased which made allowances for the effect upon the viewer.

In the Middle Kingdom this change in the meaning of free-standing statues was taken to its logical conclusion. Besides funerary sculpture there is royal temple sculpture, which has an unequivocally memorial character, both from the standpoint of its style and in regard to the way it was erected. The royal statues, which are larger than life, are placed in temple courts flooded by light to which the people have access. In the image of the sovereign it is not his deified nature that is prominent but his personality as * Pl. 40 a human being and as a responsible representative of the state.

Eleventh-Dynasty sculpture, like architecture, was mod- * Pl. XII elled upon that of the Pyramid Period. After the political unrest and troubles of the close of the Old Kingdom and the First Intermediate Period it was bound to seem important that the royal image should once again express the power and glory of the indestructible idea of divine kingship, which had been realized during the Pyramid Period. Towards the end of the Old Kingdom the effort to obtain a rendering as naturalistic as possible had led the statue to lose something of its block-like character. The relaxation of the classical laws of composition had broken off the traditions of skilled craftsmanship. Thus Middle Kingdom sculpture had to make a completely fresh start, and it is not surprising that the first attempts should still show distinct traces of the efforts that were made to cope with the new form, and that some uncertainty should be apparent in the treatment of stylistic features.

A note of concentrated power emanates from the massive and compact statue of Mentuhotep II, larger than life, with its powerful legs and crude face. The strict way in which it is contained within the cubic form, with the planes meeting at right angles, is in accordance with the style of the Pyramid Period. In spite of the ungainly stiffness of the figure, it becomes evident that sculpture in the round has returned to clear laws of form. It was soon to gain in expressive content, in conformity with the spirit of the age.

During the Middle Kingdom, and Dynasty XI in particular, private sculpture recedes into the background by comparison with royal sculpture. From nomarchs' tombs only a few relics of funerary statues have survived, although these no doubt once existed in large number. Several small statuettes, usually of mediocre quality, follow the Old Kingdom tradition; others show traces of groping towards a new form. In models and wooden statuettes placed in the tomb of the deceased one can readily see the impact left by the traditions of the Old Kingdom and the First Intermediate Period. Some female statuettes from the end of Dynasty XI, with slender and elaborately modelled bodies, give proof of a fresh austerity and sensitivity.

In relief sculpture, too, the old traditions had been broken off during the period of anarchy. The Upper Egyptian nomarchs continued to embellish their tombs with reliefs and paintings, but the stylistic treatment is so varied, and owes so much to local peculiarities, that it is hardly possible to attempt a comprehensive characterization. The motifs represented display some stark individuality, which continues the tendency at the end of the

Pl. 42 Princess Kawit at her toilet. Detail of a scene on the limestone sarcophagus of Princess Kawit. From Thebes, Deir el-Bahari. Dynasty XI, c. 2000 B.C. Cairo Museum.

Pl. 43 Processional temple of Sesostris I at Karnak. C. 1950 B.C. The blocks of stone were re-used in the New Kingdom to build Amenophis III's pylon. Those found were removed and the temple re-erected.

Pl. 44 Statuette of King Sesostris I. Wood. From Lisht. Dynasty XII, c. 1950 B.C. Height 59 cm. Contribution from Edward S. Harkness and the Rogers Fund, 1914, Museum Excavations 1913-1914; Metropolitan Museum of Art, New York.

Old Kingdom to depict life on this earth in a naturalistic manner and to relax the rules governing artistic style. Thus, for example, unique events of importance in the life of the deceased may be placed on record in the picture. The occupant of the tomb occasionally casts aside his role as a motionless observer of events and takes a hand in the action. In the case of motifs showing complicated movements the artist's delight in experimentation is apparent. All these details point to the fact that to an ever-increasing extent account is taken of the effect upon the viewer, before whom all the events in the deceased's life are proudly displayed. This interesting progress toward a new pictorial concept, which must be understood as a further development of the artistic intentions voiced in Dynasty V, found no emulators among the artists of the pharaoh's court during the Middle Kingdom.

Official relief sculpture at the royal residence was concerned not with experiment and variety but with a new attempt to consolidate the style that had disintegrated during the First Intermediate Period. A means of doing so was provided by the introduction, at Thebes during Dynasty XI, of a network of squaring lines for drawing the outline. Its proportions correspond to the units of measurement in use in the Old Kingdom. The network of squaring lines that was drawn on the surface of the stone made it possible both to determine the total proportions and to fix all the details exactly. With the aid of this system a balanced clear style of relief sculpture could develop with surprising speed during Dynasty XI. Already in the relief sculpture and paintings of Mentuhotep II, in which the lines are drawn with elaborate care, there is a harmonious relationship between the inscription and the image, which gives proof of a new sense for the ordering of forms and a new solidity of composition. Pl. XIII

Particularly exquisite and elegant are the delicate reliefs, only slightly raised, which have survived from the temples

of Mentuhotep II at Tod, Armant and Elephantine. They likewise evidence a feeling for a balanced, decorative arrangement and treatment of the plane, as well as a sensitive expressiveness of line.

The subject-matter depicted in the reliefs of royal buildings is limited. As in the Old Kingdom, they are confined to representations which portray the king associating with the gods or performing rites. In spite of the formal austerity a new sensitivity and dignity are noticeable in these images, and occasionally one can detect a faint expression of emotion, a mood of lyricism.

Of the reliefs and paintings in the tombs of the court aristocracy little has survived. But from the few examples we have it can be ascertained that here, too, the new style, to which we owe such impressive works of art in Dynasty XII, came into being already during Dynasty XI.

In Upper Egypt from the First Intermediate Period onward scenes were frequently carved on the outer walls of sarcophagi. A relief on the limestone sarcophagus of Princess Kawit, from her tomb at Deir el-Bahari, shows the princess at her toilet. The servant standing behind her arranges her hair and pins down her curls with a bone needle; Kawit herself is shown holding a mirror in her left hand and lifting up a drinking-cup to her mouth with her right hand; another servant standing in front of her fills up a second cup. The civilized, rather mannered elegance of this representation elevates an everyday event almost to the level of a ritual ceremony. In this relief, as in many others, it is evident how far man has departed from the naive *joie de vivre* of Dynasty V. Its place has been taken by a cool and noble dignity. On the spiritual and artistic foundations created during the reign of the first Middle Kingdom pharaohs there developed, in the ensuing Dynasty XII, a remarkably mature artistic style, which inaugurated the second great flourishing period in Egyptian art.

After the death of Mentuhotep II the problem of the * Pl. 41, Cat. 40
succession to the throne seems to have caused some trouble. Mentuhotep III, whose name is not mentioned in the later king-lists, seems not to have been a legitimate heir. During his brief reign an expedition was sent to the quarries in the Wadi Hammamat in order to procure blocks of stone for his sarcophagus. This task was entrusted to the vizier Amenemhat, who is probably identical with Amenemhat I, the founder of Dynasty XII, who came to the throne in 1991 B.C. Although historical sources do not provide any detailed information about the circumstances in which the new dynasty came to power, some clues are afforded by the 'Prophecies of Nefertin':

'A king will appear in the south / by the name of Ameni (Amenemhat). / He is the son of a woman from Nubia, / he is a child from Upper Egypt: / rejoice, O mankind, at his time. / This son of a . . . man will make his name immortal.'

If one goes by this prophecy, Amenemhat was not of
royal birth, but was a usurper who deposed the last pharaoh * Pl. 42
of Dynasty XI. After Amenemhat had consolidated his power, he moved his residence north to Lisht, south of Cairo. The removal of the seat of government may have seemed to him expedient for a variety of reasons. The building of a belt of fortresses on the eastern edge of the Delta, the so-called 'Prince's Wall,' shows that the protection of the eastern border and the relationship with eastern neighbours had become a major political problem, which could much better be assessed from the northern part of the country than from Thebes. But by moving his residence the pharaoh also no doubt sought to demonstrate his intention to resume the great tradition of the Old Kingdom. He himself and his successors had a pyramid tomb built not far from their new residence, and the court aristocracy also had themselves interred there, near the pyramids of their sovereigns. In order to guarantee

Pl. XIII King Mentuhotep II. Painted limestone relief. From Thebes, Deir el-Bahari. Dynasty XI, c. 2000 B.C. Length 98 cm. Gift of Egyptian Exploration Fund, 1917; Metropolitan Museum of Art, New York.

continuity of succession, in the twentieth year of his reign Amenemhat appointed his son, Sesostris I, co-regent. His concern to ensure a smooth succession of the royal office was justified, for in the thirtieth year of his reign he fell victim to an assassination attempt. A literary text, handed down in several copies, 'The Instruction of King Amenemhat,' in the form of an instruction to his son and successor Sesostris, contains the following passage:

'Hearken to what I say to thee that thou mayest be king and hold sway over the land and shores, and be more successful than I. Beware of subordinates, do not encounter them alone, do not trust a brother, acquaint thyself with no friend and find thyself no confidant, (for) this leads to no good. When thou sleepest watch over thy heart, for on the day of calamity man is without any trusty follower.

It happened after dinner, when night had fallen. I had allowed myself an hour's relaxation and had fallen asleep upon my bed, for I was fatigued. My heart had gone to sleep. At that moment it seemed as though weapons were being seized and as though someone had asked for me, and I leapt up like a snake in the desert. I roused myself to engage in personal combat. I discovered that there was a scuffle among the bodyguard. Quickly I seized weapons and drove the scoundrel back, but there is nobody who is strong during the night and one cannot fight alone successfully without a helper. See, thus this abomination happened when thou wast not with me and the court did not yet know that I wish to hand over the sovereignty to thee.'

At the news of his father's death Sesostris I hastened to the residence to assume power. The succession question was satisfactorily settled by raising the son of the ruling

pharaoh to be co-regent. The kings who followed him during Dynasty XII adopted this method of bolstering the royal authority and so assured the dynasty of a long and glorious tenure of power, in the course of which a number of important rulers guided the fortunes of the country.

Apart from its literary form, 'The Instruction of King Amenemhat' is a political document which contains critical observations on problems of the day and provides an insight into the fundamental change which had taken place in the position of the monarchy. Royal sovereignty, which is still now seen as divine, rests upon the human shoulders of the king as an individual and is regarded by him as an obligation to be borne in a responsible manner.

The tremendous demands which this view made upon the king to display discernment and energy in his policy have left their imprint upon the royal sculpture of the Middle Kingdom. It affords a picture of the king's frightening isolation, heroic greatness and maturity, conscious as he must be of his place in eternity, with all the scepsis and
* Pl. xiv, Pl. 44, Cat. 31 inner tragedy to which this knowledge must lead. Sesostris I does indeed emulate earlier sovereigns in emphasizing his divine origin, and in later generations too the
* Pl. 47 ruler's legitimacy rests upon the claim to have been
* Pl. 50 appointed by the gods. But his divine nomination to kingship has more of a practical political significance: it is
* Cat. 4 a means of consolidating the throne by taking into account
* Pl. 45 the religious ideas of the people. The pharaoh of the Middle Kingdom is far removed from the divine monarchy of the Pyramid Period with its claims to a timeless eternal existence. In lieu of this idea we have a king who bears responsibility for the problems of earthly existence; these are no longer borne by a god, but by man.

Sesostris III was venerated by contemporaries and by posterity as one of the most important rulers of antiquity. In the picture left us of this ruler by Herodotus (II, 102–110) and Diodorus Siculus (I, 53–58, 94) there may well have been traits drawn from the tradition about other pharaohs; nevertheless the fact remains that it was due to his shrewd and energetic foreign policy that Egypt regained her international prestige. There is little about his personality in contemporary records, except in the hymns sung in his praise. Far more revealing are works of sculpture, in which one can detect a trace of dignity and human greatness that cannot but deeply affect the viewer.

Amenemhat III was able to retain the full majesty of the authority he inherited from his father. During his long reign he continued the conquest of the Faiyum, begun by his grandfather, and made it one of the most fertile areas of Egypt. It was on the edge of this oasis, near Hawara, that he built his tomb, the 'Labyrinth' much admired in antiquity (Herodotus, II, 148).

After the brief reign of Amenemhat IV his sister Sobek-Nofrura brought the rule of Dynasty XII to an end.

Twelfth-Dynasty sculpture in the round follows the ancient rules governing structure and form, but the modelling of the surface is more exquisite and subtle than was the case in the Old Kingdom. The decisive change in the style of Middle Kingdom sculpture is manifest in the expressive rendering of the human face, which takes on an inner spiritual content and reflects the character of the subject. During the reigns of Sesostris III and Amenemhat III all the lines and individual forms are imbued with a new sense of plasticity. The highly accentuated modelling of the cheek-bones and the eyebrows indicate the bone structure. The upper eyelids are broad and heavy, giving the eyes a cryptic and melancholic look. A narrow, sensitive but forceful mouth, often pulled down slightly at the corners, and a firm chin are combined with flabby cheeks. The wrinkles around the bridge of the nose and the lachrymal bags under the eyes help to give the impression of a likeness taken from life. The tense plasticity of the individual forms conform to the inner tensions revealed in the

Pl. 45 Sesostris III. Brown stone. Dynasty XII, c. 1860 B.C. Height 16 cm. Gift of Edward S. Harkness, 1926, Carnavon Collection; Metropolitan Museum of Art, New York.

Pl. 46 Amenemhat III. Granite. Dynasty XII, c. 1820 B.C. Height 86.5 cm. Hermitage, Leningrad.

expression. The portraits of this ruler convey visually an awareness of the transitory and dubious character of worldly things. In place of the timeless ideal pharaoh of the Pyramid Period, which portrays the ruler in the prime of manhood, in the Middle Kingdom we have the portrait of a man who has grown old with time and who is conscious, in his dignified isolation, of the heavy spiritual responsibilities he bears. * Cat. 7

Occasionally, especially in the case of portraits of Amenemhat III, doubt and melancholy are the predominant emotions expressed by the royal portrait. There is a hint of weary resignation, springing from the knowledge that the political and spiritual order is once again about to disintegrate. * Pl. 46, Cat. 5

Pl. 47 Head of a female sphinx. Green stone. Discovered near Rome. Dynasty XII, c. 1900 B.C. Height 38.9 cm. Brooklyn Museum, New York.

In private sculpture, too, a new style was created at the beginning of Dynasty XII. Although the free-standing sculptures, which are usually of small proportions, are not of such importance as the life-size private statues of the Old Kingdom, there are nevertheless among them some very impressive works of art, which suggest that a style was developing capable of expressing the spirit of the age. The funerary statue recedes into the background, since the simple shaft-tombs and *mastaba* of the court officials at Lisht had no room for such a statue. Of the sculpture in the round in nomarchs' tombs very little has survived, and it is entirely absent from the reign of Amenemhat III onwards. On the other hand in temple sculpture a variety of new motifs and types was developed. Already towards the closing phase of the Old Kingdom the pharaoh had occasionally given a senior official permission to have a statue of himself put up in the temple. In the Middle Kingdom the king used to honour meritorious officials by presenting them with a statue and granting them the privilege of erecting it in the temple court. With this donation came a bequest from the proceeds of which the priests met the expense of the rites connected with the statue. Members of the upper-middle class also found for
* Pl. 48, Cat. 22, 25
themselves a place in the temples of the gods and thus ceased to be dependent on their descendants for performance of the funerary rites. They could also enjoy in this way the privilege of prayers by the priests and visitors to the temple. The inscriptions on these statues appeal to passers-by to say a prayer for the deceased. This shows how much vitality there still was in the old concept that the image had the character of reality.

The austere compact structure of the statues forms a striking contrast to the animated outline of the private sculpture of Dynasties V and VI. It also appears to be
* Pl. 49
more intensified and consolidated than it had been during the Pyramid Period. Some new types of free-standing sculpture appeared which were suited to this trend toward a simple austerity of form. Male standing or seated figures are clad in a long kilt reaching down from the chest or waist to the ankles, or alternatively wear a cloak covering the whole body. In the Old Kingdom the garment was not distinguished from the silhouette of the body; now it acquires a significance in its own right and the bodily forms can be made out beneath it. The fact that the costume is treated in large planes contrasts effectively with the plastic modelling of the face and accentuates the austere compactness of the figure.

Intensification to create a compact form was accomplished most tellingly in the block-statue, a type which evolved at this time. The subject is depicted wrapped in a cloak,

Pl. XIV Head of statuette of Imeret-nebes. Wood. Dynasty XII, c. 1900 B.C. Height 86 cm. Rijksmuseum van Oudheden, Leyden (cf. Cat. 31).

squatting on the ground with the knees drawn up to the body, the back and the lower part of the leg both forming vertical planes. The arms, raised to shoulder level, form the forward limit of the upper edge of the cube. Only the head and occasionally the hands (shown crossed over the knees) and feet project from the cubic form. The rigid geometric form into which the figure is placed acquires dynamism from the fact that the external planes are assimilated to the organic outline of the body. Thus the block-statue does not give the impression of a mathematical construction; instead, the abstract form and naturalistic figure are blended in a marvellous way to form a homogeneous whole. The result is a telling realization of the principles of composition basic to Egyptian art. Characteristically enough, right up to the final phase of Egyptian civilization the block-statue is one of the established types in the repertoire of free-standing sculpture.

The motif of the scribe statue comes to be modified to conform with the style of the period. In the case of the scribe Sebek-em-imu, now in Vienna, who is still depicted wearing a short kilt, the typical drawing up of the legs beneath the body is barely suggested. The arms are held close to the torso, the right hand rests upon the upper part of the right thigh, and the left hand is upon the chest. There is nothing in this posture to suggest that the man is a scribe. The facial expression points rather to an introspective person, who keeps his knowledge to himself. In the Old Kingdom statues of scribes wore an expression of candour and critical intelligence; in the Middle Kingdom they bear an imprint of contemplative seriousness, of the dignity conferred by learning.

* Cat. 28

In relief sculpture, which at the beginning of the Middle Kingdom developed a new balanced style thanks to the device of the network of squaring lines used in the preliminary drawing, the trend to refinement continued during Dynasty XII. Temple reliefs display, in the harmony

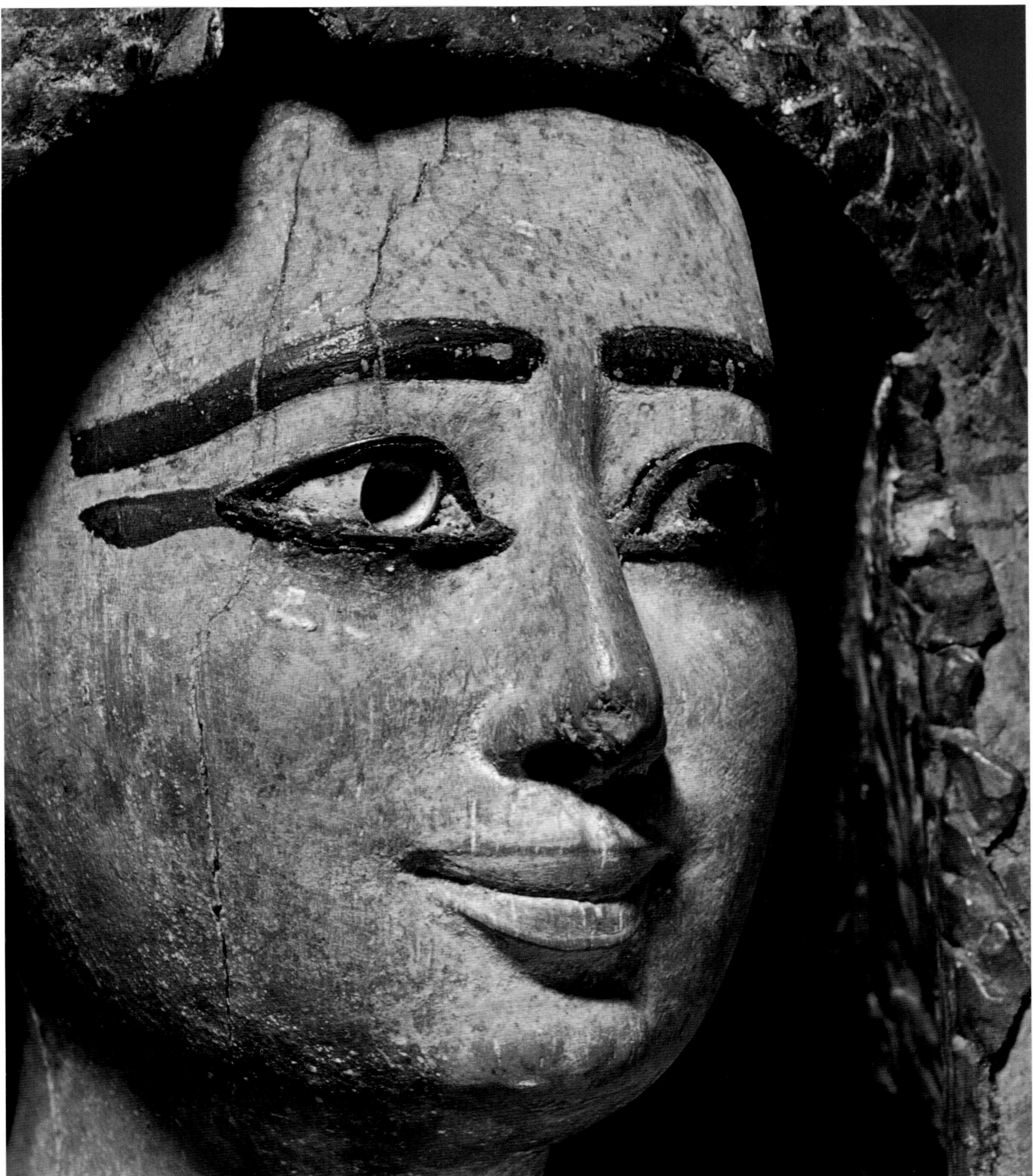

◁ *Pl. 48 Prince of Athribis. Grey granite. From Benha. Dynasty XII, c. 1820 B.C. Height 63.5 cm. British Museum, London.*

Pl. 49 Block-statue of Sesostris-senebef-ni. Brown quartzite. Dynasty XII, c. 1870 B.C. Height 68.5 cm. Brooklyn Museum, New York.

Pl. 50 Statuette of Khnum-hotep. Basalt. Dynasty XII, c. 1850 B.C. Height 19 cm. H. O. Havemeyer Collection, Bequest of Mrs. H. O. Havemeyer, 1929; Metropolitan Museum of Art, New York.

between figures and written characters, a sense for the decorative arrangement of the plane. The symmetrically placed decorative inscriptions seem to blend the image and the script into a single whole. The details of the individual characters are elaborately executed and with their austere pictorial quality add much more to the representation than would a mere explicatory sign. They have the same degree of importance as the image itself. Occasionally they are not distinct from each other at all in form, and only the content of the picture sets it apart from the characters. In the modelling of the body the relief follows the natural contours with a fine sense of plastic values. The relation between the figures is imbued with new meaning. During the Old Kingdom they were simply placed alongside one another; or if they were arranged in a group, their relationship was determined by the external action portrayed. During the Middle Kingdom an inner relationship occasionally is expressed as well—one that belongs to the emotional sphere. The austere and dignified style, the balance in the segmentation of the plane, the sureness of touch and the sophistication in the treatment of line, the plasticity of form and the restrained introspective expression—all these features are characteristic of relief sculpture during Dynasty XII.

* Pl. 51

Pl. 51 Sesostris I presenting a votive gift to the god Min. Detail of a pillar relief in Sesostris I's temple at Karnak. Dynasty XII, c. 1950 B.C.

Pl. 52 Statue of the royal keeper of the seal, Gebu. Black granite. From Thebes. Dynasty XIII, c. 1700 B.C. Height 93 cm. Ny Carlsberg Glyptotek, Copenhagen.

Pl. 53 Funerary stele of Amenemhat. Limestone relief. Dynasty XII, 1917 B.C. Height 69.5 cm., width 39 cm. Kestner Museum, Hanover (cf. Pl. 54).

The reliefs and paintings in the nomarchs' tombs of Middle Egypt have a vital contributory part to play in Twelfth-Dynasty relief sculpture and painting, even though their style is often conservative and provincial. The variety of motifs, some of which depict particular events as well as the themes commonly chosen during the Old Kingdom, shows that the nomarchs were far more concerned with handing down to posterity the memory of their own persons and of significant events in their lives than they were with the magic effect which the images would have upon the deceased in the after-life.

Characteristically enough, the representations also frequently relate to a unique event which occurred at a particular moment, which is indicated precisely, and thus diverge greatly in content from the timeless eternity suggested by the funerary images of the Old Kingdom,

Pl. XV Pectoral of Amenemhat III. Gold and semi-precious stones. From Dahshur. Late Dynasty XII, c. 1820 B.C. Height 8 cm. Cairo Museum.

Thus in the tomb of Khnum-hotep at Beni Hasan a Beduin prince is depicted accompanied by his retinue seeking permission from the nomarch to settle in his region. This significant event is ascribed by the accompanying inscription to the sixth year of Sesostris II's reign. The representations and inscriptions in the nomarchs' tombs are an informative historical source. In the tomb of Prince Ameni, for example, there is an account, ascribed to the forty-third year of Sesostris I's reign, which records that the prince took part in the king's Nubian campaign and that later he also accompanied Amenemhat II on his expeditions to Nubia and Coptos. The

ensuing statements about the administration of the area show that the nomarch had already then lost his independence and become a faithful vassal of the king, who collected taxes and other revenue on behalf of the crown.

The effective arrangement of reliefs on the walls of ceremonial pillared and columned halls in tombs, together with their clear balanced style, are in conformity with the tendency at this time towards a new feeling of consistency and order in relief sculpture and painting.

In painting on reliefs and especially in painting proper
preference is given to delicate colours rich in nuances,
* Pl. 55 which correspond to those found in nature. Landscape,
Cat. 52, 53 plants and animals are rendered in elaborately differentiat-
ed shades. A new attitude develops towards living things. Landscape gains in importance as a frame for the action depicted. The indication of time and the incorporation of the pictures into an enclosing space give them a clearly defined connection with this-worldly existence.

A particular type of relief sculpture is that of funerary
Cat. 74 stelae, which are of very varied artistic quality. They
were even commissioned by the poorer classes of the
* Pl. XV population and by means of pictures and inscriptions serv-
* Cat. 101 ed to ensure eternal life for the deceased and his family.
Pl. 53, Cat. 59 They depict the deceased and his relatives seated in front
of the offering-table, which is covered with funerary gifts.
Pl. 54 The inscriptions record, as well as the formulae used when
rendering sacrifice and the explicit request for prayers addressed to passers-by, details about the life of the deceased—either particular events or merely an enumeration of his good deeds. On his stele Amenemhat, master of cattle throughout the country, states the following:

'I was father to the orphan, husband to the widow, windbreak to the frozen. I gave the hungry bread and the naked clothing. I took the man from the mouth (judgement) of the judge by pleading for him without his knowledge. I did not humiliate a man before his superior. There were no dead under my supervision. O, ye who live upon this earth, who pass this grave, say the prayer for the dead. . .'

From this examination of the varied development of relief sculpture and painting during the Middle Kingdom it will be evident that the image is no longer bound up with some magic meaning for the viewer but places before his eyes a likeness of conditions on this earth, determined by time and space.

In mobiliar art, too, the trend towards a realistic style is apparent. Of course popular art, whenever and wherever it is encountered, tends to an unsophisticated rendering of the visual image and is largely independent of artistic principles and stylistic norms, which it only adopts unconsciously as it becomes assimilated to the style of the period. This explains why these works are of such remarkable realism and freshness, so that one cannot do justice to them by a critical evaluation of their style.

In goldsmiths' work the Middle Kingdom's cultivated sense for a decorative arrangement of forms, for elegance of line and nuances of colour, is combined with technical perfection. In the diadems and pectorals produced during this period coloured semi-precious stones are attractively combined with glittering gold to create works of unsurpassed excellence and beauty.

After initial troubles which could never be entirely quelled, power was seized for fifty-five years by the kings of Dynasty XIII, whose names alone have been preserved for posterity. They are listed together with the name o the provincial god of the Faiyum, Sobek. The political conditions during this period bear great resemblance to the symptoms of decline at the end of the Old Kingdom. The state is partly fragmented into petty kingdoms, the internal administration is weakened, and necessary tasks in the field of foreign policy are not performed. In the south the province of Nubia was lost. Towards the end of

Pl. 54 Detail of inscription on the funerary stele of Amenemhat (cf. Pl. 53), lines 4 to 6.

Pl. 55 Roaring hippopotamus. Blue glazed faience. Middle Kingdom. Height 15.2 cm. British Museum, London.

Dynasty XIII the southern border of Egypt was again located near Elephantine, as it had been at the beginning of the Middle Kingdom. In the north, especially in the eastern part of the Delta, an immigration had taken place of Semitic tribes. These soon formed such an important element in the population that some of their leaders acquired royal dignity during Dynasty XIII. Towards the end of this dynasty's tenure of power Xois in the western Delta was ruled by independent princes, who in Manetho's list are referred to as Dynasty XIV, while the representatives of Dynasty XIII withdrew to Upper Egypt. During this 'Second Intermediate Period' the unity of the state collapsed and cultural standards also declined; artistic style degenerated and facial expressions took on a rigid character. Cat. 16

One Thirteenth-Dynasty work is the statuette of Gebu, the keeper of the royal seal, in which the form of the squatting scribe is further abstracted. Gebu is depicted as an old man crouching on his heels. His hands rest flat upon his knees which, enveloped in the long kilt, form a Pl. 52

level plane. The facial expression conveys the wisdom of age but also traces of weariness, of a resigned awareness that he is subject to an immutable destiny and must endure it in the solitude which human nature imposes.

Cat. 23 The almost life-size granite statue of Sebekemsaf, now in Vienna, is a typically impressive late work of private sculpture from the Middle Kingdom. The person portrayed, a high-ranking court official and relative of one of the Thirteenth-Dynasty kings, is shown in a rigid posture with his kilt protruding stiffly and his arms held tightly to the body. Whereas during Dynasty XII the realistic style was confined to plastic treatment of the face but was never employed in rendering the body, so that sometimes the style of the two parts seems discordant, the realistic representation of Sebekemsaf, in full figure, forms an interesting exception.

The overaccentuation of the formal element and the hardening of individual facial features, which are no longer combined to form a unity according to a single principle of modelling, give the face a rigidity and raggedness which suggest that the style was gradually dissolving.

In spite of the perfect technique evident in the working of the hard smoothly-polished stone, the spiritual emptiness of the expression cannot be overlooked. These are characteristic features of a late phase of art and herald spiritual decline.

While the collapse of the Egyptian state continued, in the Near East groups of peoples had been set in movement by the immigration of Indo-Aryan tribes into the Euphrates area, and they were pressing against the northern border of Egypt. In Egyptian sources the leaders of these groups are referred to as 'the rulers of foreign lands'; writers in antiquity transcribed this designation as 'Hyksos.' They should not be regarded as a homogeneous tribal group but as a relatively thin Hurrite upper class that had succeeded in seizing power in Palestine and Syria, whence they advanced to the Egyptian border. In about 1650 B.C. the Hyksos founded their capital in the Delta near Avaris and as a new dynasty claimed dominion over the whole country. Only in the south, especially in Thebes, were indigenous princes tolerated as dependent petty kings. The Hyksos are accounted by Manetho as Dynasty XV, whereas Dynasty XVI probably comprises the dependent rulers in Upper Egypt.

Like all immigrants who set foot on Egyptian soil, the Asiatic rulers adopted the ancient traditions of Egyptian culture.

The innovations which these foreigners made were in the technical field—especially in the introduction of the horse-drawn war-chariot and an improvement in military weapons. Their contribution to Egyptian culture had a most significant impact upon political life and military technology during the subsequent period.

PHARAOH - MAN AND KING

Pl. 56 Funerary figure of Iy, scribe responsible for keeping account of the corn in the royal barns. Wood. Dynasty XVIII, c. *1500 B.C. Height 28 cm. Kestner Museum, Hanover.*

THE NEW KINGDOM

During the Second Intermediate Period a princely family from Thebes had come to power and gained importance in Upper Egypt, which laid claim to the royal title and was accounted as Dynasty XVII. While the Hyksos king Apophis reigned over the Delta, in 1560 B.C. the royal dynasty at Thebes became strong enough for Sekenenra Taa II to risk a campaign against the alien rulers. After his father had been killed in battle, Kamose continued this war of liberation and succeeded in reconquering the country as far as the Faiyum. But it was not until the reign of King Ahmose, his brother, that the Hyksos were finally expelled and the unity of the Egyptian state restored. He is the first ruler of Dynasty XVIII. An encroachment upon southern Palestine secured access to the copper mines in the Sinai. In the south Lower Nubia was recovered and to administer it a viceroy was appointed who bore the title 'Son of the King of Kush.'

The tasks that the first rulers of the New Kingdom faced were in many respects comparable to those undertaken by the founders of the Middle Kingdom, although of course the political situation in the Near East had in the meantime changed radically and the pharaohs now had to reckon with external pressures. In order to consolidate the unity of the new state a rigid centralized aministration was formed, with two viziers at its head, whose seat of government was at Thebes and Memphis respectively. They were supported by military leaders, for the army, which included foreign mercenaries, played an influential role in New Kingdom history. The officials were generally appointed on a hereditary basis, which had some advantages but occasionally raised problems as well. In addition to the military and the civil bureaucracy, the priesthood also attained far-reaching influence. The generous endow-

ments of the national temple of the god Amun at Karnak gave the priests economic independence. The close bond between the monarchy and the national god, Amun, also afforded them an opportunity to influence political decisions and so gradually to develop their secular power, until towards the end they became rivals of the monarchy. The aristocracy had ceased to play any role by this time. Just as at the beginning of the Middle Kingdom, now too it was thought necessary to provide the king with a legitimation of his authority in terms of divine descent. The ancient dogma whereby the pharaoh was declared the son of God is taken up again in a modified form. The queen becomes the 'wife of God,' who from a union with the national deity Amun, in the guise of the king, begets the heir to the throne.

Religion and above all ritual play an important part in the New Kingdom; they centre upon the figure of Amun. It is difficult to interpret the original character of this deity. During the Old Kingdom Amun emerges in the Hermopolitan cosmogony, where his name means 'the hidden (god).' His qualities are not indicated; in the context of theological speculation he appears as an abstract idea, an effective but invisible force. At the beginning of the Middle Kingdom Amun is worshipped in the nome of Thebes and during Dynasty XII he is associated with the ancient sun-god Rē of Heliopolis, as Amun-Rē. During the New Kingdom he is the central figure in religious life as 'Amun-Rē, the great king of the gods.' His original abstract nature is overlaid by his interpretation as the sun-god. In the great hymns to Amun-Rē it is only his qualities as sun-god that are mentioned. But it may be that the meaning of the name Amun—'the hidden (god)'—promoted more strongly than we know the tendency towards a spiritualization of the deity and so laid the foundations for the attempted reforms of King Akhnaton.

Amun-Rē is the god of the living, the mighty king of gods of the Egyptian empire. Religion and ritual are almost exclusively oriented towards the monarchy and the political power it exercises.

In the interpretation of the theologians Amun becomes the senior deity. He is considered the creator of the world and of all the gods of nomes and towns in the land. The common people of course never abandoned the worship of the animal and hybrid deities who had a firm place in their hearts, and in particular remained faithful to Osiris, the great god of the dead. In the official theology Osiris became a nocturnal form of the all-encompassing sun-god, to whom is ascribed not only the creation and preservation of the world but also dominion over the beyond. 'Guides to the beyond' give a description of man's path through the dangers of the nether world, where demons and spirits lie in wait for him, and against whom he must protect himself by magic formulae and occult knowledge.

The source of authority in religious matters is the national temple at Karnak. Here all the great gods of the land acquire a temple or chapel in which they are honoured. The name of this national temple (*ipet iset*, or 'collector of the places') expresses this focussing of all religious notions.

The most important function of the rulers of the New Kingdom lay in the field of foreign policy, not only because they thought it necessary to reconquer the areas that had been lost during the Hyksos period, but also because for the first time there now developed an ambition to play a leading role among the peoples of the Near East, an ambition which led Egypt into wars of aggression.

This can be explained by the changes that occurred in the Egyptian world-outlook at this time. The actions, thoughts and life of the individual were now given far more attention than they had been in former ages, so that we can also gain a more personal picture of the pharaoh. No such individual features enable us to assess the kings of the Middle Kingdom. Works of sculpture reflected the spiritual experience of the age and its ethical outlook, not the personality of the pharaoh. Even literary sources, apart from a few exceptions, contained information of a general nature. The rulers of the New Kingdom, on the other hand, are markedly communicative. Their successes and deeds are handed down to posterity in representations and inscriptions.

Upon the firm foundations laid by King Ahmose, his successor, Amenophis I, was able to turn to spiritual and artistic matters undisturbed by martial exploits, and to make his court a centre of cultural life.

Whereas the works of art which have survived from Dynasty XVII still show traces of the tentative efforts then being made to evolve a new style, and in outline and in detail give a rigid and schematic impression, during the reign of Amenophis I a well-established idiom soon Cat. 15, 32, 34 developed. Relief and sculpture, as well as architecture, were influenced by the austere style and measured clarity of the early Middle Kingdom. Such works show that a Pl. 56, 63 new endeavour was being made to apply the classical norms of style, such as is invariably the case whenever tradition has been interrupted by a period of chaos. By looking back and concentrating upon essentials, the innovators can obtain a foundation upon which a new style expressing the spirit of the age may develop.

THE THUTMOSID ERA

Thutmosis I is the first New Kingdom ruler to embark upon a policy of expansion. Passing through Palestine and Syria, he reached the Euphrates to do battle with the Mitanni, who remained for the next century Egypt's chief adversaries in the east. Great importance is attached to the equipping and training of the army, in particular to the provision of war-chariots. The military headquarters are located at Memphis. Also in educating the heir to the throne much attention is given to the inculcation of martial virtues.

Of great importance, too, for the splendid achievements to follow was the fact that the reigning pharaohs were not only first-class military leaders but also had a marked talent for the wise administration of the country, at the centre as well as in the provinces.

These political successes apart, the power of the state and the monarchy finds expression in a vigorous upsurge of building activity in all parts of the country. In the national temple to the god Amun at Karnak almost all the New Kingdom rulers erected temples, both large and small, chapels, obelisks and statues.

From the reign of Thutmosis I onwards the royal tombs are located in a rocky defile on the western bank of the river at Thebes, now known as the 'Valley of the Kings,' the mortuary temple being situated some distance away on the edge of the fertile strip of land. From the outside the entrance to the tomb lacks any kind of architectural features. The disposition of the chambers inside the tomb varies; they consist of passages, either winding or with right-angled turns, which broaden out into a number of rooms or pillared halls. The walls feature exclusively representations of a religious content, most of which have some relation to the 'guides to the beyond.'

Pl. 57 Terraced temple of Queen Hatshepsut at Deir el-Bahari, Thebes. Dynasty XVIII, c. 1480 B.C.

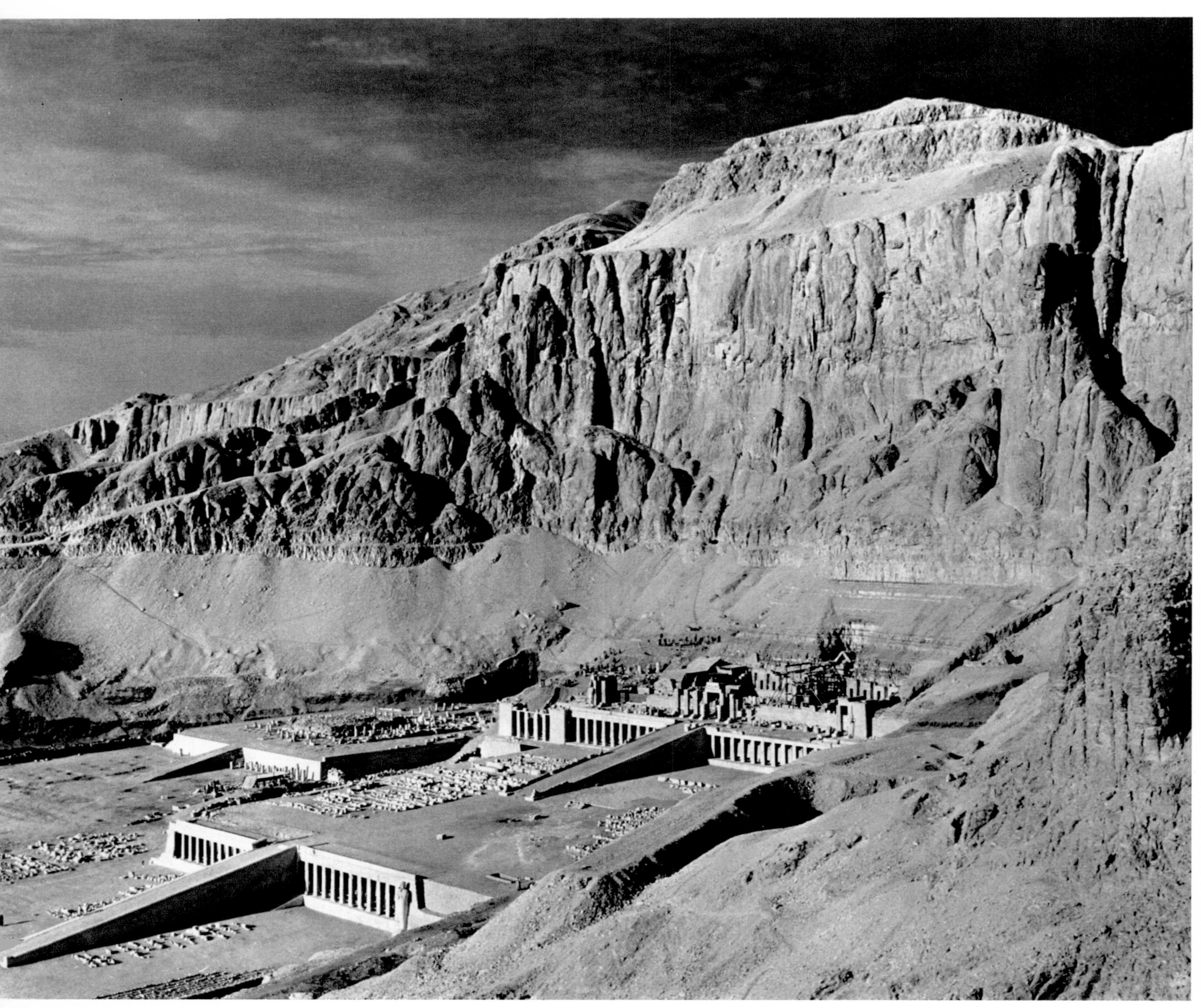

Pl. 58 Statue of Thutmosis III. Greyish-green stone. From Karnak. Dynasty XVIII, c. 1450 B.C. Height 90 cm. Cairo Museum.

The brief reign of Thutmosis II is followed by that of Queen Hatshepsut, who at first acts as regent during the minority of the heir to the throne, Thutmosis III, but soon becomes herself the reigning pharaoh. The fact that a woman can take over the function of sovereign illustrates the great change that has occurred in the idea of kingship. Whereas during the Old Kingdom significance is attached to the deified royal office, not to its bearer, and during the Middle Kingdom institution and holder become one, during the New Kingdom matters are reversed: now it is the energy and shrewdness of the ruler which confer significance upon his office.

Pl. 57 The fine terraced temple of Queen Hatshepsut at Deir el-Bahari, which is fairly well preserved, affords an excellent idea of early Eighteenth-Dynasty architecture. An avenue flanked by more than two hundred sphinxes led from the fertile land to the enclosure wall of the temple, which thrusts itself into the rocky mountains; it had three terraces and adjoining pillared halls, chapels and courts; surrounding it were gardens containing exotic trees brought from Punt, the land of fragrant incense. To the viewer it presents an attractive sight, combining as it does landscape and architecture into a harmonious whole. The entire complex, as well as the use of square and hexagonal pillars, point to the influence of the nearby Middle Kingdom temple of Mentuhotep II.

In relief sculpture there is an effort to simplify the structure of scenes and to clarify and intensify form and line; this too follows the tradition of the Middle Kingdom, above all of Dynasty XII.

With their bright aspect and delicate colours, the reliefs in the temple of Queen Hatshepsut radiate *joie de vivre* and serene calm. Best preserved of all are the representations depicting the divine procreation and birth of the queen, and the sequence showing the expedition to Punt, the land of incense; in the latter one can see, portrayed with minute accuracy and obvious delight, the exotic trees, plants and animals, the huts of the inhabitants, and the corpulent Queen of Punt. This elaborate precision and the freshness indicate an intense preoccupation with the natural world and an almost scientific eagerness to render the subject with as much authenticity as possible.

At the time a considerable number of statues were erected in the queen's mortuary temple, which portrayed Hatshepsut standing, seated or as a sphinx. Already during the Middle Kingdom other statues had been added to that of the king in the temple court. The delight in artistic expression, the desire to be as versatile and exhaustive as possible, led to an accumulation of statues in temple courts. The significance of the individual statue as a monument thus recedes into the background; the aim of conveying spiritual or religious content gives way to an aesthetic conception of the statue as a work of art.

From the standpoint of structure and style the free-standing sculpture of the Thutmosid Era, with its austere rigidity of form, is entirely bound up with the ancient tradition. On the other hand in the facial features the statues of Hatshepsut are less rigid and display a tendency towards a charming open-heartedness.

As a woman, Hatshepsut was spared the necessity of fighting foreign foes. Only during the last years of her reign was the internal peace of the country somewhat troubled by the prince regent, who finally sought to assume the power from which he had been debarred. Whether Hatshepsut met a violent end is not certain. The fall of her confidant, the vizier Senmut, suggests that there was opposition to her rule, in which Thutmosis III, who was nominally co-regent, probably had a hand. After her death the statues of the queen were smashed and her name erased from the monuments. In later king-lists this shrewd woman's tenure of the pharaonic throne is not recorded.

For Thutmosis III it was not easy to assert his claim to power, and the divine oracle of Amun was called upon to confirm him as the legitimate ruler. Such confirmation may have been secured by exerting pressure upon the priests. The oracle, which later attained great importance, undoubtedly gave the priests of the national temple the opportunity to influence both the choice of royal heir and other political decisions. The officials, too, among whom there were some forceful personalities, had to be taken into account by the pharaoh. In the course of time entire * Cat. 3
dynasties of officials developed.

During the peaceful years of Hatshepsut's reign the princes of the city-states of Syria and Palestine had united under the prince of Kadesh and concluded a treaty of friendship with the Mitanni. The united armies of these allies threatened the few military bases the Egyptians had left in the Near East. Immediately after his accession to the throne Thutmosis III succeeded in stopping the enemy advance by a bold counter-attack, and then in sixteen further campaigns recovered and consolidated the lost territories, whereupon he concluded a treaty with the Mitanni delimiting their respective spheres of influence in the Near East. In Nubia Thutmosis III was able to advance the southern border as far as the Fourth Nile Cataract. It was due to this eminent general on the pharaonic throne that Egyptian hegemony in Syria remained uncontested. With the other great powers diplomatic relations were maintained with statesmanlike skill; embassies from the Hittites, Babylonians and Assyrians presented the Egyptian court with gifts to symbolize their amity. The reconquered city-states in Syria and Palestine were divided into provinces and brought under strict administration. Reliefs and paintings in private tombs depict the presentation of rich tribute by representatives of the occupied territories.

Both contemporaries and subsequent generations regarded Thutmosis III as the first military genius of antiquity, an astute politician characteristic of a new kind of world. Pl. 58

Pl. XVI Men driving along a flock of geese. Detail of a wall-painting from a private tomb at Thebes. Dynasty XVIII, c. *1370 B.C. British Museum, London (cf. Cat. 51).*

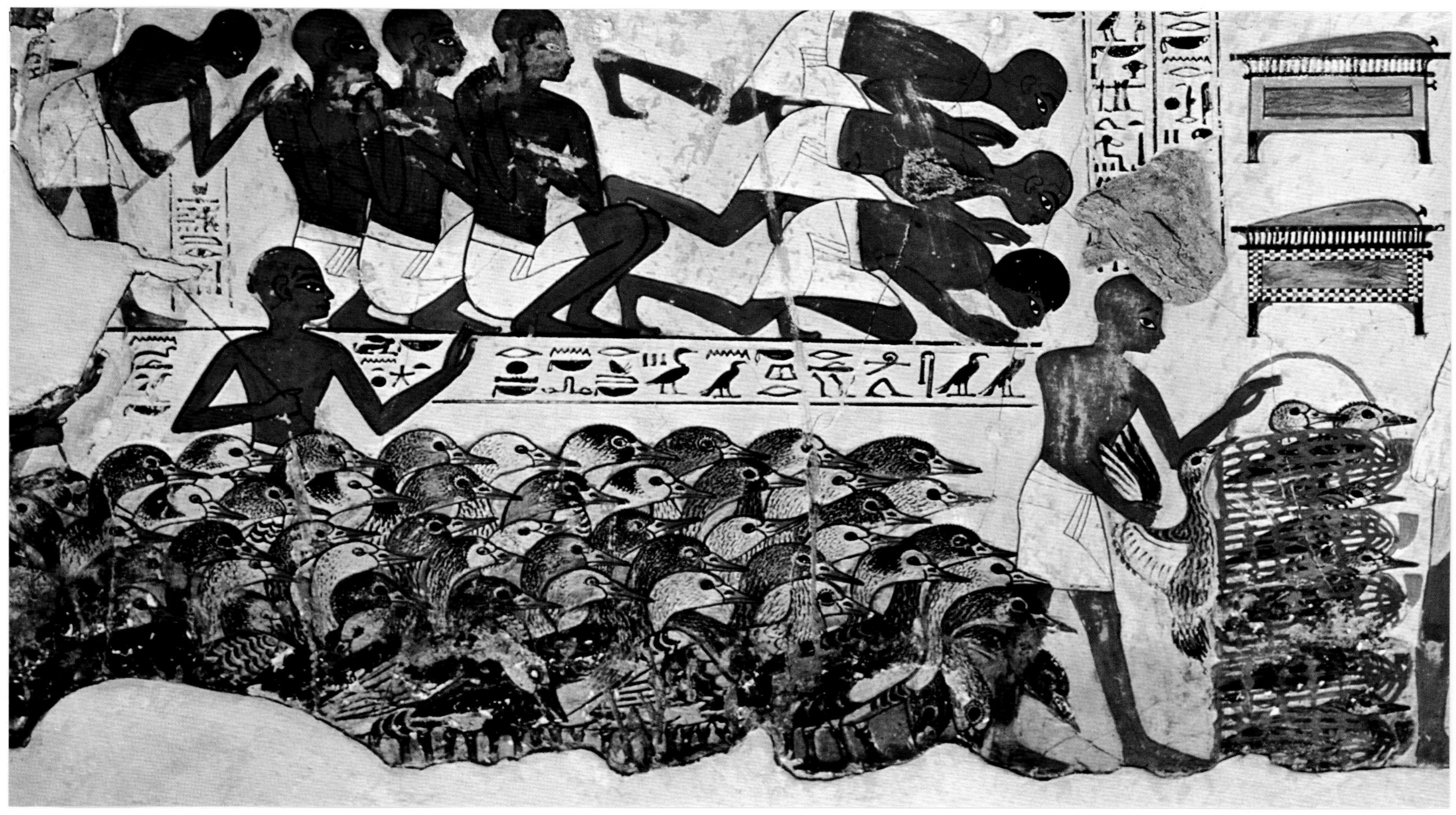

The king himself left an account of his campaigns in a hall of the Karnak temple. In contrast to similar records from earlier times, which were limited to formulae glorifying the pharaoh, and in most cases bore little relation to his actual achievements, the annals of Thutmosis III are of value as a reliable historical account of actual events. The gradual awakening of a sense of time gave rise to a sense of history. The artists of the period produced statues of
Pl. 58 Thutmosis III portraying him as a robust young man. His face, with the wide-awake eyes, conveys the impression of an alert energetic ruler, open to influences from the outside world. The vital tension of this royal image is just as remote from the self-sufficient, dignified seriousness of royal portraits during the Middle Kingdom as it is from the ageless sublimity of the divine pharaoh during the Pyramid Period.

The official reliefs in the New Kingdom temples show a tendency towards stiffness in their motifs, towards a dogmatic and stereotyped representation of the king before the gods, a tendency which had no relation to contempo-

Pl. 59 Head of a statue either of Thutmosis III or of Hatshepsut. Slate. Dynasty XVIII, c. *1450 B.C. Height 45.7 cm. British Museum, London.*

Pl. 60 Plants and animals brought back from Thutmosis III's campaign to Syria. Detail of a relief from the so-called 'Botanical Garden' in the temple at Karnak. Dynasty XVIII, c. *1450 B.C.*

rary events. On the other hand, in the festival hall of Thutmosis III at Karnak there is a sequence of reliefs
Pl. 60 highly characteristic of the spirit of the age, showing plants and animals which the king brought back with him from his campaigns in Asia. The life-like accuracy of these pictures and the life-affirming joy in the phenomena of an alien world are the product of the open-minded spirit which prevailed in the Thutmosid era.

After the death of his father, Amenophis II continued his work. His upbringing, together with the military spirit of the age, directed his interests to the fields of warfare and sport. On one stele we read the following lines:

'His majesty ascended the throne as a king, / as a handsome self-controlled young man, / who had completed

Pl. 61 Amenophis II. Small head of a sphinx. Granite diorite. Presumably from Karnak. Dynasty XVIII, c. 1430 B.C. Height 9.3 cm. Ägyptische Staatssammlung, Munich.

eighteen years, / standing on his own feet, full of power. / He was versed in the art of the war-god, / on the battle-field he had no equal. / He was acquainted with the art of riding, / in this great army none was his match. / None could bend his bow, / none could overtake him in the race. / He is one with a strong arm / who does not tire when at the helm.'[7]

The small sphinx's head depicting Amenophis II, now in Munich, seems to illustrate this inscription. Its delicate and mature style conveys the youthful power and charm of the king, who conforms to the ideals of chivalry. Pl. 61

With the reign of Amenophis II the period of aggressive foreign policy comes to an end. His successor, Thutmosis IV, seeks to regularize the relationship with the Mitanni kingdom. For purposes of state he contracts a marriage with a Mitanni princess, whereby for the first time a foreigner becomes a king's consort, although not officially a queen. There is evidence of energetic building activity during his reign. The reliefs and paintings executed at this time are among the finest achievements of Egyptian civilization.

Whereas in royal buildings the mural representations continued to be executed in relief, in private tombs it is paintings that prevail. The reason may have been that the brittle limestone in them is little suited to working in relief, whereas it formed an excellent ground for painting when rendered smooth with the aid of clay and chaff and coated with stucco. Apart from this no doubt the aesthetic approach, the striving for optic appeal, will also have encouraged the trend towards painting, which afforded much more varied possibilities of representation than relief sculpture did. Thus during the New Kingdom painting becomes the artistic idiom that best portrays the new attitude to life.

Tribute from the provinces, access to sources of gold in Nubia, and vigorous foreign trade all helped to make

Pl. 62 Plucking and salting away of geese. Detail of a wall-painting from a private tomb at Thebes. Dynasty XVIII, c. *1410 B.C. Height 19 cm., overall width 45 cm. Kestner Museum, Hanover (cf. Cat. 50).*

Pl. 63 War-chariot drawn by two horses. Preliminary drawing by means of a network of squaring lines. Limestone in black and red. Dynasty XVIII, c. *1500 B.C. Height 39 cm., width 27.5 cm. Kestner Museum, Hanover.*

Egypt a wealthy country. The upper classes, the court officials in particular, developed a generous, free-and-easy style of life, characterized by pretentious elegance. The paintings in the officials' tombs in the national necropolis, situated on the western bank of the river near Thebes, give an impressive idea of this age of splendour and the civilized society it bred.

* Pl. 62 The burial-chambers are entered through an open entrance-hall, whence one reaches first a hall placed at an
* Cat. 49, 50 oblique angle, which in turn adjoins a long corridor; this leads to the chapel containing the statue of the deceased. The scenes depicting life on earth are located in the transverse hall, whereas the religious scenes are reserved for the long corridor and the chapel. The traditional religious motifs are enriched by detailed renderings of preparations for the funeral and the ritual which accompanies it. One
Cat. 64 relief, now in Hanover, shows some *muu* dancers wearing tall crowns of reed, such as usually led the funerary procession, in a hall of the deceased's homestead. In the middle register is the garden, with date-palms and sycamores, and on the right, in another building, two women, possibly female mourners, as well as the *muu* dancers waiting for the funerary ceremonies to begin.

In the scenes of everyday life a large number of new motifs appear, which reflect many facets of social life in this imperial age. In addition to those depicting life and activity on the great royal and private estates, there are scenes showing foreigners bringing tribute from the occupied provinces and embassies from distant lands. Other scenes depict with dramatic dynamism events that occur when hunting game, birds and fish. The ladies of the court are shown wearing fashionable draped garments and artistically worked wigs, the latter lavishly decorated with jewellery. Every detail is elaborately rendered, and

Pl. 64 Ointment jar in the shape of a girl swimming with a duck. Wood and ivory. Dynasty XVIII, 14th cent. B.C. Length 26 cm. Musée du Louvre, Paris.

Pl. 65 Ointment bowl in the shape of a bound antelope. Yellowish serpentine. Dynasty XVIII, 14th cent. B.C. Length 14.7 cm. Kestner Museum, Hanover.

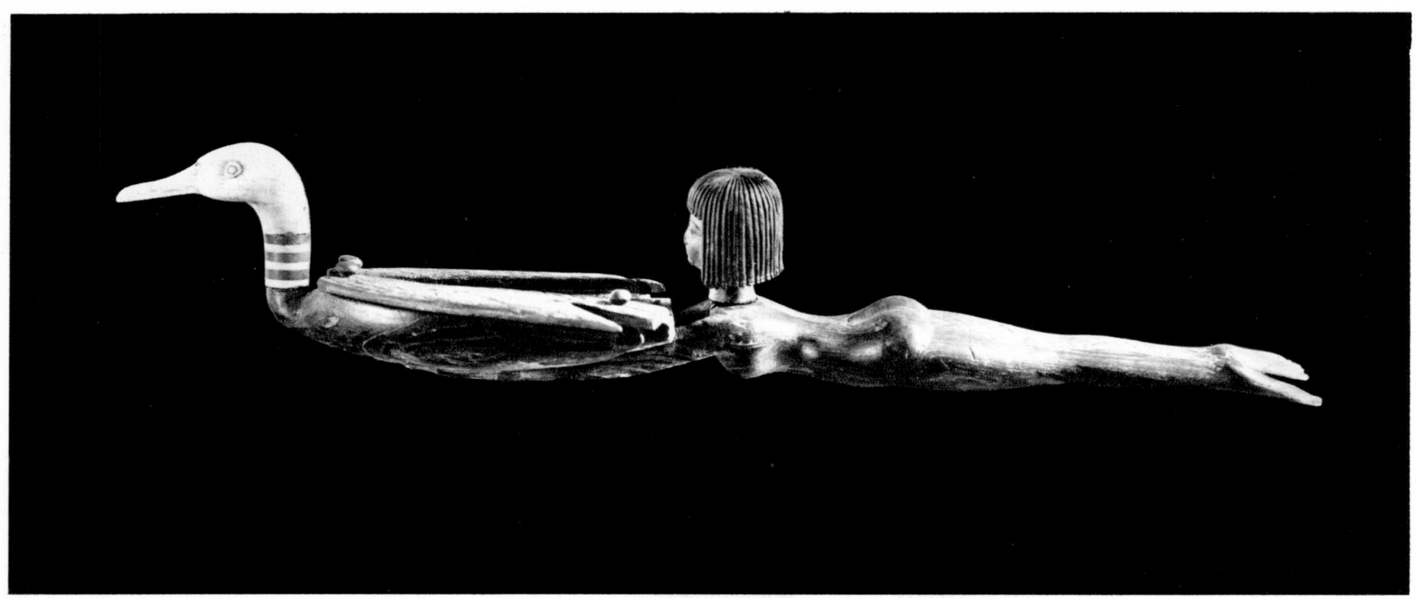

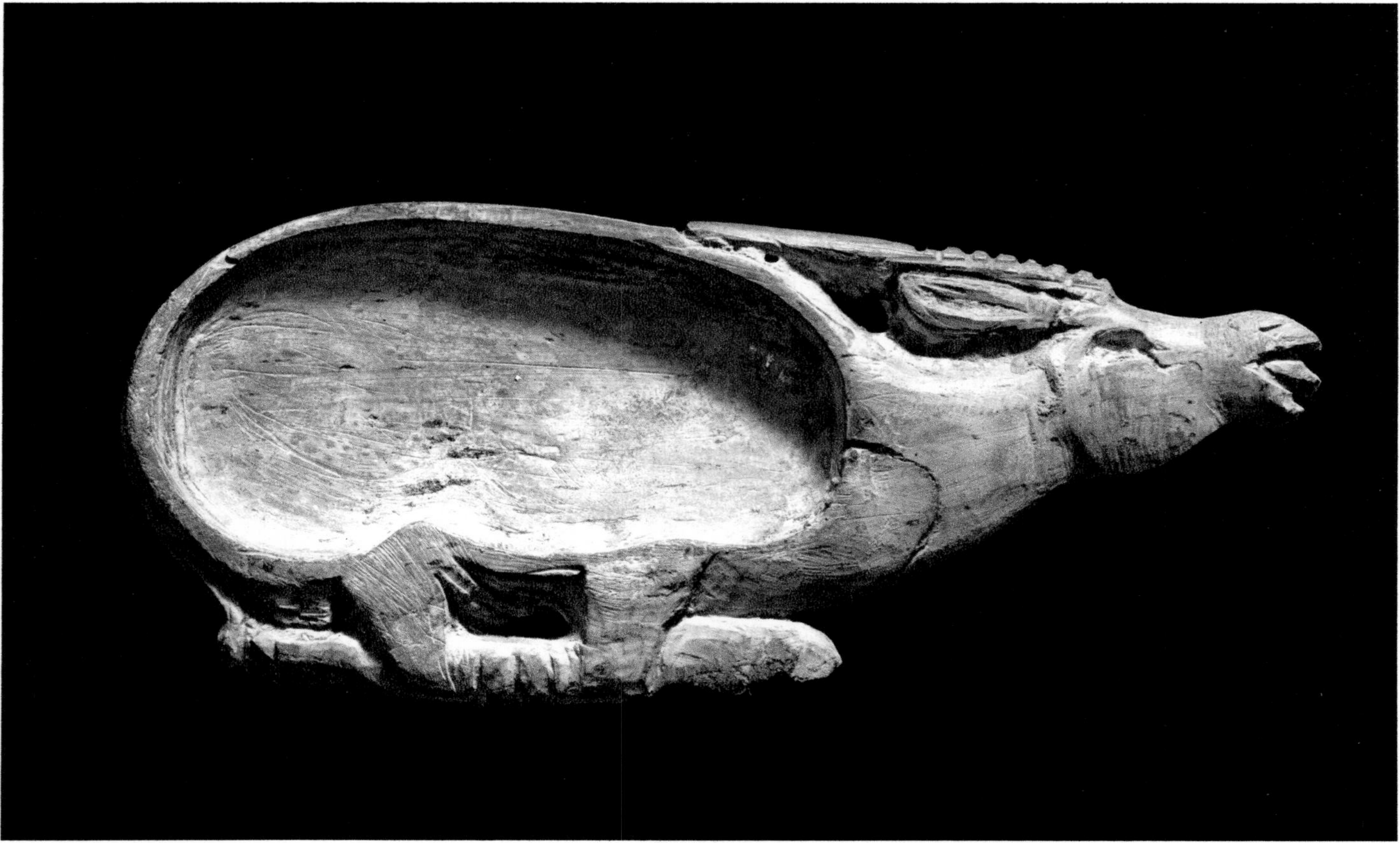

Pl. XVII Banqueting scene. Wall-painting from Neb-Amun's tomb at Thebes. Dynasty XVIII, c. 1370 B.C. Height 61 cm. British Museum, London.

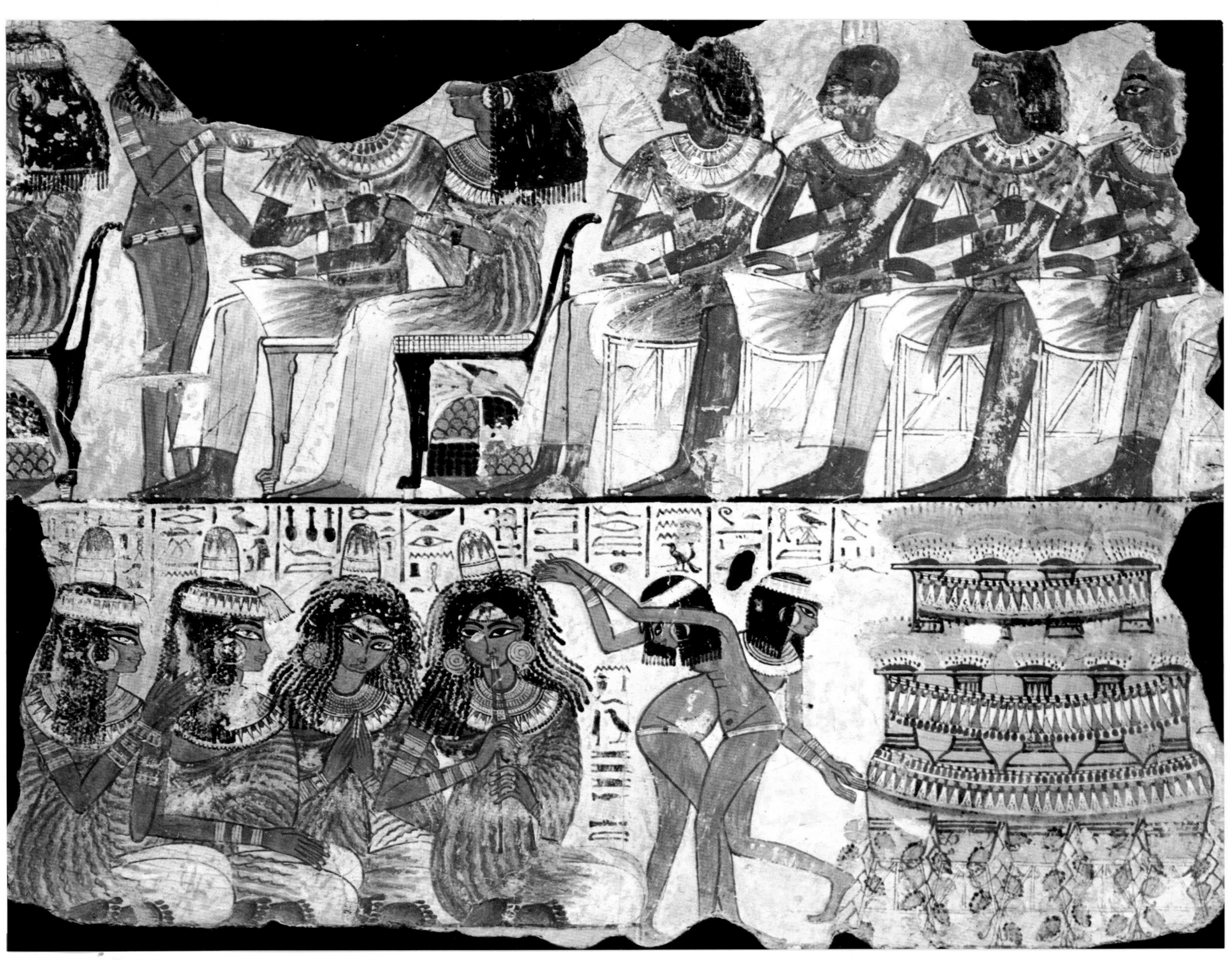

the artist takes an obvious delight in portraying every nuance in the clothing and other precious materials. The occupant of the tomb appears in the majesty of his office, and frequently the image of the pharaoh during whose reign he attained honour and standing also has a place in his tomb.

During the reign of Amenophis II it is the restrained nobility of a courtly world that we find expressed in the clear outlines of the figures, the loose way in which they are arranged in the plane, the austere plain style and the bare suggestion of gestures. Under Thutmosis IV the style becomes looser, the lines are drawn with greater verve, and the colours are soft and fluid. The gestures speak a more significant idiom. The figures are combined to form groups, in which they are related to one another by shared experience; and occasionally this is taken to a point where it conveys atmosphere.

A characteristic innovation is the artistic embellishment of utensils by means of human figures. On mirrors, Pl. 64, 65, Cat. 97–99 ointment jars and receptacles these play an aesthetic role subordinated to the practical purpose. Here too the imaginative and attractive treatment of these objects makes it clear that a work of art no longer begins with an ideal image of ritual significance; instead the image has come to serve a decorative purpose.

Cat. 70 The body of a war-chariot of Thutmosis IV features a scene depicting an encounter with hostile Asiatics. This compact work, with its overlappings and distortions of perspective, describes with astonishing virtuosity and sureness of touch the turmoil and excitement of the battle. The pharaoh is featured on the chariot as a general annihilating his enemies with bow and arrow. The accurate rendering of the Asiatics' characteristic ethnic features and costume deepens the impression that this is not a symbolic glorification of the triumphant pharaoh but a portrayal of an actual battle.

It may be assumed that during this period artists decorated pylons and temple walls with monumental scenes of campaigns and battles, and that these served as models for the scene on Thutmosis IV's war-chariot. The whole conception of the scene seems more suited for a large composition, so that this pictorial motif may be regarded as a replica of battle-scene reliefs which have not survived; for the earliest we have dates from the Ramessid Era.

In free-standing sculpture, as in relief works, the style becomes looser and more polished during the time of Amenophis II and Thutmosis IV. The tense vitality of the early phase of Dynasty XVIII gives way to a greater suppleness of form in the reign of the first of these two rulers; during the second the royal image occasionally has a coarse look, almost like that of a common citizen. This points to the transition from courtly chivalrous idealization of the sovereign to a realistic interpretation of his earthly existence. From a stylistic point of view private sculpture, too, follows this line of development. As was the case already during the Middle Kingdom, the statues of dignitaries had their place not only in the tomb but above all in the temple. They are for the most part life-sized, in conformity with the enhanced importance enjoyed by court officials, military leaders and priests. The favourite form for a free-standing work of sculpture was the block-statue or that of a '*naos*-bearer,' in which the figure carries a chapel with a divine image. During the Middle Kingdom the aim of the person represented was still to take part in the temple cult by way of his statue, for which he besought the sovereigns to make provision.

In the New Kingdom private sculpture becomes a monument to the deceased. The inscription describes his achievements on earth and the favourable points in his character, thereby expressing the growing self-confidence of the upper classes.

Pl. 66 Singer of Amun. Ebony, with layer of gold and silver over plaster. Dynasty XVIII, c. *1490 B.C. Height 39 cm. Pushkin Museum, Moscow.*

Pl. 67 Amenhotep, the priest. Ebony with remains of a layer of plaster. Dynasty XVIII, c. *1490 B.C. Height 40 cm. Pushkin Museum, Moscow.*

This world that had become so prosperous, which sought to rest from the burdens it had assumed and the battles it had fought in its rise to greatness, was yet to produce another age of splendour and beauty.

THE AGE OF MATURITY

Amenophis III inherited from his father a kingdom which extended from the Euphrates in the east to the Fourth Nile Cataract in the south. The immense wealth that Egypt obtained from the occupied provinces enabled him to keep court and to build on a majestic scale. During the first years of his reign he went on campaign to Nubia and took part in the traditional hunting expeditions which from time immemorial had been among the ritual functions of the pharaoh; but before long he withdrew completely from the extravagant splendour of life at court. In the field of foreign policy he continued the matrimonial alliances initiated by his father and sought to maintain friendly relations with Asiatic rulers. He paid court to the Mitannian princess Gilukhipa and later to Tadukhipa, and these overtures were welcomed by the Mitannian king Tushratta; her rich dowry was outweighed in value by gold from Nubia. The correspondence which has survived provides interesting information about the conventions of diplomatic intercourse and the political situation.

In times of political isolation, when the power of the sacrosanct kingship had been inviolate, the eastern neighbours were contemptuously referred to as 'these miserable Asiatics.' Now the rulers mix with one another on terms of equality. In letters the form of address is 'my brother,' signifying mutual recognition of the royal authority of each. At first, of course, the Egyptian pharaoh still has a position of seniority.

When the king of Babylonia, who had himself sent one of his daughters to the Egyptian court, for his part also asked for the hand of an Egyptian princess in marriage, his request was obviously regarded as unreasonable on the grounds that he was a foreigner, and in a haughty reply he was told that an Egyptian royal princess had never been

Pl. 68 Temple of Amenophis III at Luxor. Dynasty XVIII, c. 1380 B.C.

given in matrimony to a foreign court. The Babylonian resigned himself to this answer without protest and reduced his request to one for 'any good-looking Egyptian girl.'

On the other hand a liberal attitude of mind during Amenophis III's reign is reflected in his marriage to a commoner, the daughter of an official from Akhmim, whom he made his principal wife and queen. The significant role played by this forceful and shrewd woman, Queen Tiy, is apparent from the diplomatic correspondence discovered at Amarna and dating from the closing years of Amenophis III's reign and that of Amenophis IV (Akhnaton). It appears as though Queen Tiy, supported by some of her wise advisers, exerted a decisive influence upon foreign policy. While the ageing king indulged in the extravagant life at court a threatening change was taking place in the balance of power in the Near East. The Mitanni were harassed by the rising Hittite kingdom, to which the princes of the Syrian city-states adhered one after another. The archives at Amarna and the diplomatic correspondence discovered at Ugarit, in northern Syria, give an insight into the dangerous situation that resulted.

Pl. XVIII Lady-in-waiting. Wall-painting from a private tomb at Thebes. Dynasty XVIII, c. *1370 B.C. Height 39 cm. Kestner Museum, Hanover.*

The appeals for Egyptian military aid by the Mitannian king and the prince of Byblos were met with reserve at the Egyptian court. Finally, during the last years of the king's reign, a small number of troops were sent, but they could only impose a temporary and fragile peace. Amenophis himself never set foot on the soil of his Near Eastern provinces; he was quite alien to military matters and probably hardly noticed the approaching danger. The last years of his life were overshadowed by illness and debility, from which even the healing image of Ishtar from Nineveh, sent by his brother, the Mitannian king, could not cure him. It is, however, most revealing that foreign deities should have been called in to effect a miraculous cure.

In spiritual and artistic life Amenophis III's reign is a flourishing period. In architecture, as in painting and sculpture, the simple restrained Thutmosid style is superseded by curvature of form and elegance of line. A typical example of the architecture of this era is the temple at Luxor, which is in a good state of preservation, and served above all as a processional temple. A colonnade with seven papyriform columns on either side, the shafts and capitals of which follow the vegetal form of the papyrus plant, leads the visitor into a court surrounded on three sides by two rows of papyrus-bundle columns. The adjoining columned hall, in which the closely-packed columns draw the procession together and concentrate it, so to speak, provides access to the sacred area, the chapels containing statues of the gods. * Pl. 68

The architectural design systematizes and unites the various elements into a harmonious whole, in regard both to proportion and to form; it shows sensitivity and does justice to the cultic purpose of a processional temple. The buildings of Amenophis III show a striving toward large size and monumentality which, however, does not detract from the elegance of their general conception and the

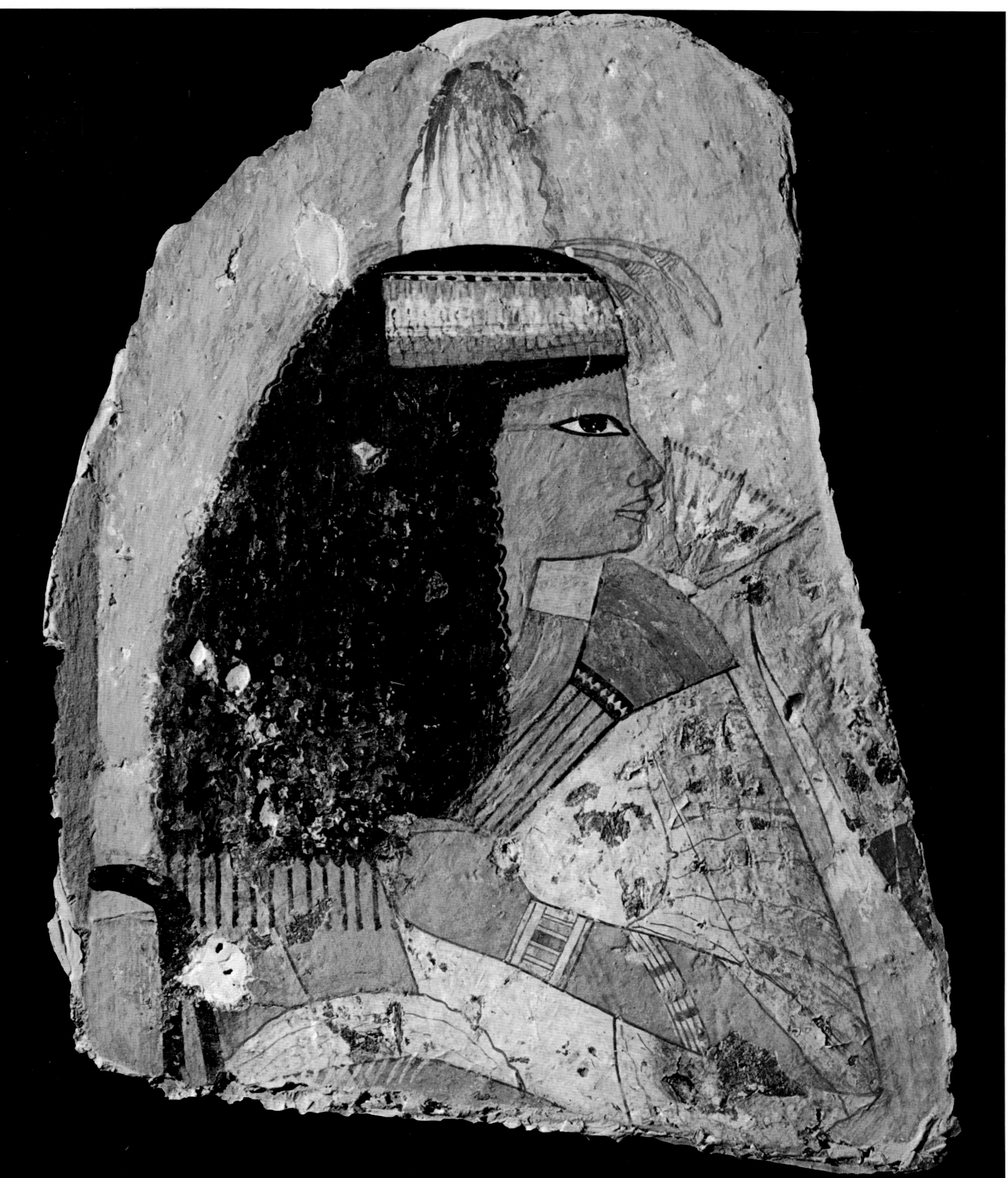

◁ *Pl. 69 Head of a statue of Amenophis III. Detail. Quartzite. From Thebes. Dynasty XVIII, c. 1370 B.C. Overall height 117 cm. British Museum, London.*

Pl. 70 Statue of the scribe Amenophis Hapu. Black granite. From Karnak. Dynasty XVIII, c. 1370 B.C. Height 130 cm. Cairo Museum.

Pl. 71 Statuette of Neferet-mau. Detail. Painted wood. Dynasty XVIII, c. 1380 B.C. Overall height 20.5 cm. Museo Egizio, Turin (cf. Cat. 33).

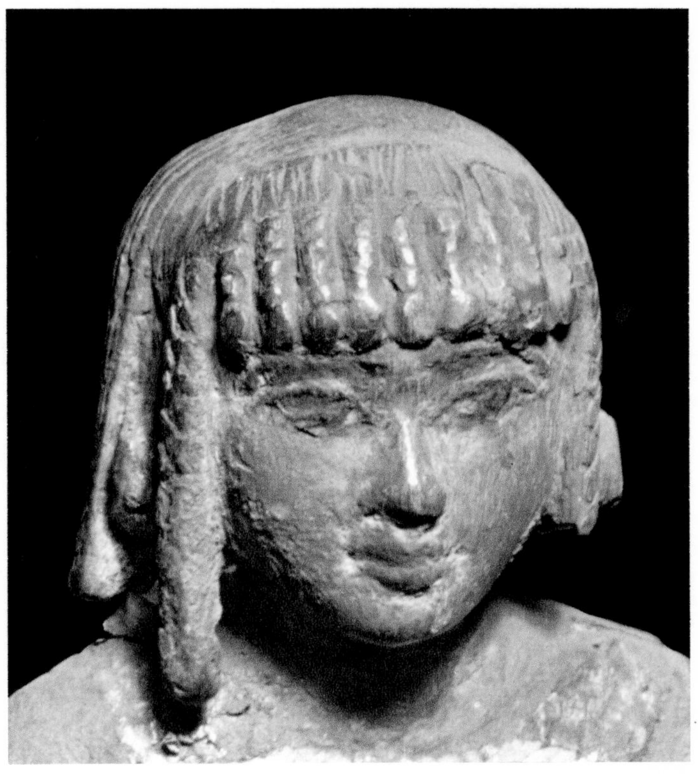

subtlety shown in the execution of details. Despite all the endeavours that have been made over the last few years, only an inadequate impression can be gained of what must once have been a magnificent mortuary temple built for the pharaoh on the west bank. That this temple was a centre of monumental splendour is evident from its dimensions and from the two colossi of the king, the 'colossi of Memnon.'

The free-standing statues of the age of maturity continue the efforts made in the closing phase of the Thutmosid era to develop a style true to nature and idealized by an aesthetic sense. These two apparently contradictory tendencies coexist side by side. The refined psychological interest in the outward shape and the nature of things has deepened since the time of Queen Hatshepsut and calls for a realistic treatment. But most of the works that have survived express the new aesthetic sense in graceful lines and gently curving forms; art has broken loose from the canonical scheme and in most cases also from the connection with ritual, and generates its meaning from within. The delight in outward splendour finds expression in the very elaborate rendering of elegant fashionable garments and lavish jewellery. In the image of the king we again
* Pl. 69 encounter a new concept, characteristic of the satiated state reached in this age of maturity, but some statues also anticipate the introspective spirituality that springs from the psychological experiences of the imperial period.

Cat. 8 The official monumental temple statues of Amenophis III follow the traditional manner of representation and have little to show in the way of inner spiritual content; in statuettes, on the other hand, stress is laid upon the human features. The king sometimes appears as a thick-set corpulent figure, in the easy-going posture of a commoner.
Cat. 17 The ebony statuette of the king, now in Brooklyn, has a delicately rounded elegant body and a full flabby face; the expression is of one lost in thought; it suggests a personality which tallies with the picture of Amenophis III handed down to us in the written sources. Particularly impressive are two quartzite portrait heads of the king, larger than life, originally from his mortuary temple and now in the British Museum. In these heads one can glimpse a little of the sophistication and sensitive spirituality of the age. The broad upper eyelids give the impression of a cryptic look, not of this world.

The full lips and refined cheeks suggest an almost decadent sensitivity and make the portrait an idealized one, rich in inner content. From it there radiates as much dignity as from the royal images of the Pyramid Period or from the portraits of the Middle Kingdom.

One of the most important personages at Amenophis III's court was his namesake Amenophis, son of Hapu, who

Pl. 72 Queen Tiy. Limestone relief from the tomb of Userhet at Thebes. Dynasty XVIII, c. 1370 B.C. Height 42 cm. Musées Royaux d'Art et d'Histoire, Brussels.

held various offices in the administration, among others that of chief architect of the royal buildings. Like Imho-
*Pl. xvi, Cat. 51 tep, the architect of the Zoser pyramid, he was remembered by the people as a sage right down to Ptolemaic times. The pharaoh gave him permission to build a mortuary temple of his own, a privilege normally reserved to sovereigns. Among the many statues of Amenophis Hapu which at one time stood in the Karnak temple there is one
Pl. 70 showing him as a scribe.

In contrast to the abstract forms which this figure was given in the Middle Kingdom, he is here again depicted squatting on the ground, the position of the hands indicating his occupation. In lieu of the tense alertness that characterized scribes in the Old Kingdom, we have here a figure sunk in meditation, wrapped up in his own concerns, as the tilt of the head suggests. The gentle well-cared-for look and the expression of emotional spirituality convey the psychological mood of the country's intellectual élite during the age of maturity in the New Kingdom. Wherever it was not just a matter of achieving artistic effect by representing the over-sophisticated ostentatious society of the period, an effort was made to grasp
* Pl. 72 the psychological problems that beset people of the day, and in this we can sometimes see portents of the decadence to come.

Pl. 21, Cat. 33, 35 Smaller statuettes in wood or ivory, some of them of first-rate quality, reflect the artistic taste of the age. The wigs and fine jewellery are rendered with elaborate care. The gracefully shaped figures express the cultivated noble attitude adopted in this age of maturity.

In the wall-paintings of private tombs it is the buoyant *joie de vivre* of spoiled aristocratic society that is the most
Pl. xvii, xviii conspicuous feature. Banqueting scenes in particular afford the artist a gratifying opportunity to achieve a painterly effect of line and colour. Dainty female musicians and dancers enliven those participating in the feast, who are seated in noble composure. This delight in representation, in the potentialities of the medium, lends these pictures a new dynamism; with their overlappings, foreshortenings of perspective, composite groups and even their *en face* views they seem to approximate more and more closely to the natural movement of the figures.

Representations of funerals afford the possibility to express the stirring ecstasy of grief by vehement gestures and gesticulations. Shared experience gives the figures in these scenes inner tension and unity. The art of this period enjoys a wide range of possibilities for expressing the innermost emotions of joy and grief. The same intensity which the artist shows in penetrating the human psyche is evident in his treatment of the world he lives in.

Temple art has little to show of the stirring beauty and profundity of these new experiences, even though the delicate touch with which the lines are drawn in relief works is in conformity with contemporary style. In the temple at Luxor Amenophis III had carved a sequence of scenes depicting his divine procreation and birth following the model provided in Hatshepsut's mortuary temple. A relief from the tomb of Userhet at Thebes, portraying Queen Tiy, despite all the delicacy and fluidity of line, keeps to the tradition of official court art, which seems quite appropriate for a member of the royal dynasty who is here to be found in the tomb of an official.

The differences of style which develop between official temple art, bound as it is by tradition, and free artistic activity become ever more evident. They show how far religion and politics have moved away from the living contemporary world and the changes taking place in men's outlook. But it is precisely this law of change, to which all life is subject, that provides the impulse to artistic creation. In Egyptian art, too, this was to lead to new possibilities of self-expression and further stylistic changes.

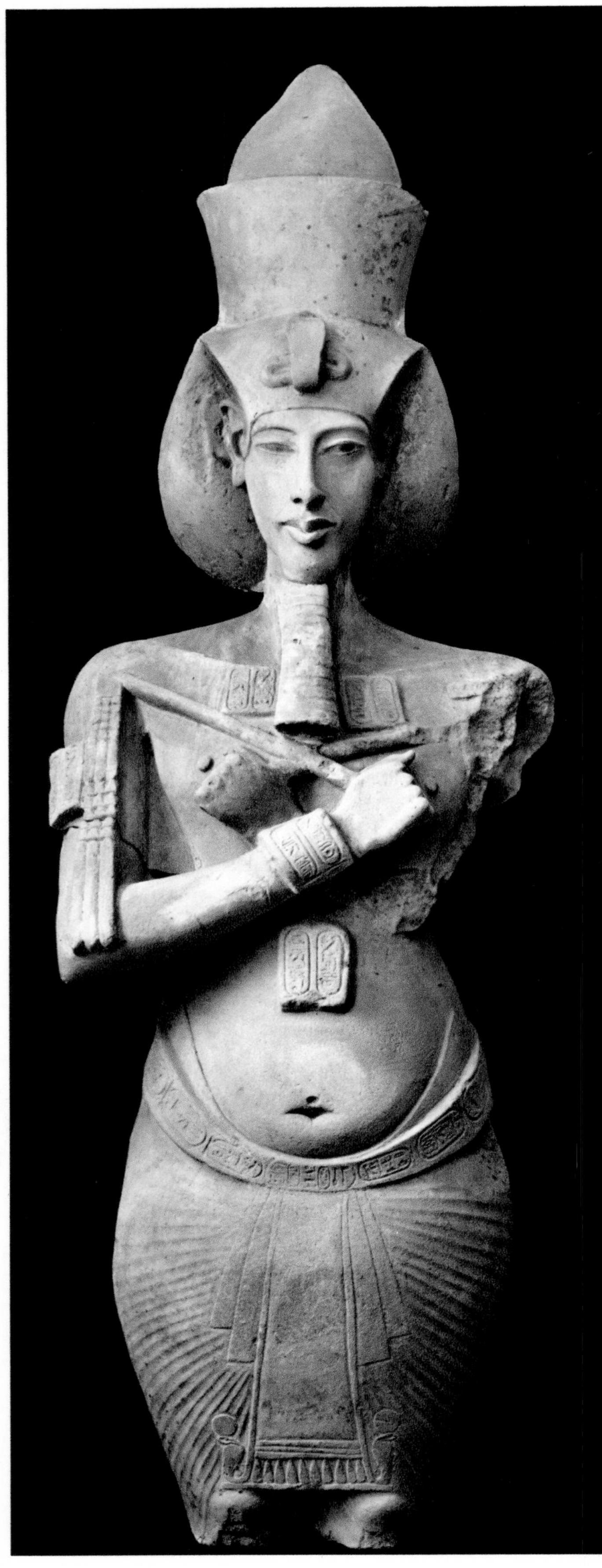

Pl. 73 Amenophis IV (Akhnaton). Reddish-brown sandstone with remains of colour. From the pillared court of the Aton temple at Karnak. Dynasty XVIII, c. *1360 B.C. Height* c. *400 cm. Cairo Museum.*

THE AMARNA PERIOD

During the age of maturity the interconnection between politics, economic life, social structure and the religious concepts embodied in the national cult was particularly close; accordingly a change in any of these spheres was bound to affect them all.

At the beginning of his reign King Amenophis IV was supported by two persons with lively critical minds: Queen Tiy, who exercised a major influence upon affairs of state, and the military commander, Ay, formerly tutor to the young king. But it soon became evident that Amenophis IV possessed neither the inclination nor the talent to be a pharaoh of the traditional type who would fulfil the functions expected of him. His character was fundamentally different from that of his predecessors on the throne of the pharaohs. In evaluating his personality, little importance need be attached to his significance as statesman and king; on the other hand already as a young man he felt very certain that he had a vocation to reform the faith.

Amenophis IV's revolutionary changes in religious life were wholly rooted in the social, political and spiritual circumstances inherited from the preceding period; nevertheless they produced a violent upheaval in Egyptian culture. The reason for this may have been that for the first time in Egyptian history an individual personality, with all the self-confident passion of a reformer, intervened in the domain of religious beliefs, which had become outdated and no longer corresponded to the requirements of the day.

Amun, the great king of gods, with his characteristics borrowed from the sun-god Rē, had never been a clearly defined figure. In his capacity as national god of the Egyptian empire the political aspects of his character had

Pl. 74 Hand of Amenophis IV (Akhnaton). Limestone relief. From Hermopolis. Dynasty XVIII, c. 1350 B.C. Height 23.5 cm., width 27.5 cm. Norbert Schimmel Collection, New York.

Pl. 75 Courtiers bowing before the queen. Painted limestone relief. From Hermopolis. Dynasty XVIII, c. 1360 B.C. Height 22.5 cm., width 54 cm. Norbert Schimmel Collection, New York.

been uppermost. Contact with Asiatic cultures was bound to lead Egyptians to compare critically their gods with those of others. This enlargement of their horizon made them feel the need for a god that was universal in scope. The prerequisites for such a universal god were present in the cosmic qualities of the ancient sun-god Rē.

The reform of Amenophis IV may in the first place be seen as an attempt to liberate the sun-god from the interpretations and distortions that had accrued over the centuries, with the object of elucidating the proper nature of the sun cult and approximating as closely as possible to the truth. This intention Amenophis announced by taking at his accession the name: 'he who lives in truth, the only one of Rē.' In reliefs he first appears, like his predecessors, as a worshipper of the national god Amun, to which was soon added the figure of the falcon-headed Rē under the term 'Aton,' which occurs from time to time in the Old Kingdom as an expression denoting the disc of the sun. Soon afterwards the falcon-headed sun-god Rē is superseded by Aton, the sun's round disc, whose rays Pl. 76 terminate in hands holding the written character for 'life.' This transformation of the image of the sun-god signifies a renunciation of the ancient traditions of Heliopolitan doctrine, with its elaborate mythological interpretation of

Pl. XIX Two daughters of King Akhnaton. Detail of a wall-painting from the palace near the Aton temple in Amarna. Dynasty XVIII, c. 1350 B.C. Ashmolean Museum, Oxford.

the creation and of the cosmic system. The Aton cult is restricted to worship of the sun as the life-giving and life-sustaining force. No longer bound by its former human or animal guise, the sun cult acquires a monotheistic character appropriate to a universally effective force. On the other hand, of course, the exposition of this doctrine and its proclamation were closely linked with the person of the king, who is the only one to recognize the nature of the god. As a consequence Aton is only depicted in combination with the king and his family, who are shown worshipping him and making offerings to him. The conception underlying the Amarna cult is a contradictory one: on one hand, it represents a striving after eternal truth, an effort to discover the one great god, which is deeply moving; on the other hand, it contains an inherent weakness that explains why it remained only an episode in Egyptian religious history. In earlier times the mythological interpretation of the gods had given man a readily comprehensible idea of the way in which they functioned. Because this was completely lacking in the Amarna Period, the new doctrine did not satisfy the common people.

The revolutionary concepts of the king find visible expression in the artistic layout of the Aton temple which

Pl. 76 King Amenophis IV (Akhnaton) as a sphinx under the rays of the sun, Aton. From Amarna. C. 1357–1354 B.C. *Height 59 cm., width 93.2 cm. Kestner Museum, Hanover.*

Pl. 73 he built at Karnak. The colossal statues of the king which he erected there make a breach with previous artistic tradition. Among the portraits of sovereigns from past centuries, depicted in all the dignity of their office, that of Amenophis IV appears as a terrible distortion. His body is infirm and deformed, with a swollen abdomen; he has a narrow ascetic face, with a sagging chin, full lips, and narrow slanting eyes. The exaggeration of the features indicates that artistic form was subordinated to purpose, the purpose being to convey spiritual content. This expressionistic tendency suggests that these statues were consciously designed to propagate the Aton doctrine. The king was no doubt aware of this possibility, for contemporary sources record that he himself sought to create a new artistic style. The fact that the statues were erected in the sacred temple area of the national god Amun may have seemed monstrous to the priests of the great temple at Karnak, who could only take this as a challenge.

Pl. 77 Two daughters of King Akhnaton. Sunk limestone relief. From Hermopolis. Dynasty XVIII, c. 1350 B.C. Height 19.5 cm., width 20.5 cm. Kestner Museum, Hanover.

Pl. 78 King Semenkhara (?). Plaster. From Amarna, House P. 47.2, Room 19. Dynasty XVIII, c. 1350 B.C. Height 21 cm. Stiftung Preussischer Kulturbesitz, Staatliche Museen, Berlin.

We cannot show in detail the extent to which the king's reform may be regarded as a rebellion against the religious and temporal ascendancy of the Theban priests. During the sixth year of his reign the breach with spiritual tradition was completed outwardly as well. The king changed his name from Amenophis ('Amun is satisfied') to Akhnaton ('pleasing to Aton'). At the same time preparations were made to move the court and government to Amarna in Middle Egypt. This decision may have been prompted in part by a desire to avoid the opposition of the Theban priests and senior officials and in part by a desire to give the god Aton a temple of his own in an area free from different religious traditions.

The new concept of the deity is elucidated in the formulation of the sun-god's title: 'Rē, lord of the two horizons, who rejoices on the horizon, lives in his name of Rē the Father, who has appeared as Aton.' No attempt was made to interpret the doctrine dogmatically. King Akhnaton's well-known hymn to the sun in the tomb of Ay and the hymns to the sun in other private tombs at Amarna provide no clues as to the theological content of the Aton cult. They sing of the all-embracing creative power of the sun manifest in all living phenomena:

'Beautiful is thine appearing in the horizon of heaven, / thou living sun, the first who lived. / Thou risest in the eastern horizon and / fillest every land with thy beauty.... / When thou goest down in the western horizon, / the earth is in darkness, as if it were dead. / The sleepers in their chambers / rest with their faces hidden and / no eye seeth the other.... / The beasts come forth from their caves / and the worms begin to bite.... / The earth is silent, for its creator / resteth in his horizon.... / When dawn breaks and thou risest in the heavens, / thou dispellest the darkness and sheddest thy beams. / The Two Lands keep festival, they awake / and stand on their feet. They wash their bodies / and take their garments. Their

◁ *Pl. 79 Plaster mask of a man. From Amarna, House P. 47.2, Room 19. Dynasty XVIII, c. 1350 B.C. Height 13 cm. Stiftung Preussischer Kulturbesitz, Staatliche Museen, Berlin.*

Pl. 80 Upper part of a statue of a woman. Limestone. Dynasty XVIII, c. 1320 B.C. Height 50 cm. Museo Archeologico di Firenze, Florence.

Pl. XX King Akhnaton. Painted plaster. From Amarna, House P. 47.2, Room 19. Dynasty XVIII, c. 1350 B.C. Height 25 cm. Stiftung Preussischer Kulturbesitz, Staatliche Museen, Berlin.

arms / are lifted in praise of thee and / the whole land doeth its work. / All beasts are content with their pastures. / The trees and herbs are verdant. The birds / fly down from their nests and lift their / wings to praise thy person. . . . / Thou hast fashioned the earth according to thy desire. / Thou alone, with men, cattle and / all wild beasts that are upon the earth / and go upon feet, and all that soar / above and fly with their wings. / Thou puttest every man in his place and / suppliest their needs. . . . / Thou makest millions of forms of thyself alone. / Thou art in mine heart and there is / none other that knoweth thee save / thy son, Neferkheprure, Sole one of Rē, / to whom thou revealeth thy nature and power. . . .'[8]

In the expression of the sun cult fanatical reformatory zeal is superseded by a hymn of lyrical poetry.

In the seclusion of the royal residence at Amarna it was possible for artistic style to develop on consistent lines. In the case of cult scenes showing Akhnaton and his Pl. 74, 76, 77
followers under rays terminating in hands, the distorted expressive style remains obligatory. Whether they are in temples, on free-standing stelae or in private tombs, these official images have the meaning of a religious and political manifesto. They no longer contain any harmony of proportion, or the gentle fluid lines of the preceding period; they give the impression of being unbalanced in structure; the style in which they are executed reflects a distorted and nerve-wracked decadence.

The reliefs in the tombs of court officials contain almost without exception motifs which bear a relation to the king, his teaching and his life. In inscriptions court officials and servants bow low in obeisance before their Pl. 75, Cat. 66
sovereign and boast that the king himself has instructed them in the Aton cult. Akhnaton's claim to be the sole interpreter of the god created a wide gulf between the royal prophet on one hand and the people on the other, who approached him only in humble submission and veneration. Alternatively, people may have been attracted by the charm of the motif, which occurs in the Amarna style, of officials bowing down humbly before the king and even prostrating themselves with their faces in the dust.

The very human and personal atmosphere which emerges toward the end of the Amarna Period in reliefs depicting the royal family corresponds to the joyous, friendly character attributed to Aton in the hymn to the sun, as one who grants man a life free from all dangers and problems. This intimacy of feeling, the belief that all natural phenomena enjoyed Aton's loving solicitude, led in

Pl. 81 General Horemheb receiving foreign ambassadors. Detail of a limestone relief from the tomb of Horemheb at Saqqara. Dynasty XVIII, c. 1330 B.C. Rijksmuseum van Oudheden, Leyden.

Amarna art to a deepening of intellectual and spiritual content and to a graceful style. In the delicately coloured murals of palaces and dwelling-houses an unconstrained, truly artistic effect was achieved. This dispensed entirely with the preliminary drawing or outline; every link with the canons of composition and style was abandoned. In place of guide-lines we have delicate shadings of colour which give the picture a harmonious fluidity and gentleness. Darker tones are employed for the outline of the torso, which produce a plastic animated effect. A detail from a mural in the town palace at Amarna shows the new possibilities that were opened up in painting. Two daughters of the king are depicted squatting upon high leather cushions. The shape of their bodies, the thin necks and protruding bulge at the back of the head are in conformity with Amarna style. The affectionate relationship between the young nude girls, with their delicately modelled limbs, evokes a lyrical mood. Overlappings and nuances of

*Pl. XIX

Pl. 82 Head of a statue of an unknown person. Grey quartzite. Dynasties XVIII/XIX, c. 1300 B.C. Height 23 cm. Museo Egizio, Turin.

Pl. 83 Dancer. Painted limestone sherd (ostracon). Dynasties XVIII/XIX, c. 1300 B.C. Height 10.5 cm., width 16.8 cm. Museo Egizio, Turin.

colour produce an illusion of depth, bounded by the ornamented background.

The artists' delight in the picturesque also leads them to represent living things. Nature no longer forms a mere Cat. 54 backcloth against which some event takes place. In the Aton cult all creatures—'everything that grows, everything that flies and everything that crawls'—enjoy the sun-god's blessing; and so nature itself appears worthy to be depicted. In the colourful landscapes on the palace floor birds can be seen frolicking in the jungle, and fish playing in the water. The representation of the limitless abundance of nature does not require the elements portrayed to be combined to form a single scene. In one room of the pleasure palace at Amarna there is a painting which ★ Pl. xx, Pl. 78, 79 extends freely across all the wall surfaces, without any interruption by the corners of the room or any apparent articulation, producing the illusion of a spacious, smiling and animated landscape.

With most Amarna sculpture we are dealing either with Pl. 78, 79 plaster models from workshops or with unfinished parts of free-standing statues, which must be considered preliminary or intermediary stages in the fashioning of the final product. A number of heads of princesses have a large protuberance at the back which has led to the much-discussed problem whether this feature represents a physical deformity, a current fashion, or a stylistic effect. It may be assumed that some deformity of the body hereditary in the royal family was the reason why this striking peculiarity was represented. This would conform completely to the effort made to render a true image both inwardly and outwardly. But no doubt artists soon succumbed to the temptation to exaggerate this sweeping curve, so that in the subsequent period the reasons for the deformed heads will have been chiefly stylistic. This hypothesis is corroborated by the fact that many court officials who certainly did not all suffer from the same complaint had themselves portrayed with this bulge at the back of their head.

The naturalistic shape of head and the individual facial features of a number of plaster masks have raised the question whether they might be masks modelled on living persons, and whether the intention may have been to produce a true portrait. From all that we know about the underlying spiritual principles of the period this theory does not seem very convincing. In the Amarna Period the aim was not to produce a portrait-like resemblance. The personal expression of the face masks may be much more plausibly explained by the endeavours made during this period to attain inner truth. Apart from this, in these plaster masks the natural portrait was doubtless already stylistically modified. The plaster portraits of the king and of unknown private persons express a spiritual content which does not reveal any inner connection with the problems of everyday life, but instead suggests devotion to a religious and spiritual outlook; on the other hand in the

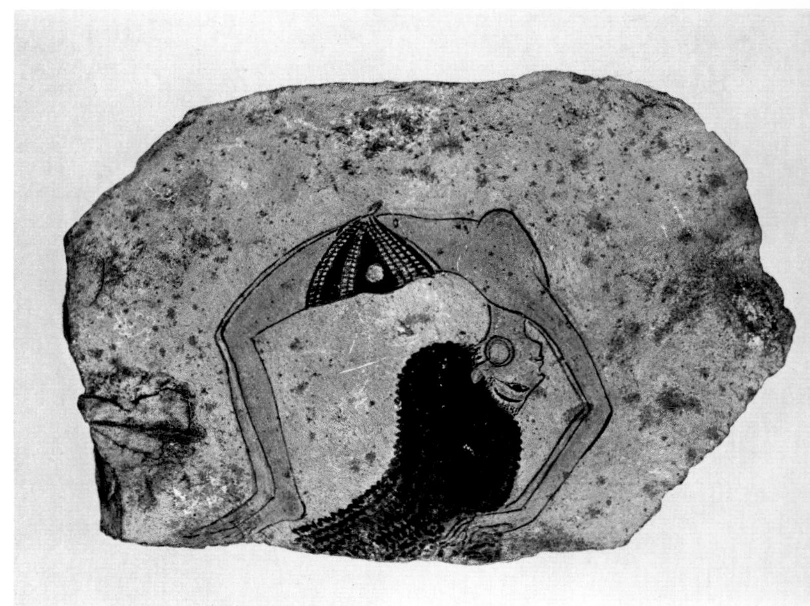

little yew wood head of Tiy an entirely different world lies before us. This impressive sculpture also indicates the spiritual attitude of this humbly-born queen: the slanting almond-shaped eyes, with their critical and censorious stare, look out from beneath lowered eyelids; the corners of the mouth are turned down, and the furrows leading to the nostrils evoke an impression of haughty disdain for the things of this world—an attitude which reveals her inner feelings about the life of her time. The king's portrait depicts him as a reformer, a seeker after truth, a prophet convinced of his mission, a man carried away by his praise of the deity; Tiy, on the other hand, wears an expression befitting this shrewd woman, who has achieved maturity from her bitter experience of intrigue and is more than a match for the responsibilities that have fallen to her. * Pl. XXI

While the king, in the isolation of his residence at Amarna, devoted himself to religious and philosophical contemplation, and revelled in the exuberant emotional atmosphere of life at court, a critical situation was developing at home and abroad that heralded the gradual collapse of the Egyptian empire. When he had transferred his residence to Amarna, the king had dismissed most of his officials of long standing and had chosen courtiers and administrators from among supporters of the Aton cult, upon whose devotion he could reckon. Most of them came from the lower classes of the people or from abroad. It may be assumed that they were not so much shrewd far-sighted officials with political experience as ambitious loyal courtiers who were unable to exert any influence upon the pharaoh. But the king left matters of foreign policy to these officials and watched passively as a menacing situation developed in Asia. The valuable Egyptian possessions in Syria and Palestine fell victim to the assaults of the Amorites and Hittites. Throughout the country there were conflicts and divisions of opinion. In this period of discontent and weak government two power groups emerged which

Pl. XXI Queen Tiy. Detail. Yew wood, gold and paste. From Medinet Gurob. Dynasty XVIII, c. 1350 B.C. Overall height 10.7 cm. Stiftung Preussischer Kulturbesitz, Staatliche Museen, Berlin.

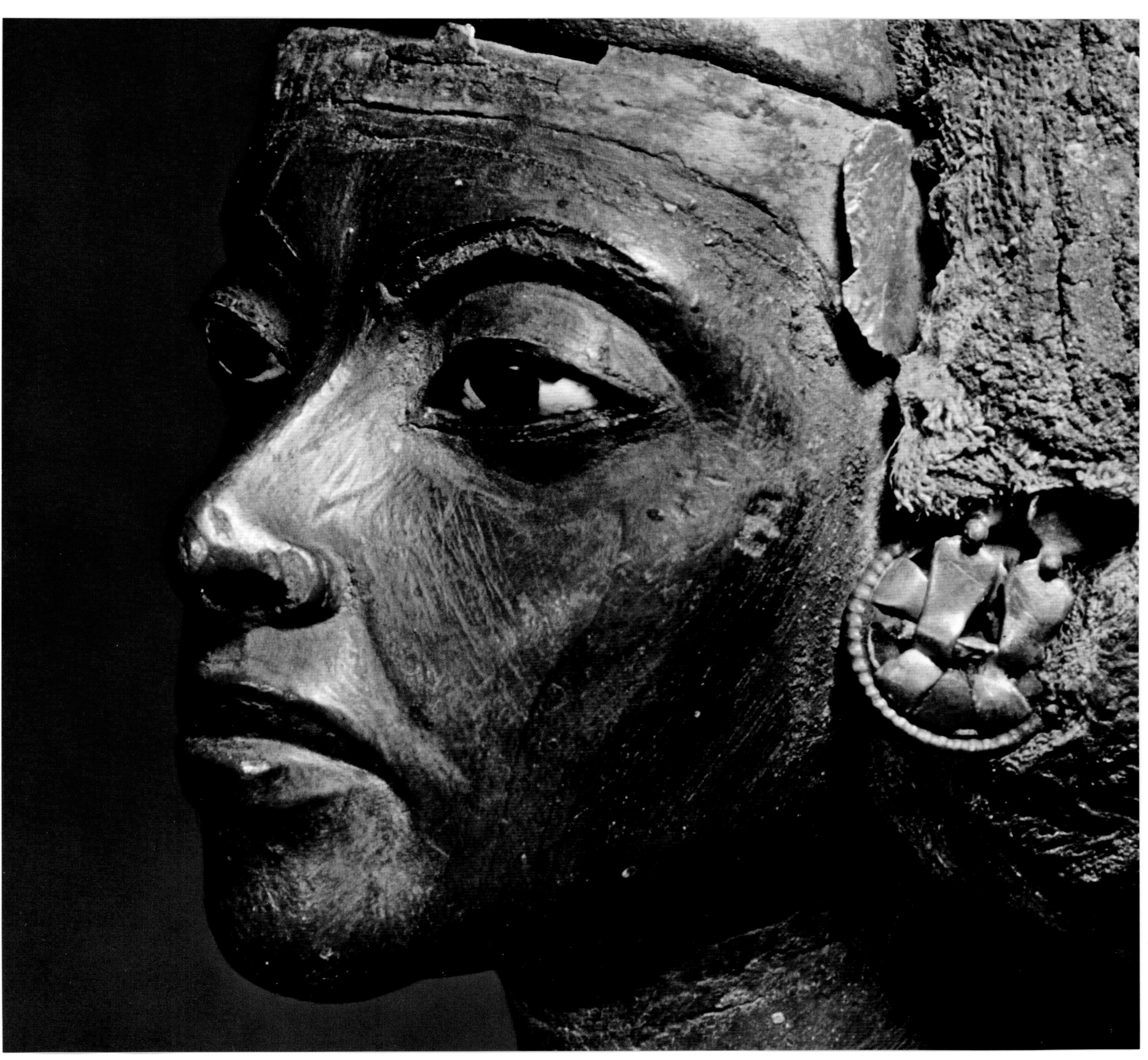

* Pl. XXII, Cat. 93

were to play a significant role in future developments. The priests of Amun were able to consolidate and expand their spiritual and above all their temporal influence; and simultaneously the military leaders also gained in esteem and importance.

The succession to the throne was in doubt. Since Nefertiti, the chief consort of the king, had not born him a son, Amenophis (Akhnaton) appointed his son-in-law Semenkhara as co-regent. Many of the actions which they took during their four years of joint rule suggest a realization on their part that the revolutionary venture at Amarna had failed. Probably with the approval of the king, Semenkhara built a mortuary temple at Thebes which was simultaneously used for the Amun cult; and in temples throughout the country Amun and the other provincial deities regained their ancient rights. After both the king and the regent Semenkhara had died, the throne passed to Tutankhaton, likewise a son-in-law of Akhnaton. Since he was so young, Ay, one of the most important personalities at court from the beginning of the reign of Amenophis IV (Akhnaton), managed affairs of state for approximately ten years. During this period a gradual restoration took place. The residence was transferred back from Amarna to Thebes. With this step and the change in the king's name to Tutankhamun the Amarna Period officially came to a close; the god Aton speedily fell into utter oblivion. Amenophis (Akhnaton) passed into history as the heretical king of Amarna. In antiquity people were scarcely aware of his tragic life, which we can sense when we study the history of the Amarna Period and examine the works of art that it produced.

* Pl. 80, 81, Cat. 61–63, 72

In the monuments of this transitional period the attractive style of the Late Amarna Period was continued in a graceful, if sometimes also mannered, form. Idyllic genre scenes, which also occur on objects of everyday use, display the elegance of a cultivated and somewhat decadent age. The rich treasure in the tomb of Tutankhamun, who died early in life, provides an insight into the material and artistic wealth of royal funerary furniture during this period. Tutankhamun was succeeded on his death by Ay, who as we have seen had been in charge of state affairs for some years. His accession to the throne was contested, but he gained the support of a general named Horemheb, whom the elderly Ay appointed his deputy and successor.

For the developments that followed it proved important that the successor to the throne was an energetic person with military experience. From the reign of Amenophis III onwards the dynasty had become visibly weary and decadent; much of Egypt's former glory and prestige had been gambled away; the state was on the brink of collapse. The new ruler, Horemheb, brought in fresh blood and a martial spirit which reinvigorated the monarchy. He undertook internal reforms in an attempt first of all to extirpate corrupt and inefficient administrative practices, and launched a campaign into Syria and another to Nubia designed to improve the security of the remaining Egyptian military bases. He built his tomb at Saqqara, not far from the residence at Memphis, in the ancient city of the dead; and here, too, high officials of Tutankhamun's time found their last resting-place. In the reliefs of these tombs Amarna art finds final mature expression. Their introspective style, which penetrates into the innermost recesses of psychological experience, translates the creative spiritual and artistic achievements of the Amarna Period into a balanced harmony appropriate to a world that once again appears to be stable.

The reliefs in the tombs of Horemheb and of the high priest Neferronpet have figures grouped dynamically, which seem to display a profound psychological insight into the events of their time; they reflect the spiritualization to which the Amarna Period had led.

Pl. 84 Head of a statue of Sethos I. Granite. Dynasty XIX, c. 1300 B.C. Height 24 cm. Roemer-Pelizaeus Museum, Hildesheim.

Pl. 85 Portico of the rock-cut temple of Ramses II at Abu Simbel. Dynasty XIX, c. 1250 B.C.

Pl. 86 Hypostyle hall of Ramses II in the temple at Karnak. Detail. Dynasty XIX, c. 1250 B.C.

THE RAMESSID ERA

Horemheb's measures to restore the political order and safeguard the kingdom against foreign enemies were continued by Ramses I, who at first held office as a general, vizier and deputy to the king and then assumed the throne on Horemheb's death. After a brief reign he was succeeded by his son Sethos (Seti) I, who managed to recover Palestine and the Lebanon. He also endeavoured to reconquer Syria from the Hittites; his efforts in this direction were continued by his son, Ramses II, who fought the famous battle at Kadesh, but was unable to secure a decisive victory. On the other hand, a little later Hattusil, the Hittite king, showed himself prepared to conclude a treaty of peace and friendship with Ramses II, because he felt threatened by the rise of the mighty Assyrian empire. The amicable relations between the two empires were consolidated by vigorous commercial exchanges and by the marriage of Ramses to a daughter of the Hittite king.

To protect the border against the Libyans, who during the reign of Sethos I had attempted to invade the western Delta, Ramses II built a belt of fortifications. The southern border was secure and peace prevailed there. Thus all the

prerequisites were created for the economic and cultural efflorescence which Egypt experienced during the reign of Ramses II.

Under Merneptah, a son of Ramses II, and his successors trouble flared up again in the Near East and the Mediterranean lands. The so-called 'Peoples of the Sea,' among whom were Sherden, Tyrsenians, Philistines and Acheans, harassed towns on the Egyptian coast, and the Libyans also renewed their inroads upon the western Delta.

It was in this dangerous situation that internal troubles developed over the succession to the throne, and it was not until Dynasty XX that Egypt was in a position to resume her struggle against hostile invaders. Nothing is known about the origin of the founder of Dynasty XX, Setnakht. His successors bear the name of Ramses and carry on the tradition of the Ramessid Era in every respect. With Ramses III, a son of Setnakht, a strong ruler once more accedes to the ancient throne of the pharaohs. In the west he succeeds in driving out the Libyans and on the eastern border fights a great naval battle against the immigrants to whose pressure the Hittite empire had succumbed. Towards the end of his reign, and after his violent death, internal opposition and economic difficulties, which his weakened kingdom could not counter effectively, led to a disruption of political unity.

The political task of the Ramessid Era was to protect the heritage of a great epoch, the fruit of the natural supremacy of the Egyptian state, which had made it the leading power in the Near East. The time of aggressive wars is over and the attempts to recover the jeopardized areas and to protect the frontiers take on an increasingly defensive character. Just as in their external and internal policies the Ramessids were pre-eminently restorers, so also in their cultural activity they must be seen as endeavouring to return to ancient traditions. The immense amount of construction in which the sovereigns of Dynasties XIX and XX engaged al-

Pl. XXII Queen Ankheseamun and King Tutankhamun. Gold-plate mounting from a wooden shrine. From Tutankhamun's tomb. Dynasty XVIII, c. 1340 B.C. Height 49 cm. Cairo Museum.

◁ *Pl. 87 Statue of Ramses II. Black granite. From Thebes. Dynasty XIX, c. 1250 B.C. Height 194 cm. Museo Egizio, Turin.*

Pl. 88 Ramses II fighting the Hittites in the battle of Kadesh. Detail from a relief on the outside wall of the great pylon of the temple at Luxor. Dynasty XIX, c. 1270 B.C.

Pl. 89 Tilling the soil in the world beyond. Detail from the 'Book of the Dead' compiled for the priest Anhai. Papyrus. Dynasty XXII, c. 1100 B.C. British Museum, London.

most suggests that they wanted to make visible once again the entire grandeur and power of the pharaonic state.

Architecture and sculpture follow the traditional style. The new contribution which is made in this period is limited to two apparently contradictory tendencies, evident above all in the monuments from the reigns of Sethos I and Ramses II. On the one hand sculpture reverts to the elegant and graceful style of the late phase of Dynasty XVIII, developing an extra-refined, highly sensitive idiom both in form and in expression. On the other hand there is a greater fondness for monumental proportions, which serve to enhance the effect of works of architecture and sculpture. Both trends are characteristic of the final phase of artistic development, based upon a great creative tradition. Both possibilities contain the danger of rigid formalism, such as does indeed develop at the close of the New Kingdom. Nineteenth-Dynasty architecture and art, however, usually succeeds in avoiding decadent over-emphasis, which turns artistic form into empty mannerism or finds fulfilment purely in mastery of the colossal.

Apart from these creative achievements, springing from the contemporary spirit, there develops during the Ramessid Era a historical consciousness which goes beyond the immediate past to embrace the cultural legacy of which the Ramessids were the heirs. It is this spirit that leads men to protect and restore the monuments of the Pyramid Period and occasionally to have recourse to the artistic forms of the past. Inscriptions by visitors on the walls of temples show that at this time they were regarded quite literally as 'historical sights.' Temples were built in all parts of the country by the Ramessid pharaohs, and in

*Pl. 82, 83, Cat. 29, 75

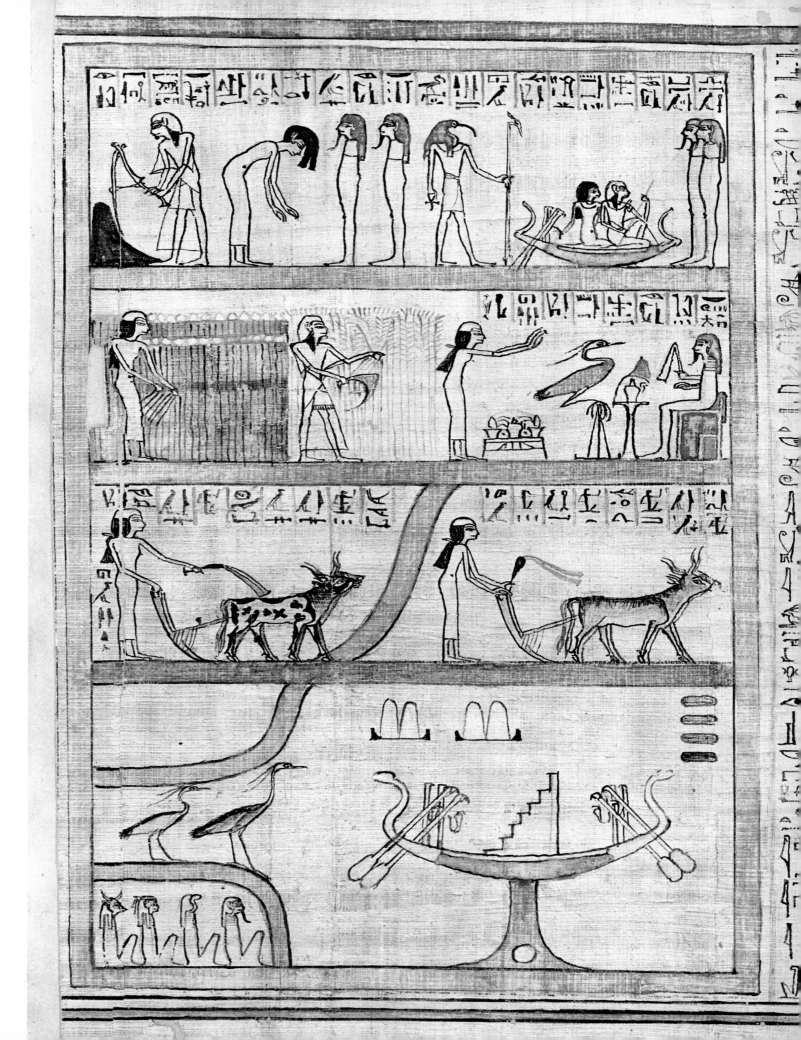

Pl. 90 The priest Niajj and his wife obtaining food and drink from the tree-goddess. Under the tree their souls appear in the guise of birds. Painted limestone relief. From Abu Sir. Dynasties XVIII/XIX, c. 1310 B.C. Height 56 cm., width 59.5 cm. Kestner Museum, Hanover.

particular by Ramses II. At Abydos, sacred to Osiris, god of the dead, Sethos I built for himself a dummy tomb. The mortuary temple which belongs to it follows completely in its architectonic style the tradition of the Old Kingdom. It is clear that here preference was consciously given to the venerable historical form rather than to the contemporary style, such as was employed, for example, in the temple at Abydos, where various deities were worshipped. This was not completed until the reign of Ramses II.

Two slightly sloping courts, situated one behind the other and enclosed at the rear by pillared porticoes, lead through two adjoining hypostyle halls to the offering-chapels of the deities. The modifications in the archi-
* Pl. 86 tecture are most plainly evident in the massive papyrus-bundle columns with their bulbous bases and thick shafts covered with inscriptions. They look heavy and clumsy; the vegetal shape, upon which columns had been based from Thutmosis III's reign onwards, is now lost. The dominant feature is their gigantic size, and there is no
* Pl. 85 longer an elegant harmonious interplay between the different elements.

Cat. 41 The reliefs of the temples at Abydos, on the contrary,
* Cat. 10 continue the graceful style of Amenophis III's reign. The outlines and the treatment of details are firmer and more clear-cut; the distinguished elegance of the figures, evident both in their attitude and expression, reveals deliberation and sureness of touch; so too do the balanced arrangement of the composition and the accurate rendering of the costume, head-dress and crowns. The natural grace of the age of maturity has been modified into a noble reserve, which occasionally has a cool and dry look about it. In plastic art similar influences and tendencies can be felt.

Pl. 84 The fine granite head of Sethos I, now at Hildesheim, is a royal portrait which displays a kingly humanity in its supple modelling, sensitive mouth and gentle features.

The number of buildings erected under Ramses II, who ruled for sixty-six years, is almost incredible. The residence of the Ramessids near Kantir in the eastern part of the Delta is embellished with temples, obelisks and statues, most of which were simply taken from earlier temples. When the government moved from Memphis to Ramses' city in 1270 B.C., within a few years a political centre came into being which did justice to the contemporary striving after monumentality. In all parts of the country there are traces of the building activity of this pharaoh, so that it is not surprising that Ramses II's name should be one of the best known in the history of the ancient world. Among the most impressive buildings of his time is the stupendous hypostyle hall in the temple at Karnak, which contains 134 columns measuring between 60 and 40 feet in height. When it was in use for ritual ceremonies and processions, the superhuman grandeur of this architecture must have aroused in those present a feeling of reverence for the eternal divine law.

Among buildings in Nubia special significance attaches to the rock-cut temple at Abu Simbel. The entire temple complex, with two pillared halls, one sited at an angle, and a chapel, is cut into the rock. On either side of the entrance are two seated figures of Ramses II, likewise hewn out of the rock. Despite their colossal size they are executed with sureness of touch and demonstrate the merits of the rigid norms governing the way in which a work of sculpture was fashioned. The effect they evoke in the viewer is far from being oppressive, massive and ponderous, as is the case with other monumental statues of Dynasty XIX. The chief reason for this, apart from the artistic quality of the statues, is the choice of site. The towering cliffs before which they stand form an impressive backdrop which deprives them of much of their unwieldiness. This effect is no doubt deliberate; it corresponds to the highly cultivated and intellectual sense of style found

Pl. 91 Sennedjem and his wife in the Elysian fields. Wall-painting in his tomb at Deir el-Medina. Dynasty XX, c. 1150 B.C.

Pl. 92 Statuette of the priest Penbui carrying on each shoulder a divine figure. Wood. From Thebes. Dynasty XIX, 13th cent. B.C. Height 60 cm. Museo Egizio, Turin.

Pl. 93 Female statuette. Wood. Dynasty XIX, 13th cent. B.C. Height 39 cm. Museo Egizio, Turin.

in the Ramessid Era. The subtlety of thought exhibited by the architects of Abu Simbel is apparent from another singular feature. The central axis of the building is
* Cat. 11 oriented towards the point on the horizon where the sun rises at the equinox, so that on this morning the light of the rising sun can penetrate into the dark recesses of the temple and for a few moments shine upon the statues of the gods, giving them a mysterious glow. The fact that in the present century it has been possible to save this unique temple from the rising flood-waters of the Nile is a first-class engineering achievement on a par with the brilliant success of the ancient Egyptian architects.

Whereas at Abu Simbel the vast dimensions of the royal statues at the entrance to the temple are offset by the grandeur of the rocky landscape, with which they harmonize, other colossi are closely bound up with elements of the architecture to which they belong. The monumental royal statues, which are invariably placed directly before a pillar, or the so-called 'Osiride pillars,' which represent the king in the guise of Osiris, are of little value as independent works of art. It is in their use as architectural members that we can see how the conception of a portrait likeness has undergone a depreciation.

Their significance therefore lies less in the field of art, or in the information they contain about the royal image of the Ramessid era, than in the effect of space they create in the building. Thus it is not surprising that little care should be devoted to fine modelling of these figures. The colossi of the Ramessid Era to be found in modern museums, torn from their former context, look coarse and unwieldy

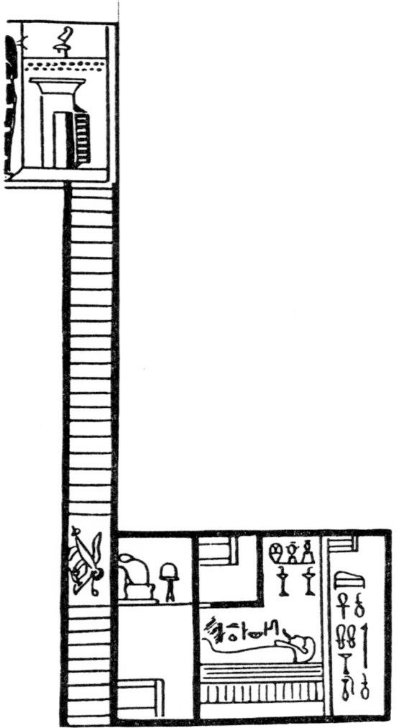

Fig. 6 'Ba,' the bird of souls, flies down into the shaft of the tomb to visit the deceased in his burial-chamber. (XXth-Dynasty papyrus, Paris.)

in their sheer monumentality, and enable one to sense the decline that had taken place, as compared with earlier ages, in rendering meaning and form.

But besides this monumental art works of an entirely different character have also survived which convey an impression of Ramessid sculpture. The fine granite statue of Ramses II at Turin fits into the long tradition of Egyptian royal images. The modelling of forms stands in a delightful contrast to the metallic hardness of individual lines and contours; the details are rendered in such a way as to form sharp edges—as for example in the folds of the draped robe. The attitude and the expression of the face suggest an amiable, kindly sovereign possessed of inner calm. Ramses II may have had something of a split personality from what we know about him and can reconstruct from the art of his time. By contrast with the pathetic idiom of the battle-scene reliefs, in which the king is portrayed as a glorious and self-confident general, he may be regarded rather as the exponent of an over-civilized, and slightly decadent, age. This was a time when men remained aware of the pettiness and transience of earthly things even as they strove with restless haste to realize a monumentality transcending human dimensions.

After the spiritual and religious upheaval of the Amarna Period, at the beginning of Dynasty XIX, the idea of sacrosanct kingship was consolidated afresh—indeed, even enhanced. Already in the lifetime of the pharaoh his statue stood in the temple on the same footing with those of provincial deities and was ritually venerated. Hitherto the king had appeared under the protection of the mighty gods; now the motif is modified and the deity is under the protection of the king, who surpasses him in greatness. This reinterpretation of the position of the deified king does not prevent Ramses II from having himself portrayed Cat. 12
in a humble attitude, prostrate on the ground, making sacrifice to the gods.

Submission to the divine will is expressed far more spectacularly during Dynasty XIX than it had been in earlier times. A morality develops which adopts as its criteria, not the laws and concepts of the contemporary world, but the desiderata of religion, the demand for total commitment by the pious believer. The people, too, developed a new intimate relationship to their deities dur- * Pl. 87
ing the Ramessid Era. The inscriptions on the funerary stelae of artisans and labourers in the city of the dead, Thebes, express this trusting attitude to the gods, this spirit of genuine piety.

In the 'instruction in wisdom' of Ani, which was probably composed already during the age of maturity but was to enjoy great popularity during the Ramessid Era, we read the following:

'But if thou prayest with a loving heart / and thy words are concealed, / then will He fulfil thy desires / and hear thy prayers, for He accepts thy offering.'

The ideas of the world beyond which from time immemorial had been ill-defined and had allowed various possibilities to coexist alongside one another, do not concentrate upon one exclusive interpretation during the Ramessid Era either. There is the hope of entering the realm of Osiris after death, of obtaining a place in the barque of the sun-god; and now a new prospect is added

to these, that of leaving one's tomb during the daytime in the guise of a bird, visiting the familiar terrestrial world,
Pl. 90 and being provided with food and drink by the tree-goddess.

In the royal tombs which continue to be built in the rocky mountains near Thebes the wall-paintings feature,
* Pl. 91 now as before, a mythological interpretation of figures from the world beyond. The novelty consists in the fact that the funerary texts which give the deceased the necessary aid on his way to the world beyond are now illustrat-
Pl. 89 ed and placed into his sarcophagus in the form of papyrus manuscripts.

Among the great creative achievements of the Ramessid
Pl. 88 Era are the battle-scene reliefs on the outer walls of the temples. These are generally in a good state of preservation. The most notable are the extensive sequences of scenes, depicting engagements on land and at sea, which Sethos I, Ramses II and Ramses III put up in sunk relief on the temples at Abydos, Karnak and Medinet Habu, the latter on the west bank of the river near Thebes. In the chronological sequence of scenes of these dynamic and dramatic compositions the actual course of the battle is shown, as a historical narrative. The pharaoh appears on his war-chariot as a victorious general, routing his enemies and destroying them. The excitement and tumult of combat in battle are well represented in the numerous details. The overlappings and foreshortenings in these dynamic scenes accord with optical perspective. But although these monumental sequences of reliefs seem to have been produced as historical documents for posterity, they are placed so high upon the temple walls that it is
* Cat. 26 impossible to see them in detail. Thus it seems that even with these reliefs the possibility that they would be seen by human eye did not play any essential part in their design. Here, too, the intention is to lend a permanent quality to the pharaoh's victory, and to place his current achievements under divine protection, by virtue of the magic power inherent in the picture. Alternatively, they may be placed so high up because the artist wished to fill with decoration the vast surface which the external walls of the temples presented.

In Theban private tombs of the period a large place is occupied by representations of funerals, the cult of the dead, worship before the gods, and the last judgment, whereas motifs drawn from life on this earth are less prominent. The individual registers frequently extend across the rounded-off corners of the room. The figures appear richly draped in fashionable robes, which billow out around their slender bodies. Often more care is given to the detailed depiction of head-dress, jewellery and costume than to the representation of the person concerned, and the cultivated elegance of his external appearance conceals the lack of spiritual content within. Whereas the wall-paintings in the Theban tombs follow the contemporary style, the Nineteenth-Dynasty reliefs in the tombs at Saqqara are noticeably under the influence of the neighbouring Old Kingdom tombs in regard both to motif and to style. A vigorous view of life in the Ramessid Era is afforded by the tombs of sculptors and artisans in the Theban city of the dead at Deir el-Medina. Their motifs and style are of untramelled freshness; they show various events and everyday customs in a manner free from schematic rules; many of the quick sketches have a refreshing directness.

Private statues revert to the absorbed expression of those from Dynasty XVIII. In temple sculpture, which is still more plentiful than tomb sculpture, we frequently encounter the block-statue. In its compact simplicity it suited the requirements of the age, which sought to express inner contemplation. The scribe statuette in its various modifications was also a popular type of work. The actual activity of the scribe receives less emphasis and attention is focussed instead upon his expression of spiritual contemplation.

Most statues of priests show them bearing a shrine or chapel with figures of deities (*naos*). The priest obviously regards himself as the keeper and protector of the provincial gods and their temples and has himself portrayed in this capacity with confident pride. For all his devout reverence and resigned acceptance of the divine will, he is aware of his mission and his privileges. As in reliefs and paintings, the draped robes and artistic wigs are rendered with care and accuracy, so that their material quality obtains an importance in its own right. In the faces the contrast between the hardening of the contour lines and the delicate expression, suggestive of a person lost in thought, occasionally verges on a stereotyped stiffness.

During Dynasty XX a gradual degeneration and rigidity in artistic style becomes more apparent. In reliefs and paintings the waning sense of form is manifest in stiff, excessively tall figures with comparatively small heads, who wear an expression of vacuous solemnity.

In sculpture the striving after monumentality gradually ebbs; the royal portrait loses its personal spiritual content, and is superseded by a cool smooth mannerism. The spirit of the Ramessid Era led on one hand to a final climax in artistic expressiveness, with the monumental colossi and vast historical scenes, executed with masterly virtuosity of technique. On the other hand the paintings and reliefs bear traces of an over-sophisticated style of life, of a society which has found self-awareness and inner peace by its close link with the will of God. Towards the close of the Ramessid Era, simultaneously with the gradual decline of political power, creative artistic talent begins to flag as well.

Repetition of motifs and uniformity in the arrangement of scenes indicate a lack of artistic imagination. The execution is frequently cursory and slipshod, the colours dull and subdued.

Under the last Ramessid rulers internal political conditions deteriorated visibly. Economic hardship led to social unrest among the common people and to corruption among the officials. In the south of the country the viceroy * Pl. 92 of Nubia and the high priest of the temple of Amun won for themselves a position of near-independence. As a result of a civil war, quelled by the army, large areas of the country temporarily came under military rule. On the death of the viceroy of Nubia, Panehsi, a devoted servant of the crown, Herihor, the high priest of the * Pl. 93, Cat. 36 national shrine, laid claim to his title and obtained extensive power over Upper Egypt. In the north Smendes, who was presumably related to the royal dynasty, assumed the pharaonic throne on the death of Ramses XI. Political unity was preserved, but contemporary sources show that in practice Herihor, who at times also bears the title of king, had no control over the Thebaïd. His political authority, which rested upon his extensive military power, was legitimized by the doctrine that Amun himself had taken over control of life on earth and expressed his will through oracular pronouncements. In this doctrine the conception of theocracy was taken to its ultimate limits, in that men were apparently doing no more than execute the will of God. The oracular statements of the god Amun, which had already played an important part both in political and private problems towards the close of the Ramessid Era, gave the high priest unlimited power. At the same time the king, who resided in the far north, lost much significance and credibility, especially since the forfeiture of the territories in Asia considerably diminished his prestige. The relationship between the rulers of south and north was nevertheless friendly, and was maintained by marital ties.

THE LIBYAN PERIOD

Already during the Ramessid Era immigrants from Libya who had settled in the Delta and Middle Egypt had secured leading positions in the army and the civil administration, and had gradually risen in importance and esteem. In 945
* Cat. 18, 80 B.C. the Libyan king Sheshonk I succeeded in winning the pharaonic throne and founded Dynasty XXII.

A marriage between his son Osorkon and a princess from the old royal house served to consolidate his position. One of his sons was sent to Thebes to take over the office of high priest and to act as governor. In this way the political unity of the country under a single ruler was restored, although in a relatively flexible form. After putting the domestic political situation in order, the Libyan king also endeavoured to resume the tradition of the pharaohs in the field of foreign policy by undertaking a campaign to Palestine, which brought rich booty. Osorkon I and his successor kept to the custom whereby the leading sacerdotal posts in the temples of the country were occupied by members of the royal house, so preventing the priests from accumulating too much power and turning against the crown.

In about 808 B.C. the Bubastite dynasty, named after its residence at Bubastis in the Delta, split into two branches. In Manetho's list Petubastis is mentioned as the founder of the Libyan Dynasty XXIII. The subsequent period was one of rapid collapse. Tefnakhte, prince of the Delta, and his son Bocchoris are listed as representatives of Dynasty XXIV. These rulers made renewed efforts to restore political unity but were thwarted by the Nubians, who had in the meantime occupied the Thebaïd and were advancing northwards.

The Libyan rulers of the Bubastite dynasty did not regard themselves as foreigners. Their families had lived in Egypt for generations and had assimilated the traditions and culture of the pharaonic state. The few works of art to have survived from the Libyan Period maintain the style of the Ramessid Era. In the field of bronze-casting such a degree of technical perfection was achieved that in the subsequent Late Period it proved possible to spread this technique far afield; it was employed to produce innumerable statuettes of deities and animals. By engraving, damascening and inlaying with silver, or electrum, semiprecious stones, glass, or a layer of gold-leaf, these elegant and graceful statuettes obtain a particular charm in their treatment of the surface, as may be seen in the statuette of Queen Karomama.

The tendency during the Libyan Period to draw upon works of art from earlier centuries by adding inscriptions, or making exact copies, was followed on a big scale during the Late Period. These practices showed that these ancient works were regarded as a form of expression valid for the contemporary era, and so that the creative powers of ancient Egypt were flagging.

PHARAOH - RULER AND STATESMAN

THE LATE PERIOD

PERIOD OF ETHIOPIAN RULE

The Late Period of Egyptian civilization lasts approximately for four hundred years, in which the destiny of the land on the Nile was to a large extent determined by alien rulers. The Nubians, whom the Greeks called Ethiopians, and who had founded a powerful kingdom at Napata on the Fourth Cataract, conquered the southern part of Upper Egypt and Thebes around the middle of the eighth century; by approximately 712 B.C. Memphis and the Delta were also in their hands. Their king, Shabaka, acceded to the pharaonic throne and founded Dynasty XXV. Like the Libyans, the Ethiopians were largely Egyptianized. They had earlier adopted the Amun cult and for a long time had been familiar with the Egyptian language, politcal system and civilization. Perhaps, as orthodox worshippers of Amun, they may have felt justified in taking possession of the main temple of this god at Karnak. The Theban priesthood offered them no resistance; they may have felt themselves closer to their Nubian fellow-believers than to the royal dynasty which held power in the distant Delta. The Theban theocratic state proved durable. One Ethiopian princess was adopted by Shapenupet I, 'the divine wife of Amun,' a daughter of Osorkon III, and was recognized as her successor. In this peaceful way the highest priestly office was linked closely to the crown. The leading positions in the temple of Amun at Thebes were likewise occupied by members of the royal house.

The cultural achievements of the Ethiopian Period also show that the new dynasty regarded itself as implementing the glorious traditions of the ancient pharaonic state. In temple reliefs the Ethiopian kings appear before the provincial deities in the ancient royal costume and bearing the titles of the Egyptian pharaohs. This custom is adhered to not only by the Libyans and Ethiopians but also by the Persian, Ptolemaic and Roman rulers. This practice testifies to the diplomatic skill of the foreign rulers and also to the power of Egyptian traditions, which exerted a lasting influence even several centuries after the New Kingdom had collapsed. But tradition can only have a fruitful long-term effect upon a culture if it is imbued with a vital spirit and is linked to contemporary experience. If the adoption of historical form and content becomes repetitive, a copy of the past, it is evident that the spiritual insight and life of one period cannot have validity for the other. When creative power flags, a culture enters upon its late phase, one in which its disintegration becomes evident in numerous individual symptoms.

The Egyptian Late Period demonstrates these characteristic features. The tendency towards archaism in official art, in temple reliefs and royal statues is out of keeping with the varied experience and problems of the day. The chief factor in domestic political life is the ethnic diversification of the people. Libyans, Greeks and Carians, who had at one time served as mercenaries in the Egyptian army, became an integral part of the population. In addition Syrian and Palestinian merchants, Nubians and later—after the destruction of Jerusalem by Nebuchadnezzar—Jews settled in the land on the Nile. This racial motley presented many difficult problems for the rulers of the country. On the other hand it widened the horizons of the spiritual élite and made possible the emergence of a framework for the all-embracing spiritual and cultural unity that materialized in the Mediterranean world during the Hellenistic age.

Hereditary professional groups and castes also developed, which led to social stratification and crippled the creative energies of the population. In such a differentiated society the position of the king was bound to be very uncertain.

The pharaonic throne was occupied by alien rulers, who naturally adopted the venerable tradition of the ancient kingdom, followed its ceremonial, and legitimized their claims to power by reference to the oracular pronouncements of the god Amun. But this did not suffice to restore the kingdom to its former splendour and power. The most important consequence was that the idea of a close bond between the king and the national god gradually lost credibility. Already in the theocracy of the end of the New Kingdom the pharaoh had appeared simply as executor of the divine will. Even if this concept at first still preserved the self-evident unity between the god and the king, it nevertheless implied a distinction between the god, who gave the instructions, and the king, who carried them out, which made the latter's conduct liable to criticism and doubt. Failure on the king's part could no longer be explained as the result of a judgment of God; instead he was held accountable for it himself. So far as the religious ideas of the common people were concerned, this meant that they were thrown into yet greater uncertainty. During the Ramessid Era the Egyptian had sought to achieve a personal relationship with his deities and had found self-confidence and inner harmony by leading a devout and morally irreproachable life. Since the king was no longer seen as an intermediary between man and God, the Egyptians of the Late Period were made terrifyingly aware of their exclusive dependence upon the gods. Thus each individual turned to worship his local deity; Amun lost importance in favour of Osiris, the ancient god of the dead, and the local deities. The endeavour to safeguard one's own life led to the desire to identify and invoke the deity in all the many varied manifestations given to it by man over the millennia.

The vast number of statuettes of animal and hybrid deities, of amulets and magic stelae, reflect the superstition which sprang from the religious uncertainty that the people now experienced. Doubt in the veracity of the great dogmas, in kingship and in the efficacy of the cult of the dead led men in despair to resort to the magic media that had been a determining influence in Egyptian life at the beginning of their history. But the conviction which this magic had had for the unsophisticated people of early times could not be re-created; and thus every genuine religious feeling was soon stifled in rigidly stereotyped traditions, in the invocation of innumerable gods and sacred animals, which in the last resort expressed man's feeling of helplessness in an uprooted world.

The spiritual élite, too, had liberated itself from the religious dogmas and mythological interpretations of earlier times, which had been superseded by a sceptical intellectual attitude. The individual's ethical outlook springs from his awareness that ultimately he is responsible to himself.

This doubt in the gods and uncertainty as to what would happen to one after death led to the endeavour to secure for oneself by good deeds on earth a reputation which future generations would mention with reverence. Thus in all social strata there is a lack of confidence. Although the men of the Late Period are sufficiently alert intellectually to recognize how seriously their world is threatened, they lack the creative energy to stop the decline.

The art of the Ethiopian Period gives expression both to the traditional attitude to life and to the open-minded consciousness of one's personal responsibility; but these two components are not fused into a new style to suit the spirit of the times.

Thus statues of the Nubian king Taharka and a large number of private sculptures have survived which copy in * Cat. 24 every detail the Old Kingdom style. Reliefs in Theban private tombs also give preference to an archaistic style, in which the motifs and the scheme of composition are adopted from Old Kingdom works. Occasionally entire

Pl. 94 Head of a statue of King Taharka. Black basalt. Dynasty XXV, c. *670 B.C. Height 14 cm. Ny Carlsberg Glyptotek, Copenhagen.*

Pl. 95 Upper part of a statue of Mentemhet. Black syenite. For the temple of Mut at Karnak. Dynasties XXV/XXVI, c. *660 B.C. Height 46 cm. Cairo Museum.*

Pl. 96 Head of a statue of a priest. Sandstone. Dynasties XXV/XXVI, c. *660 B.C. Height 22.7 cm. British Museum, London.*

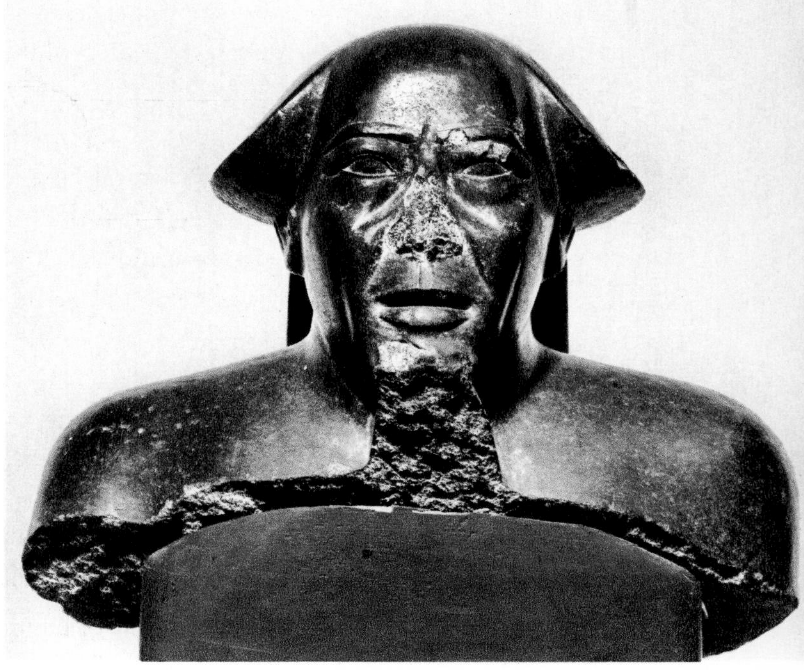

sequences of scenes are simply copied. In other reliefs the fashion of the period is taken into account in certain details, such as robes and head-dresses, but the gulf between the forms of the past and the contemporary additions remains unbridgeable. The sure perfection of line gives an impression of stiffness and artificiality, of a want of spiritual vitality.

Apart from these tradition-bound and non-creative works, there is during the Ethiopian Period one more awakening of the creative impulse, the desire to express man's spiritual predicament by an individual statement: a new realistic portraiture, which reflects the sceptical intellectual attitude of the élite. We have portrait heads
Pl. 94 of King Taharka in which the Negroid ethnic features of this member of the new dynasty are rendered in a manner true to life. The temple statues of the Ethiopian Era, too,

where they do not simply follow the ancient scheme of representation, exhibit an individual characterization which goes far beyond the efforts made earlier in this direction. A slate statuette of the steward of the sacerdotal princess * Cat. 30 Amenardis depicts clearly the old man's physical fatigue by the flabby skin and bloated abdomen. The furrowed face with its listless narrow lips reflects the critical spirit of old age, wearied by experience. Among the most impressive portraits of an elderly person is the well-known head of Mentemhet, who played an important role as * Pl. 95 governor of the Thebaïd. The stark realism in the treatment of the face, for which there was no model in earlier times, is a convincing example of the creative power unleashed during the Ethiopian Era. An alien effect is evoked by the head, executed in black granite, with the lips barely closed, the sweeping arcs of the eyebrows, the large heavy eyelids, and the pronounced wrinkles extending from the corners of the mouth to the nose and above the cheekbone. This impression is enhanced by the broad flat nose and the hair, which protrudes on either side and lies flat. The face suggests a man of intelligence and experience, who is ageing physically and spiritually.

On the other hand, the sandstone head of a priest, now * Pl. 96 in London, was based upon the Middle Kingdom model. The shape of the wig and of the face, the treatment of the eyes and mouth, and the expression of reserve recall the portraiture of Dynasty XII. But whereas during the Middle Kingdom the countenance expressed a man's solemn dignity and awareness of his responsibility for the events of his times, the work of the Late Period expresses intellectual superiority and arrogant disdain. It is by no means a coincidence that during the Late Period a particular effort should have been made to render senility in a * Cat. 27 realistic manner. Whereas the vitality of the Old Kingdom found expression in a human image that suggested timeless youth, the portraits of old age in the Late Period reflect the sceptical attitude of a world that has grown weary of life.

Pl. 97 Mourners in a funerary procession. Limestone relief from the western wall of the funerary chapel of Nes-peka-shuti. From Thebes, Tomb 312. Dynasty XXVI, c. 650-630 B.C. Height 35 cm. Brooklyn Museum, New York.

THE SAITE PERIOD

With the Assyrian invasion the peaceful years of Ethiopian rule come to an end. While King Taharka is compelled to retire to the south, where he makes vain attempts to recover the northern part of the country, the Assyrians leave the Egyptian princes of the Delta a good deal of independence. Among them Necho of Sais is the most important. He conspires with Taharka behind the back of the Assyrians and is punished by deportation to Nineveh together with other Delta princes; yet despite this he succeeds in gaining the confidence of the Assyrian rulers, to whom he owes his installation as king of Sais and Memphis.

The attempt of the Ethiopian Tanutamun to reconquer the northern areas is thwarted by resistance on the part of the Delta princes. Necho's son, Psammetichus I, seeks protection at the Assyrian court. An Assyrian army pursues the Ethiopians as far as Upper Egypt and makes Psammetichus king of the Delta and Memphis, like his father. He is the first ruler of Dynasty XXVI, also known after its capital at Sais as the Saite dynasty. By his diplomatic skill Psammetichus succeeds in uniting the land on the Nile once more into a single independent state. Toward the end of his reign Egypt becomes involved in external conflicts as a result of a change which occurs in the balance of power in the Near East and leads to the fall of the Assyrian empire. Although Necho II is able to keep the Babylonians, the new great power in the Near East, away from the Egyptian border, his attempts to recreate an Egyptian empire by undertaking campaigns to Syria and the Euphrates are thwarted. Equally vain are the efforts of his grandson, Apries, to support the Israelites in their struggle against the Babylonians, which ends with Nebuchadnezzar's destruction of Jerusalem.

A large number of Jews are taken into Babylonian captivity; others succeed in fleeing to Egypt. In the quarrels that break out between the Libyans and the Greeks of Cyrene, Apries sides with the former. After the defeat of an Egyptian army by the Greeks, Apries is deposed and the royal office passes to his general, Amosis. The struggle for power between Libyans and Greeks which has been brewing for a long time is thus decided in favour of the latter. Amosis concludes a treaty with Cyrene and finally allows the Greeks to establish a commercial settlement at Naucratis in the western part of the Delta.

Herodotus and other ancient writers relate that King Amosis adopted a friendly attitude toward the Greeks and was receptive to Greek culture.

Pl. 98 Statuette of the priest Psammetichus. Brown metamorphic slate. Dynasty XXVI, c. 620 B.C. Height 13 cm. Kestner Museum, Hanover.

Saite rule comes to a close in 525 B.C. with the invasion of the Persian king Cambyses. Egypt becomes a satrapy of the Persian Achaemenid empire, which extends over the whole Near East.

To an even greater extent than the Ethiopians, the native Dynasty XXVI sees its task as to uphold the traditions of the glorious past, which are regarded as an eternally valid manifestation of Egyptian culture. In relief sculpture elements of composition and style from the Middle and early New Kingdoms are blended with external attributes from the contemporary period. But the attempts to produce a convincing new artistic form failed, just as they had done during the Ethiopian Era. The accuracy with which the reliefs were executed shows virtuosity in producing works in a great variety of styles which meet the need for tradition. The reliefs, now in the Brooklyn Museum, from the rock-cut tomb of Nes-peka-shuti near Deir el-Bahari, on the western bank of the river near Thebes, copy the wall-paintings of the New Kingdom in regard to motif and style, but the details adopt characteristic features from Old Kingdom reliefs at Memphis. The male participants in the funeral procession express their involvement in the event by the usual gesture of mourning, whereas the wailing women are grouped dynamically: they have bared their breasts and covered their heads with dust, in an expression of the shattering effect of death and bereavement. But here, too, the facial features of the mourners display no inner feeling, except for the last figure on the left-hand side of the register, so that the general impression given is one of a cool ceremonial attitude.

* Pl. 97, Cat. 65

Toward the close of the Saite Period the wide spacing of the scenes and the accentuated curvature of the figures

Pl. 99 Apis bull. Foot-board of a sarcophagus. Painting on wood. Dynasty XXVI, 6th cent. B.C. Roemer-Pelizaeus Museum, Hildesheim.

Pl. XXIII Ibis, sacred animal of Thoth, god of wisdom and Maat, goddess of truth and justice. Bronze and gilded wood. From Tuna el-Gebel. Dynasty XXVI, 6th cent. B.C. Height including base 19.5 cm., length 20.5 cm. Kestner Museum, Hanover.

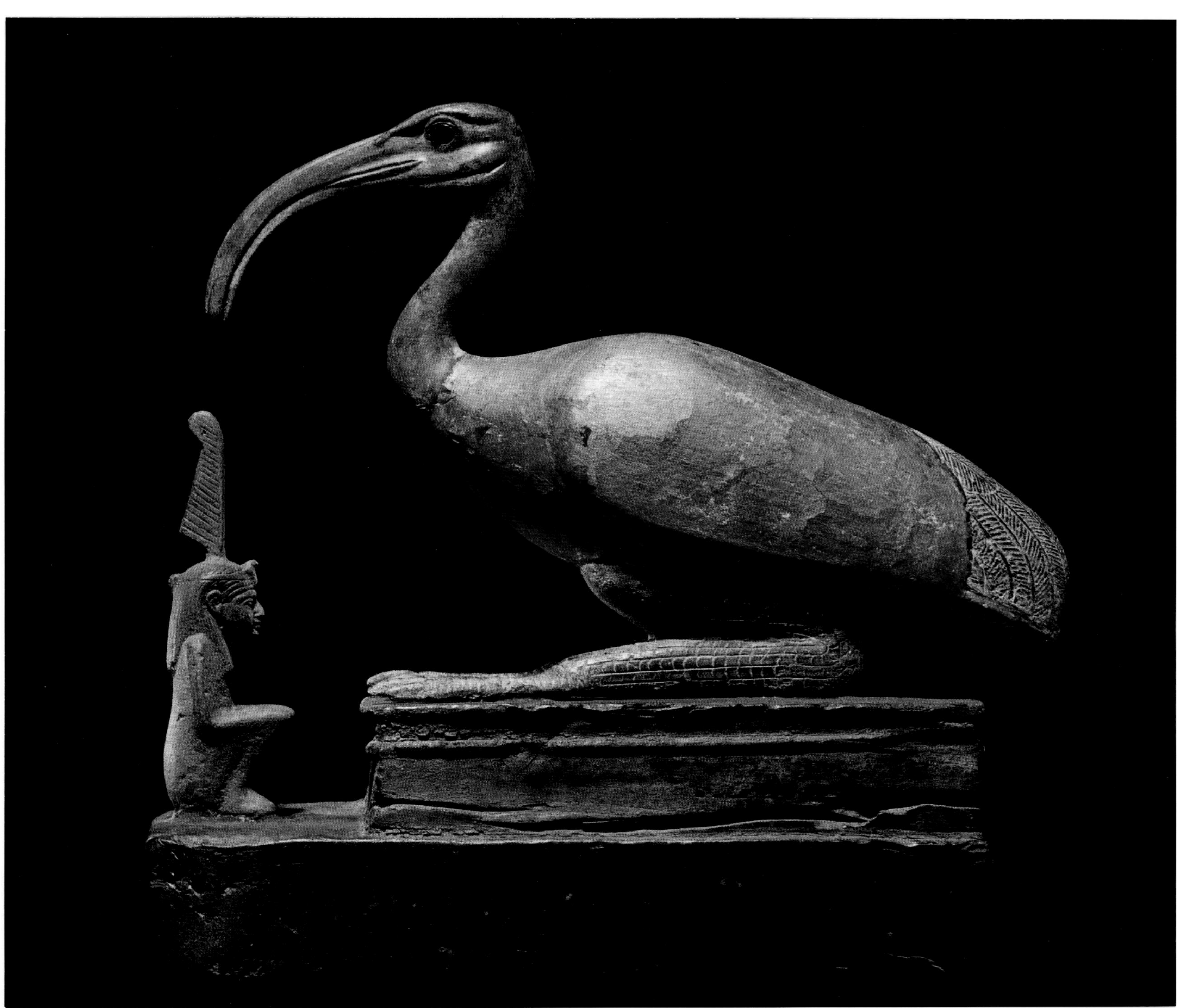

Pl. 100 Sacred baboon. Greyish-green serpentine. Dynasty XXVI, 6th cent. B.C. Height 13.3 cm. Kestner Museum, Hanover.

Pl. 101 Cat, sacred animal of the goddess Bastet. Bronze, hollow casting. Late Period, 6th cent. B.C. Height 14.8 cm. Kestner Museum, Hanover.

Pl. 102 Uraeus snake from a crown. Bronze, engraved. Dynasty XXVI, 6th cent. B.C. Height 16 cm. Kestner Museum, Hanover.

Pl. 103 Falcon. Sarcophagus of a mummified falcon. Bronze, hollow casting, engraved. Dynasty XXVI, 6th cent. B.C. Height 20.9 cm. Kestner Museum, Hanover.

point to a transformation which reveals a link with Greek art. It is hard to say to what extent this can be explained by direct influence, although Greek art was certainly known in Egypt at this time.

Since the accession of Dynasty XXVI did not at first bring about any major changes in Upper Egypt, and since no new appointments were made to the sacerdotal office, the style of life in the south remained unaltered. In temple statues the realistic portraiture of the Ethiopian Era continues down to the reign of Psammetichus I. During the subsequent period it is abandoned in favour of a strict archaism and a smooth, idealized and imitative style begins to develop. The material used is a dark green and black stone, whose hard surface enhances the formalistic coolness in the fashioning of the torso and face. Faces treated in a linear manner, with straight narrow eyebrows and pointed chin, have a youthful expression which recalls the ideal image of the Old Kingdom.

But the stiff smile that plays around the lips, which are slightly pursed at the corners of the mouth, shows that these faces lack an inner tension which could give them vitality. Despite the sure touch in execution, one gains an impression merely of vacuity and cold academicism.

Block-statues, *naos*-bearers and scribe statuettes are as before among the most popular types of temple sculpture. The large number of small bronzes and statuettes in stone and faience which have survived were intended to serve as votive gifts. They afford an insight into the variegated pantheon of the Late Period. Apart from the innumerable statuettes of Osiris, Isis and Horus, the most frequently found representations are those of sacred animals, which *Pl. XXIII, Pl. 99-103 demonstrate the Egyptian artists' talent for rendering the different species in a realistic manner. Despite the fact that these small sculptures are almost invariably works produced *en masse*, the technical and artistic level of achievement is surprisingly high. In the fashioning of such sculptures a variety of materials was employed. Thus, for example, the legs, beak and tail of Ibis, the sacred animal of Thoth, god of wisdom, are frequently worked in bronze, whereas wood or alabaster was preferred for the body. Occasionally the bronze statuettes were produced by solid or hollow casting, and then gilded or inlaid with coloured paste and semi-precious stones. It is evident that in the popular art for which the technical achievements of the Late Period were employed, creative ability is still present in the handling of new motifs and in the *Pl. 98 choice of style, whereas Saite art becomes petrified into an empty stereotype and is almost stifled in the reiteration of ancient traditions.

The tendency manifest in the Late Period to revive old art forms leads to the careful use in workshops of the network of squaring lines for the preliminary drawing, which ensures that the sculpture observes the correct proportions. From Dynasty XXVI and from the Ptolemaic Period we have a large number of workshop models on which the Cat. 76-78 units of measurement and frequently also the preliminary drawings have been preserved. Following these models, the sculptor translates the measurements to the stone, and is thus able to create by mechanical means a sculpture of balanced proportions. This method explains why finished works often display a cold academicism in the precision of their technique.

THE LAST NATIVE RULERS

The Persian rulers of the Achaemenid family, who are reckoned as Dynasty XXVII, have left relatively few traces of their hegemony over the land on the Nile. Although Darius built a large temple for the god Amun in the oasis of Khārga, generally speaking there is stagnation in cultural life. Several attempts by the Egyptians to shake off the Persian yoke were thwarted, even though Athens supported the Egyptian revolt by naval action. Herodotus, who soon afterwards undertook his journey to Egypt, found conditions there peaceful. Only after 120 years, in 404 B.C., did Amyrtaeus of Sais manage to rid Egypt of Persian domination. In Manetho's list he is mentioned as the only king of Dynasty XXVIII. He is succeeded by princes from Mendes, who rule as Dynasty XXIX; finally the princes of Sebennythos in the Delta, who rule as Dynasty XXX, bring the sequence of dynasties to a close.

The last native princes to ascend the venerable pharaonic throne made possible a final and significant revival of creative power. Successful defensive wars were fought against the Persians which brought peace and quiet to the country, and the new dynasty felt powerful enough to make a final effort to expand its power by undertaking a campaign to Syria. Several architectural monuments, free-standing sculptures and reliefs dating from the reign of Kings Nectanebo I, Nectanebo II and Tacho bear witness to the vigorous spirit of enterprise shown at this time. The energetic and ambitious sovereigns of Dynasty XXX may have felt an affinity to the spirit of the early New Kingdom. Relief works and sculpture are modelled upon the style of Dynasty XVIII. The art forms of this period are not only copied but occasionally are also modified in accordance with contemporary taste, which gives them a unique and often an attractive appearance. The rounded shape of the figures, who wear the fashionable costume of

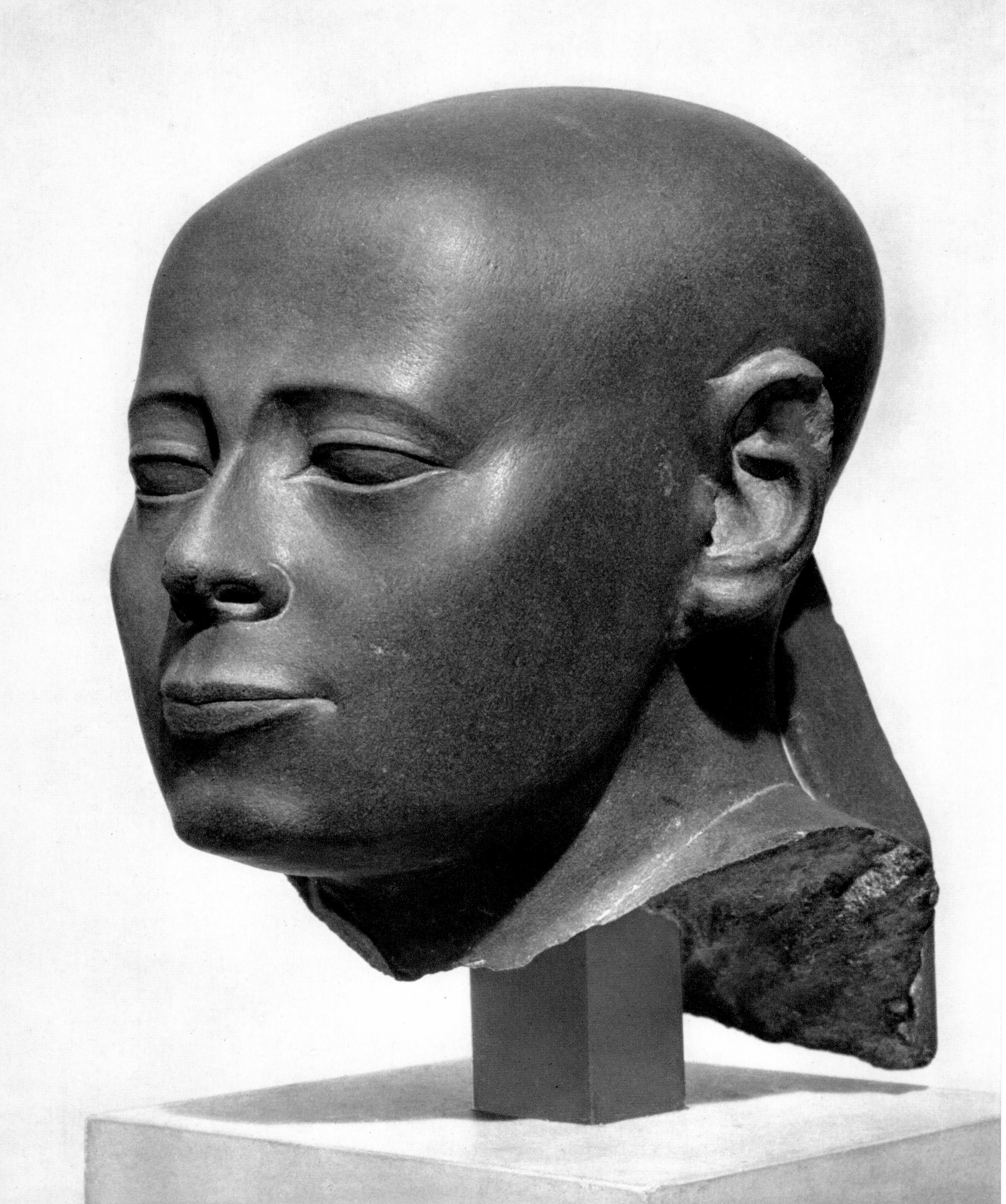

Pl. 104 Portrait head of a priest of the god Mont. Green slate. Dynasty XXX, c. 360–340 B.C. Height 15 cm. Brooklyn Museum, New York.

Pl. 105 So-called Dattari statuette (named after the former owner in Alexandria). Black basalt. Dynasty XXX, c. 365 B.C. Height 51 cm. Brooklyn Museum, New York.

Pl. 106 Reverse of Pl. 105.

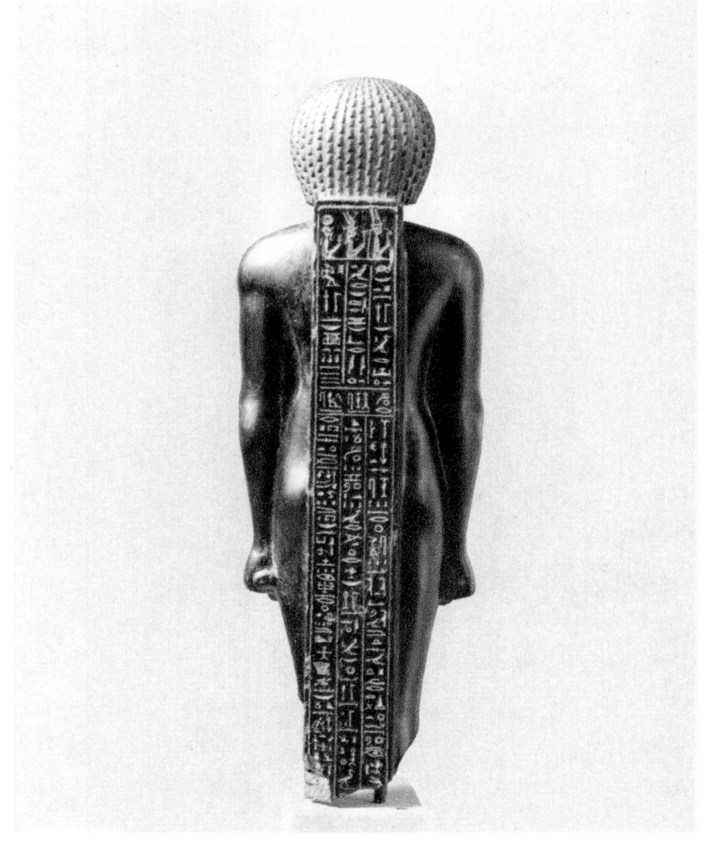

the time, and their loose disposition in the plane again point to an affinity with Greek taste, in this case to a much more pronounced degree than at the close of the Saite Period.

In free-standing sculptures, which are distinguished by
Pl. 105, 106 the glassy smoothness of the polished surface, technical perfection is combined with a form of expression that looks rigid and sterile. The faces, which are smooth and
* Pl. 104 devoid of wrinkles, give a stereotyped and lifeless impression; they suggest a frightening spiritual void which the mask-like smile cannot conceal.

And yet during this period artists were also able to probe human nature and character in the human face, and to leave to posterity portrait heads which once more present a contrast between the bloodless Egyptian ideal image and realistic features that emphasize the subject's personal traits. Beneath the skin the bone structure makes itself felt; every detail is rendered with anatomical accuracy. This new effort to depict the human face yields a human image characterized by precision and clarity, one in which form and substance achieve a unity.

The portrait head of a priest, now in the Brooklyn Museum, conveys the impression of a self-willed individual with a critical intellect and a sensitive spirit: the broad face is treated in a linear manner; the eyebrows and eyelids have clearly-defined contour lines; the lips are thin and narrow.

The shape of the face and its expression are no longer determined by features suggestive of senility, which are so inviting to the artist who attempts a realistic portrait, but by the power of inner concentration found in a man of mature years.

This new artistic form of portrait was to experience further development and reach its climax during the subsequent Ptolemaic Period.

THE PTOLEMAIC PERIOD

The expulsion of the Persians from Egyptian territory and the restoration of an independent Egyptian state under the rule of native sovereigns belonging to the last dynasties were only possible because the Persian empire had had to muster all its power for more urgent tasks. The recovery of the province of Egypt with its riches of grain and gold was for economic reasons alone a constant objective of Persian policy. In 343 B.C. Artaxerxes III succeeded in occupying Egypt once again, but shortly afterwards he was compelled to make way for Alexander the Great, into whose hands Egypt fell without a struggle in 332 B.C.

Not long after the conquest of the country Alexander founds Alexandria, soon to develop into a flourishing commercial city and a centre of Hellenistic culture. After his death one of his generals, Ptolemy, took over the administration of the province of Egypt. It was due to his ambition and political ability that the land on the Nile once again became more than just a province. In 305 B.C. Ptolemy officially assumed the title of king, so founding the Ptolemaic dynasty under whose 300-year rule Egypt was to experience a final flourishing period.

Political unrest at home and strife within the dynasty put an end to this glorious epoch. Cleopatra, the last sovereign of the Ptolemaic dynasty, needed the support of the Romans, of the mighty Caesar, to maintain her claim to the throne against her brother. By womanly shrewdness and cunning she was able to delay for some time the occupation of Egypt by Roman legions. But in 30 B.C. the fate of Egypt was finally decided. Octavian's victorious battle at Actium made the pharaonic kingdom a Roman province. Cleopatra, its last queen, died by her own hand.

The Ptolemaic rulers showed respect and understanding for the religious concepts and customs of the country. Political prudence indicated that they should try to appear

Pl. 107 Horus temple at Edfu. Large court, portico and temple. Ptolemaic period, 237–57 B.C.

Pl. 108 Ptolemy II presenting a gift. Relief in grey granite. Ptolemaic Period, c. 275 B.C. Height 62 cm, length 47 cm. Ny Carlsberg Glyptotek, Copenhagen.

Pl. 109 Work in the field. Detail from a limestone relief in the vestibule of Petosiris' tomb at Tuna el-Gebel. Ptolemaic Period, 3rd cent. B.C.

Pl. 110 The goddess Isis with a vulture's hood and a sun disc between cow's horns, holding in her hand the papyrus sceptre. Painted sunk limestone relief. From Herakleopolis. Ptolemaic Period, c. 300 B.C. Height 44 cm., width 32 cm. Kestner Museum, Hanover.

as legitimate successors of the pharaohs, and they soon won the sympathy of the priesthood and large sections of the population by erecting temples to the Egyptian gods in all parts of the country. This perceptive policy was dictated not only by tactical calculation but also by the irresistible appeal exerted upon these alien rulers by the ancient traditions of the country, its glorious history and ancient culture, and finally the legendary figure of the pharaoh. The magnificent temples at Edfu, Dendera, Kom Ombo and on the island of Philae followed the architectonic style of the New Kingdom in regard both to their layout and their style. The ancient forms were adopted from a pronounced sense for fine balanced proportion and line, but only a few new architectural ideas were developed. Between the vestibule and the large court a wall was now usually incorporated, half the normal height and placed between columns; this was an idea encountered for the first time during Dynasty XXII, in the temple of Amun at El Hibe. The columns now obtain composite capitals in the shape of clusters of plants, which allow the architect full freedom to use his imagination and to modify them in various ways.

Pl. 107

Temple reliefs adopt the style of the New Kingdom and manifest the same rigid tradition which had characterized such reliefs for centuries past. In an austere stereotyped form the Ptolemaic and Roman rulers are depicted in the

Pl. 108, Cat. 42

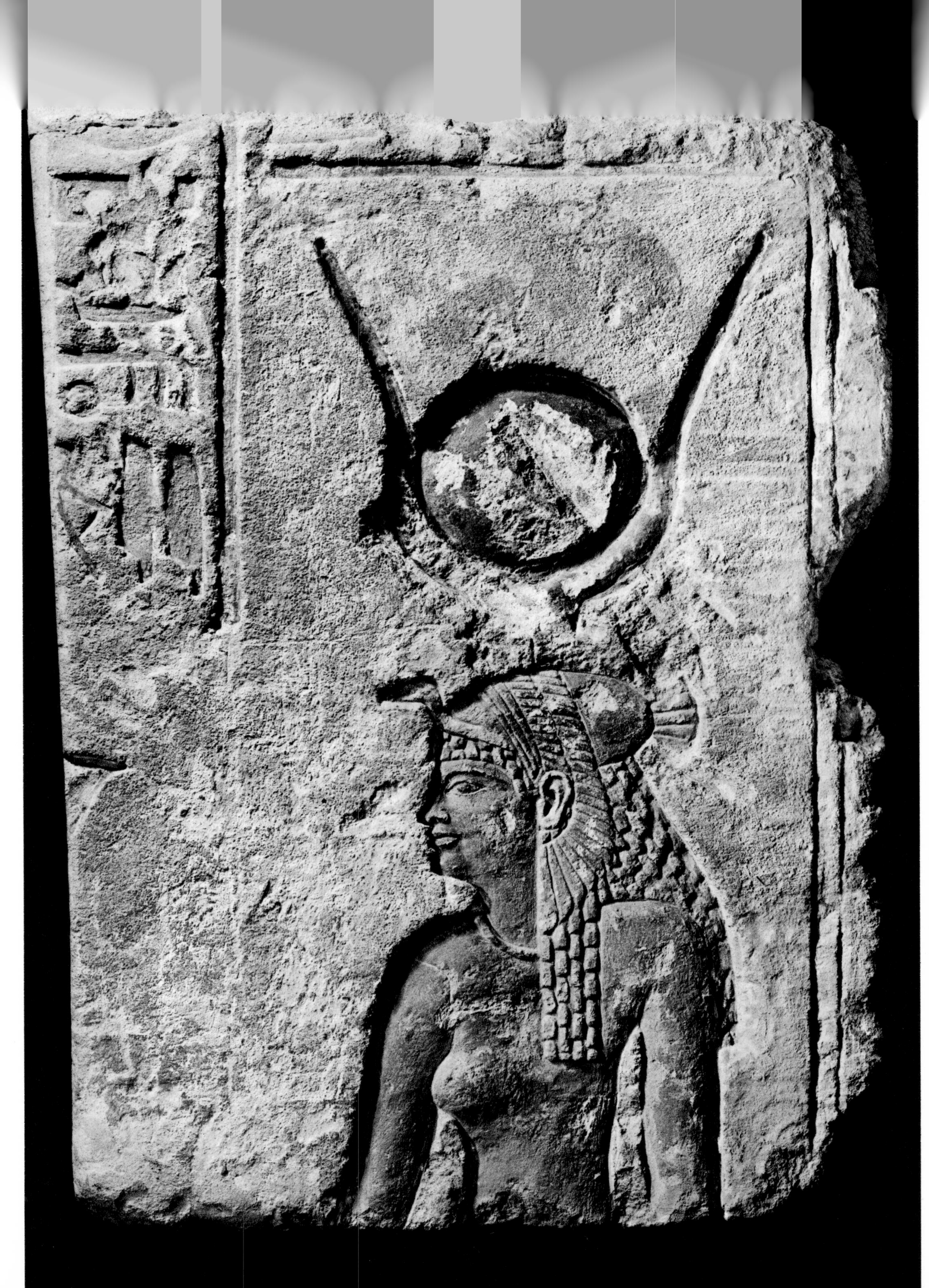

Pl. 111 Block-statue of the priest Petamenophis. Granite. Ptolemaic Period, c. 220–180 B.C. Height 31 cm. Stiftung Preussischer Kulturbesitz, Staatliche Museen, Berlin.

Pl. 112 Torso of a goddess or queen. Syenite. Ptolemaic Period, c. 280 B.C. Height 65.5 cm. Kunsthistorisches Museum, Vienna.

posture and costume of the ancient pharaohs, worshipping their gods. The regular monotonous repetition of these ceremonial scenes, enhanced by the rows of hieroglyphs used to divide the registers, gives them an almost ornamental character. In the treatment of the figures, on the other hand, a new style does develop. The differentiated plasticity of the human body points to a new feeling for form, which makes for suppleness in modelling and gives the lively expression a dignified beauty. The sensual receptiveness to voluminous forms and the fine feeling for harmony and balance in the details are of course demonstrated more clearly in the reliefs of private tombs than in temple reliefs.

In the representations in the tomb of the high priest Petosiris, produced towards the close of the fourth century B.C., the traditional and contemporary styles are sharply contrasted. For religious scenes the traditional Egyptian relief style was employed, whereas in the scenes of everyday life, located in the vestibule of the tomb, there is a
most interesting blend of elements of Greek and Egyptian Pl. 109
style. From the motifs, some of which show craftsmen at work, for which there is no model from earlier times, it is evident that these are realistic pictures of contemporary life. The costumes, head-dresses and attributes correspond
to the fashion of the day, as they did occasionally already * Pl. 110
in the Late Period.

Pl. 113 Head of a statue of an unknown man. Black granite. Close of 1st cent. B.C. Height 19 cm. Museo Egizio, Turin.

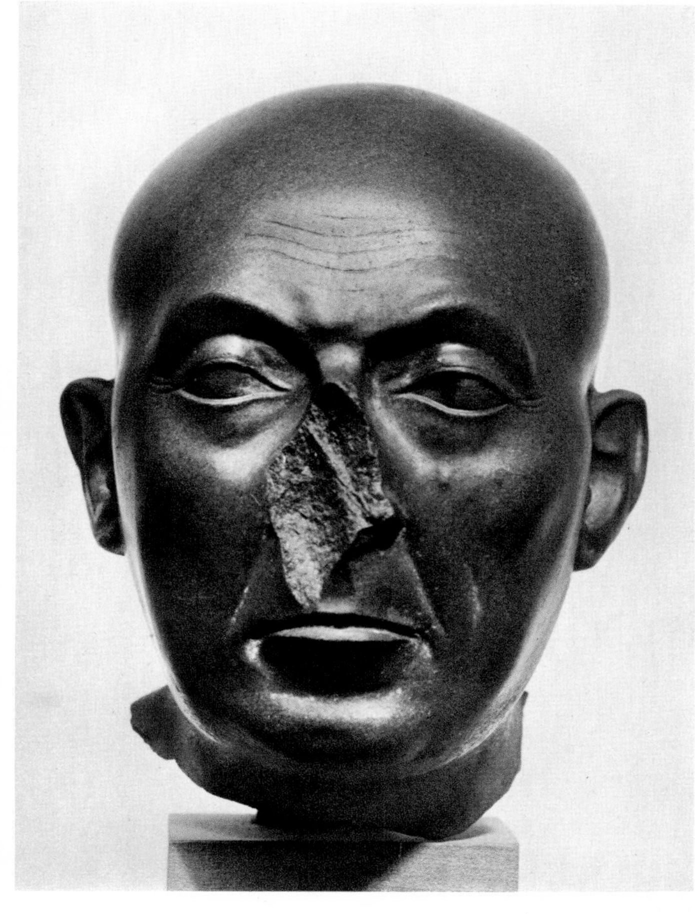

Pl. 114 Portrait head of a priest. Green slate. Ptolemaic Period, c. 220–180 B.C. Height 10.8 cm. Museum of Fine Arts, Boston.

The spirit of the Ptolemaic Period is expressed most tangibly in a highly instructive modification of relief style. The conception and first draft of the representations follow the ancient Egyptian principle, according to which the figure is spread out on the plane and divided into segments. This procedure was completely unsuited to render a figure that was regarded as an organic whole, with rounded forms and an air of dynamism, in conformity with Greek taste.

From this basic schism between two extreme possibilities of artistic conception and style there develops a style that was unique but of necessity lacked uniformity. The strict rule binding a figure to the plane is everywhere broken; instead, the figures are plastically modelled, and occasionally turned towards the viewer; the individual parts of the body have an organic dynamism which makes them appear strangely twisted—all these features convey the impression of an experiment that has not quite come off. The share of Greek taste in this relief is much greater than Egyptian, and we become aware that in the Ptolemaic Period we are not really any longer concerned with Egyptian art. It was impossible for Egyptian and Greek culture to fuse, for their underlying principles had nothing in common: whereas Egyptian art already belongs to the past, in Greek art a new world of fresh possibilities is opening up.

The Ptolemaic Period at first brought no essential change in the conventional sculptural style. As in the Late Period,

Pl. 115 Statuette of a priest holding an Osiris chapel. Black granite. Ptolemaic Period, 150–100 B.C. Height 41.9 cm. Kestner Museum, Hanover.

Pl. XXIV Mummy portrait of an elderly woman. Painting in wax on wood. From the Faiyum. Latter half of 1st cent. A.D. Height 38 cm. Ägyptische Staatssammlung, Munich.

Pl. 111, Cat. 9 ancient motifs and forms are given preference in royal imagery as well as in private sculpture. The composition of the statues is determined in this era as well by the law whereby figures are embedded in a cube (or a pillar of cubic shape), in full face or in direct profile, and the manner in which they are treated stylistically shows the idealizing tendency of the Late Period. Gradually, however, the plastic treatment of the body becomes more flexible and rounded forms appear which impart a new spirit to the ancient scheme, which has become rigid in the course of
Pl. 112 its long tradition. In the supple delicate modelling of the female body a natural beauty bursts into bloom; underlying it is an awareness of the vital organic unity of the human figure. In many of these statues one seems to be able to sense a breath of the Greek spirit.

Cat. 6 The contribution which the Egyptian style makes is to an ever-increasing extent limited to its ability to depict character by the use of lines—something that from time immemorial had been of particular importance in Egyptian art. Efforts to create a realistic image were made time and again over the millennia, but they were restricted to the characterization of individual features, which were, so to speak, imposed from without upon a form that remained within the bounds of tradition.

The religious and spiritual development of the Late Period enhanced the need felt for an individual, personal human image. But even in the case of the portrait heads of the Ethiopian Era, which were occasionally represented with a brutal realism—as, for example, the expressive head of Mentemhet—the artist limited himself to depicting external characteristics in the physiognomy of the subject, and rendering of the spiritual, psychological content took second place to rendering of the physical features. In a number of magnificent portrait heads the artists of the Ptolemaic Period revert to the creative achievements of the last Egyptian dynasty, in which, for the first time in the

Pl. 116 Late Ptolemaic king. Reddish-brown stone with black sprinklings. Ptolemaic Period, 80–30 B.C. Height 30.2 cm. Brooklyn Museum, New York.

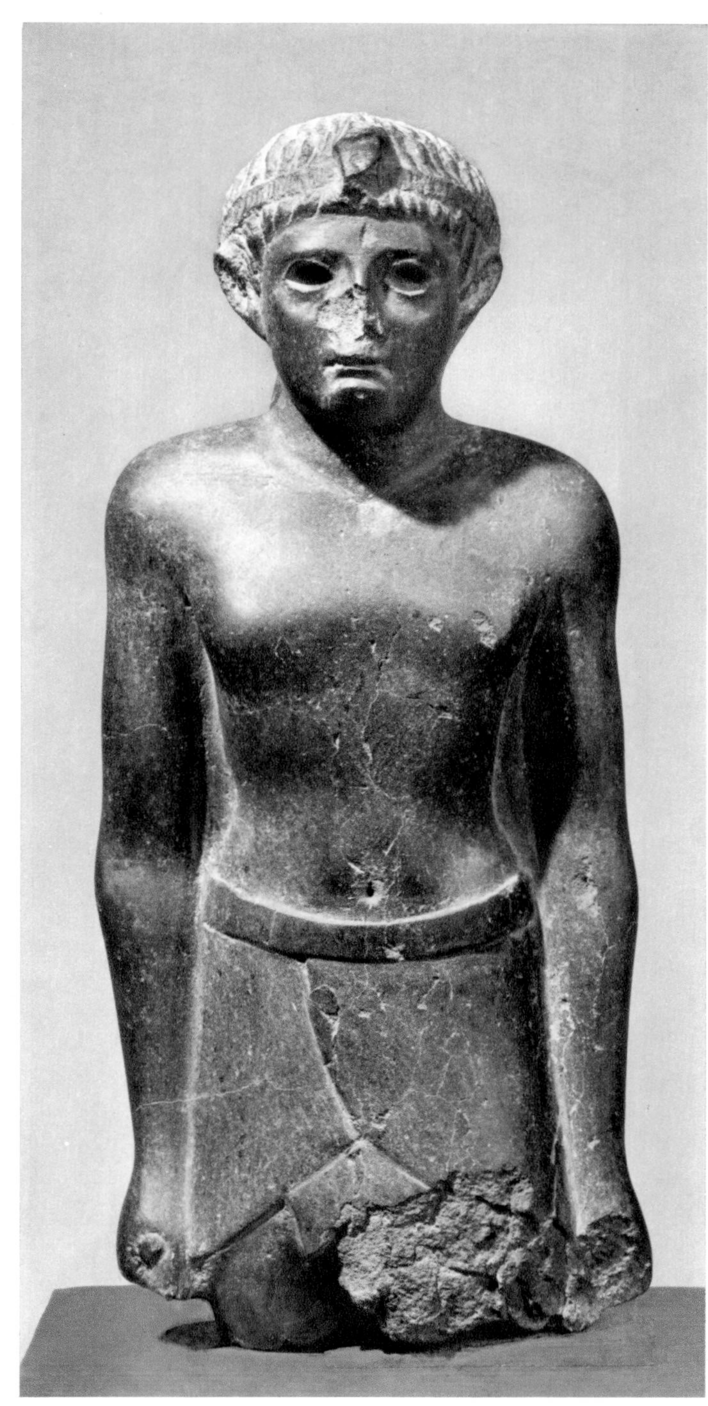

fashioning of the human countenance, a true portrait was born.

Pl. 114 The expressive 'Green Head,' now in the Boston Museum, is perhaps the most telling example of portrait art during the Ptolemaic Period. Beneath the smoothly polished bald head one can sense the anatomical bone structure. In the modelling of the facial features every detail has been brought out and combined to form a unity characterized by inner compactness, such as a true portrait requires; for a true portrait can only develop where the characteristic impress of the subject's external form is combined with an intimation of his spiritual and psychological potential. The eyebrows, slightly wrinkled at the bridge of the nose; the broad and heavy eyelids; the bags beneath the eyes; the lines extending from the nostrils to the corners of the mouth; the wrinkles on the forehead and in the corners of the eyes; the narrow firmly closed mouth and forceful protruding round chin—all these features give the face a distinct individual cachet. From it speaks the shrewd and stately personality of an ageing man who has attained maturity through experience of life. In the wonderful harmony of the plastic form and its expressive content, the 'Green Head,' which may have been produced toward the close of the third century B.C., corresponds to the open-minded spirit of the Ptolemaic Era. In the por-
Pl. 113 trait heads of the Late Ptolemaic Period plastic modelling appears to become stereotyped. The face is shown with hard emphatic lines and wrinkles, which are inscribed upon the plastic form like ornamental features. The organic unity between form and substance is broken. The accent is on the external physiognomy, and some of the heads bear an affinity to the portraiture of the Roman Republic.

Political dissension and struggles for the succession among the last Ptolemaic rulers brought the final flourishing period of Egyptian civilization to a close. In the statue
Pl. 116 of a royal prince from the latter half of the first century

B.C. we see that both the plastic sense of form and the expressive content have lost their power to convince us. The modelling of the body is schematic and flat; the facial expression remains indeterminate; the eyes were presumably at one time inlaid with semi-precious stones. The modelling of the distorted mouth, the corners of which are pulled down, suggests uncertainty. The receding lower lip is separated from the low angular chin by a deep depression. The uraeus snake on the man's brow identifies him as a member of the royal dynasty. His features, from which all tension and vitality have vanished, seem to suggest the feeble and melancholic indifference of a man who has been pushed aside.

In private statuettes it is evident that the sense of balance in the proportions has been lost. In a statuette of a priest, now in the Kestner Museum, the decline of artistic homogeneity in the portrayal of the human image is unmistakable. Above a dumpy body, which is only superficially modelled, there is a realistic head, disproportionately large, of an elderly man who wears a serious and reserved expression. Both from a formal and from a spiritual point of view the Ptolemaic Period has exhausted its creative power. * Pl. 115

Pl. 117 Mummy portrait of a young man. Wax painting on wood. From Faiyum. 4th cent. A.D. Height 35.5 cm. Kestner Museum, Hanover.

EGYPT AS A ROMAN PROVINCE

After the collapse of its political system Egypt still continued from time to time to revive its artistic potential and to develop new creative possibilities. It was only with the rise of the Roman empire that, after three thousand years of achievement, Egyptian civilization came irrevocably to an end. The influence which Egypt exerted upon ancient Rome was very slight. It was limited to the adoption of the mystical Osiris and Isis cult, which found adherents in Italy and throughout the Roman Empire. On Egyptian soil only a few individual motifs drawn from the Egyptian pantheon recall the ancient pharaonic age. The god Horus, for example, occurs in the costume of a Roman legionary, and contemporary terracottas occasionally employ Egyptian attributes and symbols, or the characteristics of Egyptian deities.

The spread of Christianity, the foundation of the Coptic Church and of monasteries introduces a new spiritual and artistic atmosphere. The last truly creative achievement on Egyptian soil are the portraits on mummies. The ancient custom of mummifying the body of the deceased appealed to the foreigners who lived in the Nile valley while it was under Roman rule. Until now the sarcophagi, with their stiff faces, had been unaffected by the vicissitudes of time. During the first centuries of the Christian era the custom grew up of giving the faces portrait-like features which were painted on, or alternatively of replacing them either by a plaster mask or by a portrait of the deceased painted with wax colours on a
Pl. xxiv, Pl. 117 wooden panel. These portraits, painted on wood, which were chiefly discovered in the Faiyum area, are of high artistic quality. The fact that the impulse for this artistic achievement, and probably their execution as well, no longer came from Egyptians but from foreigners is evident from the fact that these portraits depict Romans, Greeks, Semitic people and those of hybrid stock, whereas there are none of persons of Egyptian race. The reason for this may be that the native population was kept in a low social status, or else that the Egyptians clung conservatively to their ancient traditions, as they had done from time immemorial, particularly where matters of ritual were concerned.

Thus the realistic portrait art which developed during the first centuries of the Christian era on Egyptian soil expresses the spirit of the Greek and Roman world. Its artistic style exemplifies Roman portrait art, which is one of the most splendid achievements of Roman culture.

The Greek portrait statue in the Hellenistic period, in its organic dynamism, plunges into the freedom of the surrounding space and encompasses the living variety of the terrestrial world; the Roman portrait, on the other hand, expresses the individual ego in an impressive way and takes this as its artistic criterion. The Roman world was bound to remain far more alien to the Egyptians than the Greek—Hellenistic world, which with its open-minded spirituality offered so many more opportunities to explore. To this new world no bridge could be found.

Egyptian civilization had realized all that was latent in its nature. And so the land on the Nile steps out of the light of history. Much time was to elapse before its splendid achievements were to be properly recognized and appraised.

CATALOGUE

Cat. 1

King Chephren. Diorite. From the valley-temple in his funerary complex at Giza. Dynasty IV, *c.* 2500 B.C. Height 168 cm. Cairo Museum. (Cf. Pl. 21.)
The king is seated upon a throne with lion's legs; at the corners of the front edge of the seat is a lion's head; on the lateral surfaces is the symbol for 'to unite,' combined with the heraldic plants of Lower and Upper Egypt, which became the symbol for 'the unification of the Two Lands.' The name of the king appears on the foot-rest in an oval-shaped cartouche. The strict compactness of the statue and the ageless dignity of the king's expression convey impressively the form and content of the royal image during the Pyramid Period.

Cat. 2

King Mentuhotep II. Painted sandstone. From Thebes, Deir el-Bahari. Dynasty XI, *c.* 2000 B.C. Height 183 cm. Cairo Museum. (Cf. Pl. 39.)
The king is seated upon a smooth cubic seat with a foot-rest. He is wearing the ceremonial attire customary during the Sed (jubilee) festival, the crown of Lower Egypt and a pointed beard. The green and black colour of his skin, the dark red of his crown, and the grey and white tone of his robe seem to enhance the massive compactness of the figure. Between his feet and the front edge of the seat a fillet has been left. With its somewhat ungainly appearance, the statue shows that in the early Middle Kingdom, after the decline in artistic form during the First Intermediate Period, an effort was made to produce a valid royal image.

Cat. 3

Queen Hatshepsut. White marble. From the mortuary temple of the queen at Thebes, Deir el-Bahari. Dynasty XVIII, *c.* 1480 B.C. Height 196 cm. Contribution from Edward S. Harkness and the Rogers Fund, 1929, Museum Excavations, 1926-1928; Metropolitan Museum of Art, New York.
The queen is shown wearing a short pleated kilt, festal collar and royal kerchief with the uraeus snake upon her forehead. The graceful features express *joie de vivre* and an open-minded outlook upon the world.

Cat. 4

Upper part of a statue of Sesostris III. Black granite. From Thebes, Deir el-Bahari. Dynasty XII, *c.* 1860 B.C. Height of the surviving part 150 cm. British Museum, London.
The expression of the facial features—the corners of the mouth pulled down, broad upper eyelids and deep wrinkles—is in conformity with the royal image of the reigns of Sesostris III and Amenemhat III. At this time, unlike the Pyramid Period, the ruler was regarded as a human being caught up in the destiny of his age.

Cat. 5

Upper part of a statue of Amenemhat III. Dark grey granite. Dynasty XII, *c.* 1820 B.C. Height 39 cm. Pushkin Museum, Moscow.

Cat. 6

Ptolemaic queen. Black granite. Ptolemaic Period, 1st cent. B.C. Height 54 cm. Museo Egizio, Turin.
The queen is shown wearing a closely-fitting tunic. The gentle face is framed by stylized locks of hair, which fall down to round voluptuous breasts. Upon her head she is wearing the vulture head-dress, an attribute of goddesses and queens. Instead of the vulture's head usually featured on the forehead there are three erect uraeus snakes. The plastic modelling of the detail shows strong Greek influence. The projecting cheek-bones and the pulled-down corners of the mouth are indicative of a late work of the Ptolemaic Period.

Cat. 7

Sesostris III. Dark green slate. Dynasty XII, *c.* 1860 B.C. Height 23 cm. Kunsthistorisches Museum, Vienna.
Above the king's face is the royal kerchief with the uraeus snake. The austere and dignified features suggest a ruler of great spiritual power. The head once belonged to a sphinx. When attached to the lion's body a mysterious prophetic quality would have radiated from it.

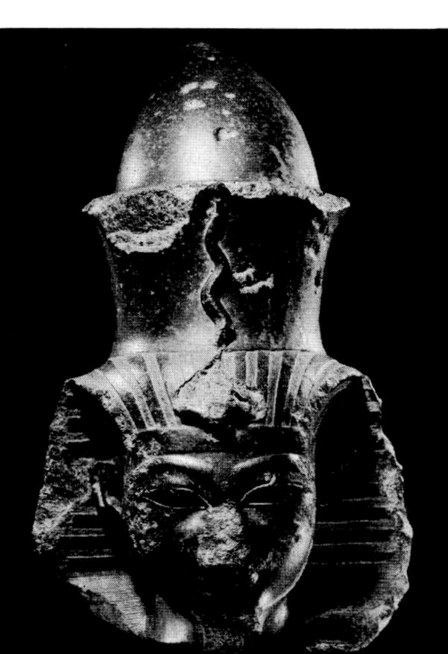

Cat. 8

Head of a statue of Amenophis III. Black syenite. Dynasty XVIII, *c.* 1380 B.C. Height 46 cm. Kestner Museum, Hanover.
Upon the kerchief with the uraeus snake stands the Egyptian double crown. Most of the pointed beard has been broken off. The back pillar bears the throne-names of Amenophis III. The slanting almond-shaped eyes, the elegantly curved eyebrows and the full soft mouth have the grace associated with the mature style of the New Kingdom.

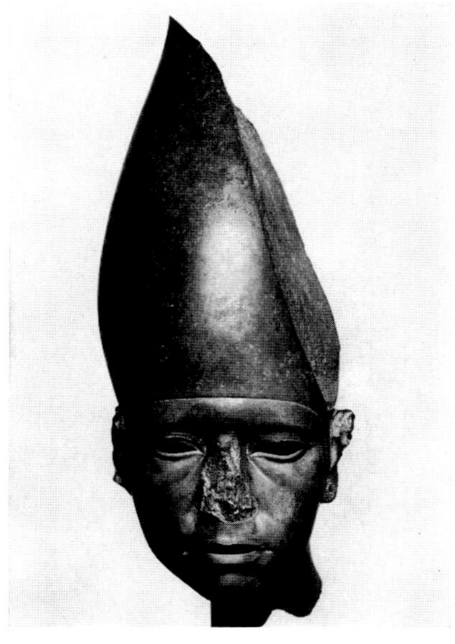

Cat. 9

Head of a statue of a king. Black basalt. Ptolemaic Period, 3rd cent. B.C. Height 46 cm. Ny Carlsberg Glyptotek, Copenhagen.
The royal head with the Upper Egyptian crown emulates in style that of the Middle Kingdom. The smoothness of the stone, the hard contour lines and the absence of inner tension distinguish it from its forerunners.

Cat. 10

Colossi of Ramses II in front of the entrance to the huge rock-cut temple at Abu Simbel.

The entrance to the temple is flanked on either side by two seated colossi hewn out of the rock, each 65 feet high. The form and stance conform to that traditional with royal temple statues.

Cat. 11

Osiride pillar in the mortuary temple of Ramses II, the so-called Ramesseum, on the west bank of the river at Thebes.

Representations of the king as Osiris in the tight-fitting mummy wrapping with flail and crook were familiar from the Middle Kingdom onwards. The pillar-like compactness of the Osiride figure matches the austerity of the pillared architecture.

Cat. 12

Ramses II presenting a votive offering. Slate. From Karnak. Dynasty XIX, *c.* 1250 B.C. Length 75 cm. Cairo Museum.

The unusual posture of the man kneeling prostrate on the ground is rendered with virtuosity. The motif suggests the humble submission made by the king to the divine power.

Cat. 13

King Pepi I. Alabaster. Probably from Saqqara. Dynasty VI, *c.* 2300 B.C. Height 26 cm. Brooklyn Museum, New York. This statuette adopts the motif of the well-known Chephren statue. The king is depicted in a cloak reaching down to his knees, with sceptre, flail and the Upper Egyptian crown. In contrast to the Chephren statue (Cat. 1), there is only a very feeble link between the falcon perched on the back support and the king on his throne. One can see the spiritual and artistic transformation which took place during the two and a half centuries separating the two images.

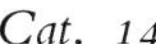

Cat. 14

King Pepi I. Green stone. Probably from Saqqara. Dynasty VI, *c.* 2300 B.C. Height 15 cm. Brooklyn Museum, New York.

The king is shown kneeling, with his body inclining forward, on a flat base slab bearing his name. In his hands, resting upon his thighs, he holds a round vessel. The motif of the king making humble sacrifice to the gods first appears during Dynasty VI. The stylistic treatment, in particular the rigidity of the facial features, heralds the final phase in artistic development during the Old Kingdom.

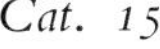

Cat. 15

King Amenophis I. Painted limestone. Dynasty XIX, 1300 to 1200 B.C. Height 65 cm. Museo Egizio, Turin.

As founder of the New Kingdom Amenophis I enjoyed great esteem among later generations. This statuette, produced two hundred years after his death, was presumably borne in processions in his memory. The royal kerchief is painted in yellow and green, the pointed beard in black. The uraeus snake on the forehead, now lost, was of metal and inlaid. The socle and cube-shaped throne with low supporting back bear his throne-name and the surname Amenophis I.

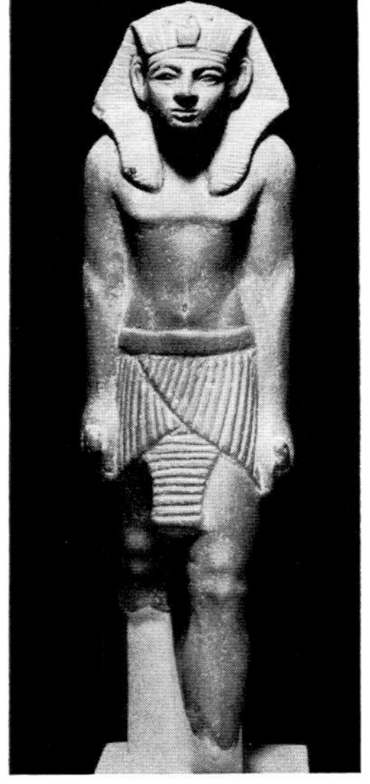

Cat. 16

King Meriankhra-Mentuhotep. Slate. From Karnak. Dynasty XIII, *c.* 1700 B.C. Height 22.2 cm. British Museum, London. This statuette represents one of the numerous XIIIth-Dynasty kings who contended for power at the close of Dynasty XII, after the dissolution of the central state administration. During this second Intermediate Period the artistic tradition of the Middle Kingdom continued.

Cat. 17

King Amenophis III. Ebony. Probably from Thebes. Dynasty XVIII, *c.* 1380 B.C. Height 26.4 cm. Brooklyn Museum, New York.

The king is depicted wearing a gilded kilt and the 'blue crown' popular in the New Kingdom. The arms of the statuette were worked separately and attached later. The ruler is represented as a young man, although this statuette was probably produced toward the end of his reign, since the inscription refers to the king as 'Lord of the Jubilees,' indicating that he had already celebrated several jubilees, or *heb-sed* festivals, during his reign.

Cat. 18

Queen Karomama. Bronze. Inlays in gold, silver and electrum. Dynasty XXII, *c.* 830 B.C. Height 59 cm. Musée du Louvre, Paris.

Karomama was the consort of a Libyan king of Dynasty XXII. This graceful figure is clad in a long robe with short pleated sleeves, over which is a top garment. The festal collar is damascened with gold, electrum and copper. The outstretched hands presumably held a sistrum, and the legs, arms, face and wig were once gilded.

Cat. 19 a und b

Sepa and Neset. Painted limestone. From Saqqara. Dynasty III, *c.* 2650 B.C. Height 165 and 152 cm. Musée du Louvre, Paris. Whereas the woman is represented with her legs together and placed side by side, Sepa appears in a striding stance, which however does not convey the impression of movement. He wears a short straight kilt and a wig of curly hair. His left arm is held at an angle across his body and in his clenched fist he holds a long staff; his right arm, which hangs down, holds the 'sceptre of power.' The woman wears the long tight-fitting robe with straps and on each wrist a number of bracelets. The wig is parted in the middle and falls down to the back and breasts.

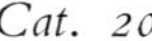

Cat. 20

King Sahura and the nome god of Coptos. Diorite. Dynasty V, *c.* 2450 B.C. Height 63.5 cm. Rogers Fund, 1917; Metropolitan Museum of Art, New York.
King Sahura is seated upon a cube-shaped throne in front of a tall back support. Beside him, in a striding posture, his left foot forward, is the nome god of Coptos, identifiable by the hieroglyphs above his head. In his left hand, outstretched and resting upon the throne, is the symbol of life; in his right hand, which hangs down by his body, he also once held the hieroglyph *ankh* (life).

Cat. 21

Memy-Sabu and his consort. Limestone. Dynasties V/VI, *c.* 2330 B.C. Height 60 cm. Rogers Fund, 1948; Metropolitan Museum of Art, New York.
An attempt has here been made to suggest the relationship of the two persons to one another, not merely by the gesture of embracing, but by rendering them in a natural attitude as well. The careful balance in the contour lines of their bodies gives the impression of a well-integrated group statue. The crude rustic faces possess a vigorous natural quality.

Cat. 22

Amenemes-ankh. Brown sandstone. Dynasty XII, *c.* 1820 B.C. Height 72 cm. Musée du Louvre, Paris.
Characteristic of XIIth-Dynasty style are the superb compactness of this elaborately modelled sculpture and the serious, dignified facial expression. The long skirt hanging down from the hips swirls out slightly at the hem. This shows that the robe no longer follows the outline of the body, as it did during the Old Kingdom, but has obtained a textural quality of its own. The vertical line of inscriptions on the seam of the skirt dates the statue to the reign of Amenemhat III.

Cat. 23

Sebekemsaf. Black granite. From Armant. Dynasty XIII, *c.* 1700 B.C. Height 150 cm. Kunsthistorisches Museum, Vienna.
This statue, produced during Dynasty XIII, illustrates the harder and more rigid artistic style of the Second Intermediate Period. The accentuation of the formal element is underlined further by the polished smoothness of the black granite.

Cat. 24

Mentemhet, governor of Thebes. Detail. Grey granite. From Karnak. Dynasties XXV/XXVI, *c.* 670/600 B.C. Overall height 135 cm. Cairo Museum.
In motif, posture and attire this statue follows the Old Kingdom style of Dynasty V. The wig has the form of those worn during the New Kingdom from the reign of Amenophis II onwards. But the modelling of the body goes beyond the usual treatment of the surface during the Old Kingdom. The facial features and expression suggest an elderly man, such as we do not find earlier. The statue of Mentemhet is a typical example of the art of the Late Period, when historical forms were copied and provided with trimmings in contemporary style.

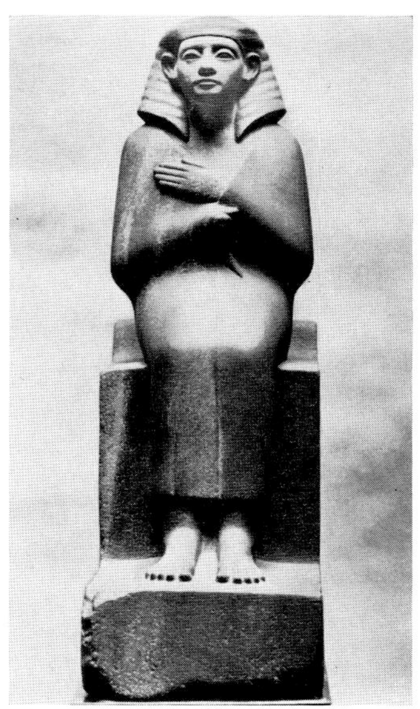

Cat. 25

Khertihotep. Brown sandstone. Dynasty XII, *c.* 1870 B.C. Height 75 cm. Staatliche Museen, Berlin.

The simple and clear structure of this cloaked figure and the broadly defined plastic treatment of the face convey the impression of inner compactness and calm. Under the cloak the forms of the body are visible.

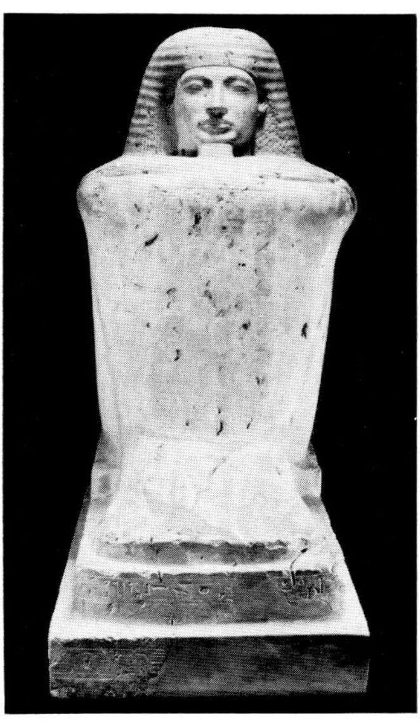

Cat. 26

Block-statue of Bek-en-Khons, high priest of Amun. Hard siliceous limestone. From Thebes. Dynasty XIX, *c.* 1220 B.C. Height 138 cm. Wittelsbacher Ausgleichsfond; Glyptothek, Munich.

The form of the block-statue, in which the squatting figure is contained within the geometric form of a cube, appears for the first time during the Middle Kingdom (cf. Pl. 49) and is encountered in very varied modifications down to the Late Period. The entire body of Bek-en-Khons as well as his feet are compressed to form a single block. Only the crossed hands appear, plastically modelled, upon the upper edge of the block. The extremely fine workmanship of the head conforms to the restrained noble XIXth-Dynasty style. The inscription states the titles and offices held by Bek-en-Khons, who occupied the highest priestly office under Ramses II.

Cat. 27

Block-statue of the priest Merneptah of Memphis. Speckled diorite. Dynasty XXV, *c.* 660 B.C. Height 39 cm. Museo Egizio, Turin.

All parts of the body of the squatting figure are rendered naturalistically. The robe clings to the lower part of the legs, between the knees and ankles, and forms a vertical straight surface. The rectangular surface of the block-statue starts from the shoulders and forms a transition to the plastically shaped arms, with hands crossed upon the knees. The characteristic individual facial features exemplify the realistic portraiture of the Ethiopian era.

Cat. 28

Sebek-em-imu. Grey syenite. Dynasty XII, *c.* 1870 B.C. Height 23.5 cm. Kunsthistorisches Museum, Vienna.
Sebek-em-imu is represented squatting on the ground with his legs crossed. His thighs are enclosed in a short kilt; the lower part of the legs, which are crossed, is visible in front and the tips of the feet at the sides. The left hand rests upon the chest and the right one is stretched out upon the right thigh. The type of scribe statuette is taken from Dynasty V in the Old Kingdom. The broadly defined thigh, as well as the stance, gesture and expression are characteristic of Middle Kingdom style (cf. Pl. IX).

Cat. 29

Iner, guardian of the temple of Hathor at Cusae. Black granite. Dynasty XIX, *c.* 1300 B.C. Height 37.8 cm. Museo Egizio, Turin.
Iner, kneeling and squatting upon his heels, is robed in a long flaring pleated Ramessid kilt. He is holding in both hands the symbol of Queen Hathor, which has a human face, cow's ears and a long wig. The protruding abdomen, the horizontal lines on the diaphragm and the unsure touch in the characterization of the face, with the narrow bridge of the nose, the weak mouth and the almond-shaped, slightly slanting eyes—all these features point to the influence of the late Dynasty XVIII, here taken over by a provincial Ramessid artist.

Cat. 30

Harwa, steward of the sacerdotal princess Amenerdas. Green slate. Dynasty XXV, *c.* 670 B.C. Height 45 cm. Cairo Museum.
The unusual attitude of Harwa, who is squatting with his right leg crossed beneath him and his left leg upright on the ground, as well as his ugly senile facial features, illustrate the endeavours of the Ethiopian Era to achieve realistic treatment.

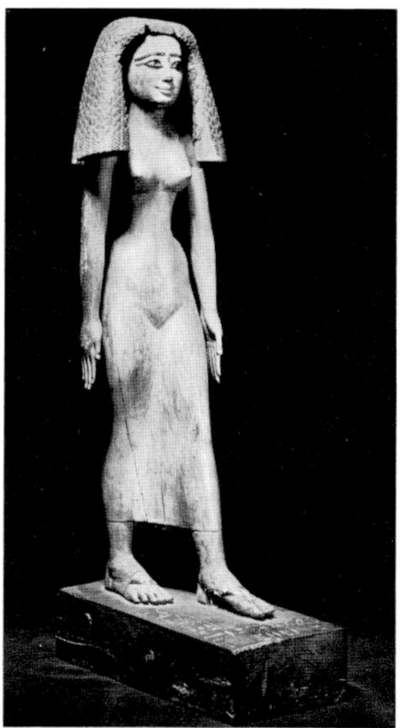

Cat. 31

Imeret-nebes. Wood. Dynasty XII, *c.* 1900 B.C. Height 86 cm. Rijksmuseum van Oudheden, Leyden. (Cf. Pl. XIV.) Toward the end of the Old Kingdom and during the First Intermediate Period wooden models were placed in the sarcophagus of the deceased and wooden statuettes representing him were placed either upon the coffin or inside it, together with the mummy. This tradition is continued during the Middle Kingdom. The arms of the statuettes are worked separately and attached; so too, frequently, is the wig; in this case the latter is affixed with wooden pegs. The delicate modelling of the slender figure is in conformity with the differentiated sensitive feeling for style of Dynasty XII in its maturity.

Cat. 32

Kha. Wood. Dynasty XVIII, *c.* 1420 B.C. From Deir el-Medina. Height 43 cm. Museo Egizio, Turin.
This fine statuette originates from the tomb of Kha, overseer of works at the Theban city of the dead, as is stated in the inscription on the long, projecting kilt. The figure is worked in a single piece. Kha's hands touch his kilt, and the back of his hands are turned outwards.

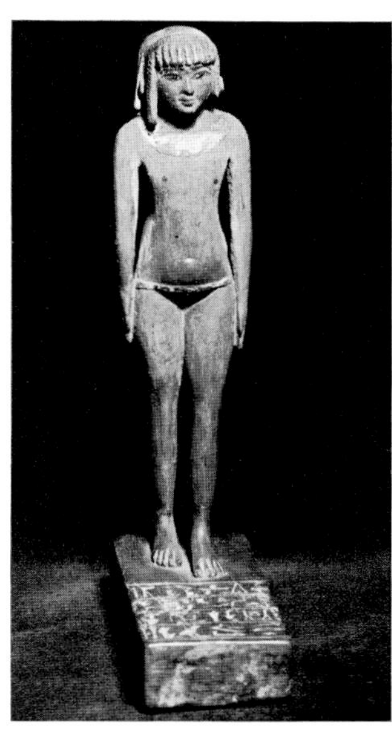

Cat. 33

Neferet-mau. Painted wood. Dynasty XVIII, *c.* 1380 B.C. Height 20.5 cm. Museo Egizio, Turin. (Cf. Pl. 71.)
As the inscription on the socle states, the statuette was donated by Nebet-hotep, the young girl's mother. Her youthful body is clad only in a gilded girdle over the loins and a collar. The hair-style emphasizes her youth.

Cat. 34

Tetiseneb. Painted limestone. From Thebes. Dynasty XVIII, *c.* 1550 B.C. Height 30.8 cm. Kestner Museum, Hanover.
This statuette originates from the early period of the New Kingdom. Tetiseneb wears a tight-fitting white robe with straps and a tripartite wig. The inscription on the side of the foot-rest and on the seat is addressed to the gods Amun and Osiris, and requests that sacrifice be made for the *ka* of the deceased.

Cat. 35

Tuty. Ebony (?). From Medinet Gurob. Dynasty XVIII, *c.* 1370 B.C. Height 25.7 cm. Brooklyn Museum, New York.
This statuette was discovered in a tomb complex containing the remains of several women, possibly members of the royal harem. From its motif and style it seems to have been produced in a Theban workshop during the reign of Amenophis III. The long robe leaves the right breast bare. The tripartite wig is crowned by an unguent cone, on which the gilding has been preserved, as it has also been preserved on the ear-rings; only traces have survived, however, of the sandals and the collar, which were originally painted in gold.

Cat. 36

Piaaï. Wood. Dynasty XIX, *c.* 1300 B.C. Height 54 cm. Musée du Louvre, Paris.
Piaaï, as is stated in the inscription on the foot-rest, was 'commander of the guard at the entrance to the palace.' His robe is in conformity with the fashion of his time.

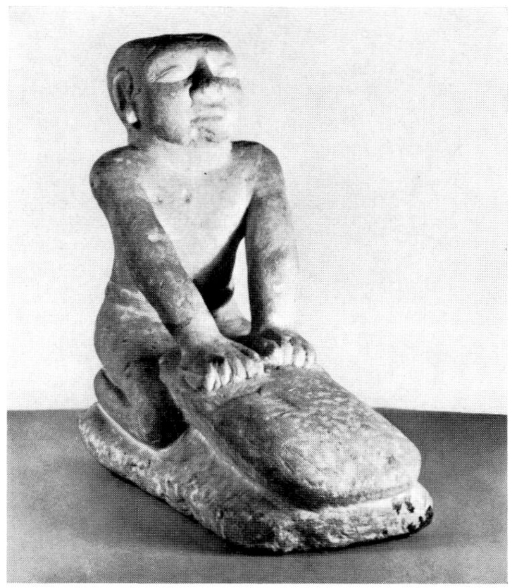

Cat. 37

Servant kneading dough. Limestone. From Giza. Dynasty VI, *c.* 2250 B.C. Height 25.6 cm. Ägyptische Staatssammlung, Munich. Toward the end of the Old Kingdom doubt whether the cult of the dead would be performed reliably led to the cessation of the practice of placing detailed representations in relief in the ritual chamber, and instead models of servants were deposited in direct proximity to the deceased, in his sarcophagus-chamber; they were shown performing tasks essential to the deceased in the after-life. The plastic form had not hitherto been used to represent movement in an action. The servant statuettes that have survived display an unsophisticated freshness in the handling of new motifs, but generally speaking they are not of high quality.

Cat. 38

Potter. Painted limestone. Dynasty VI, *c.* 2300 B.C. Height 13.3 cm. Oriental Institute, University of Chicago, Chicago. The potter from the tomb of Ni-kau-inpu differs from most servant statuettes in its theme and manner of execution. The realistic treatment of the emaciated body with the spindly legs drawn up beneath it is distinguished from the crude rustic figures of other statuettes.

Cat. 39

Rowing-boat for harpooning and trapping birds. Painted wood. From the tomb of Meketra at Thebes. Dynasty XI, *c.* 2000 B.C. Length 114 cm. Metropolitan Museum of Art, New York.

Toward the end of Dynasty VI and during the First Intermediate Period the stone servant figures deposited in the burial-chamber were replaced by wooden ones. The events formerly depicted in the reliefs of the ritual chamber afforded the prototype for models resembling doll's houses, which rendered entire slaughterhouses, granaries, sailing-boats with their crew, or an army equipped for battle.

Cat. 40

King Mentuhotep III and the goddess Uto. Detail. Limestone relief. From Armant. Dynasty XI, *c.* 1995 B.C. Height 81 cm., overall width 130 cm. Brooklyn Museum, New York. (Cf. Pl. 41.)

Mentuhotep III is depicted wearing the royal kerchief with the ureaeus snake upon his forehead, pointed beard and collar. The face, with the elaborate streaks of cosmetic paint, shows fine modelling. Opposite him is the goddess Uto, wearing a robe with straps and the vulture head-dress. The loose spatial disposition of the figures as well as the broadly defined planes give the work a dignity and symbolic power characteristic of Middle Kingdom temple reliefs.

Cat. 41

King Sethos I before Sokar, the god of the dead. Limestone relief in the temple of Sethos I at Abydos (in the hall of the gods Nefertum and Ptah-Sokar). Dynasty XIX, *c.* 1300 B.C.

The king is wearing a rich kilt with animal tail. With the handle of the censer in his left hand he is offering incense; with his right hand he is pouring from a jug a libation over the sacrificial stand. The falcon-headed god of the dead, seated upon a throne, is holding in his right hand the hieroglyph for 'life.' The sceptre in his left hand is in the shape of the hieroglyph for 'prosperity.'

Cat. 42

The Roman emperor Trajan. Detail from a limestone relief in the temple of Hathor at Dendera (the temple of Augustus' birth). Roman. 2nd cent. A.D.

The emperor Trajan is presenting the goddess Hathor with a divine barque. In motif, costume and style the representation follows the tradition of royal temple reliefs during the Pharaonic Era.

Cat. 43

Hetep-akhti. Limestone relief from the tomb of Hetep-akhti at Saqqara. Late Dynasty III, *c.* 2600 B.C. Height 100 cm. E. and M. Kofler-Truniger Collection, Lucerne.
The high and sharply incised relief originates from the wall of the receding false door in the tomb of Hetep-akhti. The deceased is shown wearing a short curly wig as well as a short tight-fitting kilt knotted in front. In his right hand, held forward, he is holding a long staff, and in his left hand a sceptre. The hieroglyphs indicate parts of a title and the name of the occupant of the tomb. Other finds from Hetep-akhti's tomb give his full titulary: Judge, Administrator of the Nome, Great One of Upper Egypt, Privy Councillor and Overseer of Works, as well as various high priestly titles.

Cat. 44

Prince Khufu-kaf and his consort. Limestone relief. From Giza. Dynasty IV, *c.* 2550 B.C. Height 60 cm., width 76 cm. Museum of Fine Arts, Boston.
Khufu-kaf, a son of the pharaoh Cheops, wearing a short kilt and panther skin, and his consort, who has taken her husband's left arm and is grasping his forearm with her left hand, are shown receiving the offerings presented to them. The simplicity and purity of line as well as the restrained composure of the expression accord with the spiritual attitude of the Pyramid Period.

Cat. 45

Ptah-hotep at the dining-table. Detail from a painted limestone relief on the western wall of the ritual chamber in the tomb of Ptah-hotep at Saqqara. Dynasty V, *c.* 2450 B.C.
Ptah-hotep, clad in a short girdle over his loins, leopard skin and cape, is seated upon a stool with lion's legs in front of a table with offerings of bread. In his left hand he is lifting an unguent vessel to his nose. Above and below the 'dining-table' other votive gifts are featured.

Cat. 46

Boats and cattle. Detail of a limestone relief from Khaemrehu's tomb at Saqqara. Dynasty V, *c.* 2400 B.C. Ny Carlsberg Glyptotek, Copenhagen.

The upper part of the relief, of which only fragments have survived, represents a haul of fish in a net. In the lower register a small calf and six oxen are seen wading through a canal, pursued by three men in a boat made of clumps of papyrus bound together. The man on the left pushes the boat off from the shore; the one on the right plies an oar. The shepherd in the middle of the boat has sat down on a chair of plaited rushes. Below the boat is a crocodile.

Cat. 47

Donkeys bringing sheaves of corn. Detail of a limestone relief from Seshem-Nefer IV's tomb. From Giza. Dynasty VI, *c.* 2300 B.C. Overall height 50 cm., width 100 cm. Roemer-Pelizaeus Museum, Hildesheim.

Detail from a harvesting scene. Two men are stacking up the sheaves brought by the donkeys.

Cat. 48

Animal life in a papyrus thicket. Detail from a limestone relief on the south wall of the entrance-hall in Mereruka's tomb at Saqqara. Dynasty VI, *c.* 2300 B.C.

Five men in a skiff are forcing their way into a papyrus thicket. One of them has picked up by its tail an ikhneumon mouse which was lying in wait for some young birds in their nest. The birds' parents, with outspread wings, are trying to attack the enemy. Various kinds of birds have settled upon the clusters of papyrus. Where the width of the papyrus blossoms was insufficient to render the brooding birds, horizontal ledges have been inserted. In the water are some hippopotamuses.

Cat. 49

Land surveying. Wall-painting from a private tomb at Thebes. Dynasty XVIII, *c.* 1400 B.C. Height 43.2 cm. British Museum, London.

To assess taxes officials were sent out to survey the fields and erect boundary-stones. On the left-hand side of this picture the tax official has just erected a boundary-stone at the end of a cornfield. A second man is standing behind him, but only fragments of this figure have survived. The inscription contains the solemn affirmation that the survey is exact. In the right-hand section, in each of two registers, one above the other, are a team of horses with their charioteers in attendance.

Cat. 50

Plucking and salting away geese. Wall-painting in ochre, reddish brown, black and white. From a private tomb at Thebes. Dynasty XVIII, *c.* 1410 B.C. Height 19 cm., width 45 cm. Kestner Museum, Hanover. (Cf. Pl. 62.)

Two men seated upon footstools are busily plucking, drawing and salting away geese. A naked boy is putting the salted birds into tall storage jars, while the overseer notes the number.

Cat. 51

Donor. Detail of a wall-painting from a private tomb at Thebes. Dynasty XVIII, *c.* 1370 B.C. British Museum, London. (Cf. Pl. XVI.)

An overseer, his writing materials tucked under his arm, is bringing a chest to be added to the gifts piled up on a stand.

Cat. 58

Female dancers. Detail from a limestone relief in Ti's tomb at Saqqara. Dynasty V, *c.* 2400 B.C.

The girls have their arms raised above their heads and are striding one behind the other in a leisurely dance step. Over the short kilt they are wearing a long skirt through which the outline of their legs is visible. The band worn around the neck is crossed upon the chest and knotted at the back. The Iba dance they are performing is one of the ceremonies of the funerary rite, but is also found in other ritual scenes.

Cat. 59

The harpist Nefer-hotep. Detail from the stele of Prince Aki. Limestone relief. Dynasty XII, *c.* 1850 B.C. Rijksmuseum van Oudheden, Leyden.

The rectangular stele, shaped like a false door, depicts in the uppermost of its three registers the deceased and his consort before the offering-table. The harpist squatting before them strikes the strings with both hands. The dull eye, without a pupil, shows that he is blind; his short thin forearms are in contrast to his corpulent body.

Cat. 60

Blind musicians with bandages over their eyes. Limestone relief. From Hermopolis. Dynasty XVIII, *c.* 1350 B.C. Height 22 cm., width 24.5 cm. Norbert Schimmel Collection, New York.

From their headgear and attire these persons may be Asiatics, possibly Syrians, grouped together around their harp. Blind men no longer fit for any work, both Egyptians and foreigners, were from time immemorial readily employed as musicians or singers. The bandaging of people's eyes has been authenticated in several instances during the Amarna Period.

FUNERARY RELIEFS: INTERMENT AND PROCESSION

Cat. 61–63 *Funeral procession and rites.* Limestone relief from the tomb of the high priest Neferronpet at Memphis. Dynasty XVIII, *c.* 1300 B.C. Staatliche Museen, Berlin.

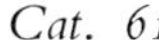

Cat. 61

Participant in the funeral procession, who by his attitude and gestures expresses various degrees of grief, mourning and despair. The stylistic treatment shows evidence of the influence of the expressive Amarna style.

Cat. 62

The posture of the man squatting on the ground expresses restrained lamentation. The outstretched arm with the hand hanging down limply conveys an impression of helplessness before the unrelenting fate of death.

Cat. 63

The deceased's servants have erected bowers for the funeral rites and decorated them with branches. Water jugs are available in wooden stands. In accordance with the requirements of ceremonial the bowers are now being demolished and the jugs smashed.

FUNERARY RELIEFS: INTERMENT AND PROCESSION

Cat. 64

Muu *dancers and wailing women waiting for the funeral ceremonies to begin.* Painted Limestone relief. Dynasty XVIII, *c.* 1410 B.C. Height 28 cm., width 68.5 cm. Kestner Museum, Hanover. (Cf. page 129.)

Cat. 65

Wailing women at the funeral. Limestone relief from the western wall of Nes-peka-shuti's funerary chapel. From Thebes, tomb 312. Dynasty XXVI, *c.* 650-630 B.C. Height 34.5 cm. Brooklyn Museum, New York.

The women's attire and gestures express lamentation for the dead. Their breasts are bare; the position of their hands, thrown back over their heads, suggests that they are covering their heads with dust.

Cat. 66

Detail from a procession scene. Limestone relief. From Hermopolis. Dynasty XVIII, *c.* 1350 B.C. Height 22.8 cm., width 54 cm. Norbert Schimmel Collection, New York.

Three men with the upper part of their bodies inclined far forward are holding in their left hands a budding stalk, splayed out at the top. The procession is presumably moving toward the king who is probably receiving the votive gifts, as in other Amarna reliefs discovered at Hermopolis. This custom may be connected with a harvest festival. (Cooney, Norbert Schimmel Collection, no. 113.)

Cat. 67

Palette of King Narmer. Slate. From Hierakonpolis. Archaic Period, *c.* 3000 B.C. Height 64 cm. Cairo Museum.
Obverse side with a depression for cosmetics. The reverse of the palette (Pl. 5) shows Narmer as the triumphant pharaoh, whilst here he appears in the upper register behind the tutelary standard-bearers (cf. Pl. 6), each of whom has between his feet the severed heads of defeated enemies. In the lower register the king, shown as a 'strong bull,' is forcing the walls of a fortress and trampling to death a prostrate enemy.

Cat. 68

Door-hinge socket with the head of a prisoner. Granite. From Hierakonpolis. Dynasties I/II, *c.* 2800 B.C. Length approx. 75 cm. University Museum, Philadelphia.
The prisoner is lying on his stomach with his arms bent back. The hollow on his back formerly served to hold the hinge of the heavy wooden door at the entrance to the main sanctuary of Lower Egypt at Hierakonpolis. The prisoner was symbolically crushed each time the door was opened, and his face seems to express hatred and disdain.

Cat. 69

Armlet bearing the name of Thutmosis IV. Ivory. From Amarna, house Q 48. I. Dynasty XVIII, *c.* 1350 B.C. Width 11 cm. Stiftung Preussischer Kulturbesitz, Staatliche Museen, Berlin.
The cut-out carving in relief shows the king taking a long stride, about to crush his prostrate enemy, whom he is holding with his right hand. On the left-hand side is the falcon-headed god Horus. This motif corresponds to the symbolic image of the triumphant pharaoh already rendered on the Narmer palette.

Cat. 70

Battle with Asiatics. Relief scenes on the war-chariot of Thutmosis IV. Detail. From Thebes. Dynasty XVIII, *c.* 1400 B.C. Cairo Museum.
This lively composition, the first realistic portrayal of the chaos and turmoil of battle, obtains dramatic tension and compactness by its dynamic movement and the unusual way in which the bodies are often entangled or overlap; every detail of the clothing and ornaments is elaborately rendered.

Cat. 71

Nubians bringing tribute. Detail of a wall-painting in Huy's tomb at Thebes. Dynasty XVIII, *c.* 1340 B.C.
Huy was viceroy of Nubia under Tutankhamun. Here three Nubian princes, with knees bent, do him reverence. Four servants carry precious gifts, above all the Nubian gold so greatly sought after in Egypt.

Cat. 72

Egyptians parading Syrian prisoners. Detail of a limestone relief from Horemheb's tomb at Saqqara. Dynasty XVIII, *c.* 1330 B.C. Rijksmuseum van Oudheden, Leyden.
While the Egyptian in command of the column of prisoners, his left arm raised in enthusiasm and veneration, goes down on his knees before his pharaoh, the exhausted prisoners, on the other hand, whom he drags behind him on a rope, seem to stumble forward reluctantly. In such psychological differentiation one can sense the after-effects of the Amarna Period.

Cat. 73

Stele of a dwarf. Limestone relief. From Abydos. Dynasty I, *c.* 2800 B.C. Height 32.5 cm., width 18 cm. Kestner Museum, Hanover.

The upper part bears the name: ser inpu ('Anubis is the prince') below, as a determinative, is a dwarf.

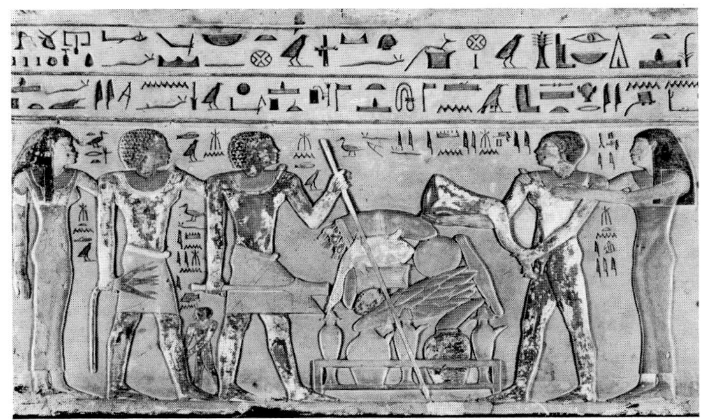

Cat. 74

Stele of Prince Khui. Painted limestone relief. Dynasty XII, *c.* 1900 B.C. Height 36 cm., width 60 cm. Rijksmuseum van Oudheden, Leyden.

Khui, wearing a short protruding kilt and holding in his hands the sceptre of power and the staff, is shown before the votive offerings. Behind him are his brother, his small son and his sister. From the right his son approaches the offering-stand, bearing the leg of an ox; behind him his mother embraces him, while the figures on the left also put their hands around each other's shoulders. The two horizontal lines of script contain the funerary prayer to the gods Osiris and Anubis.

Cat. 75

Stele of Kasa, chief of the soldiers. Sunk relief, limestone. Dynasty XIX, *c.* 1300 B.C. Height 38 cm., width 30.5 cm. Kestner Museum, Hanover.

Kasa is seated upon a chair with a low support and lion's legs; his wig and costume conform to contemporary fashion. Upon his head is an unguent cone, indicating that his hair has been anointed. In front of him the priest Imen-heru offers incense in the handle of the censer: in his outstretched right hand he holds the libation vessel with the 'water of purification.'

Cat. 76

Sculptors' trial-piece. Limestone. Ptolemaic Period, 280 to 250 B.C. Height 10.5 cm., width 11 cm. Museum für Kunst und Gewerbe, Hamburg.

From the Late and Ptolemaic Periods numerous pieces have been preserved which were produced following the ancient pattern-books and rules, and served as models for students or as the preliminary stages in a later work.

Cat. 77

Falcon upon the hieroglyph for 'gold.' Sculptors trial-piece. Limestone. From Leontopolis. Ptolemaic Period, *c.* 3rd cent. B.C. Height 15.3 cm. Kestner Museum, Hanover.

The raised edge of the square block evokes the impression of a compact sculptural work, but an attempt at a relief on the reverse shows that it is in fact a sculptors' model. The elaborate execution and the balanced way in which it is incorporated into the square plane testify to outstanding mastery.

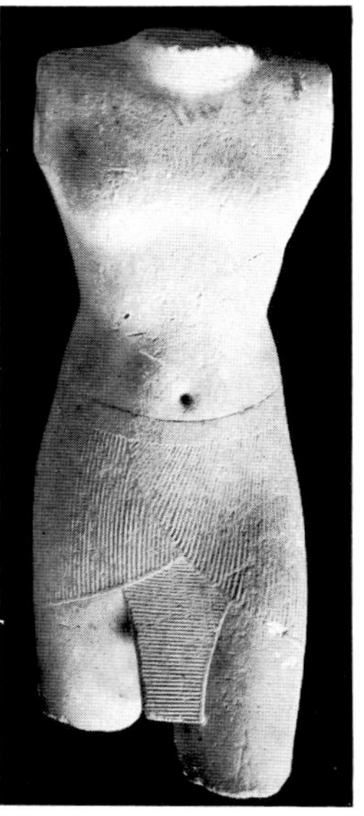

Cat. 78

Torso of a striding man. Sculptors' trial-piece. Limestone. Ptolemaic Period, 3rd cent. B.C. Height 19.1 cm., width 7.2 cm. Kestner Museum, Hanover.

The delicately modelled body is clad in a pleated kilt. On the smooth plane formed by the stumps of the arms and legs the network of squaring lines has been preserved; this helped the sculptor in calculating the proportions.

Cat. 79

Head of a baboon. Red baked clay. From Hierakonpolis. Archaic Period, *c.* 3000 B.C. Height 10 cm., width 9 cm. Kestner Museum, Hanover.
The eyeballs are worked separately and inserted; the pupil is hollowed out. In prehistoric times and during the Archaic Period the baboon was venerated as 'the great sage' represented in the 'white chapel of the Great Ones of Upper Egypt;' it may have been one guise of the *ka* of the ruler. Already at an early stage it is related to the sun-god; the calls emitted by the baboon at daybreak were interpreted as a welcome to the rising sun. For this reason it was popularly depicted raising its paws in greeting. From the Old Kingdom onwards the baboon was seen mainly as a guise of Thoth, god of scribes and of wisdom.

Cat. 80

Baboon. Bronze over core of lead with inlays of silver and electrum. Dynasty XXII, 9th cent. B.C. Height 5.7 cm. Kestner Museum, Hanover.

Cat. 81

Baboon. Painted limestone relief. Detail from a chapel of Ptolemy I. Ptolemaic Period, *c.* 300 B.C. Roemer-Pelizaeus Museum, Hildesheim.

Cat. 88

Unguent jar. Alabaster. Dynasty IV, *c.* 2500 B.C. Height 5.6 cm. Kestner Museum, Hanover.
From the Archaic Period onwards small alabaster unguent jars grew in popularity. The balanced shape of the cylindrical vessel, slightly projecting at the top and bottom, leading to a flanging lip and foot, exemplifies the composed and harmonious sense of form attained during the Pyramid Period.

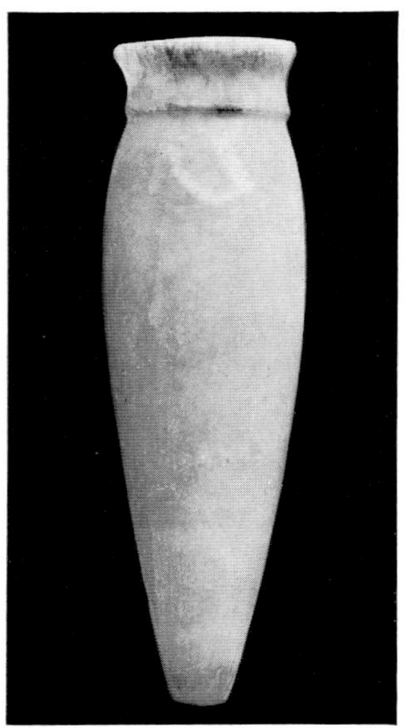

Cat. 89

Pointed vessel in alabaster. Dynasty V, *c.* 2440 B.C. Height 14.4 cm. Kestner Museum, Hanover.
These small unguent and oil flasks, tapering at the bottom, of which there are several examples, were inserted into wooden stands. With their elegant shape they conform to the relaxed spirit of Dynasty V.

Cat. 90

Head-rest of Nefermaat. Alabaster. Dynasty VI, *c.* 2200 B.C. Height 18 cm. E. and M. Kofler-Truniger Collection, Lucerne.
This piece was worked in three parts. Upon the rectangular plinth rests the fluted column, broadening out at the bottom, which supports the actual head-rest. The inscription on the column and the side of the plinth gives the title and name of the owner.

Cat. 91

Egg-shaped vessel. Alabaster. Dynasty XII, 1991-1786 B.C Height 7.3 cm. Kestner Museum, Hanover.

The material used here was a particularly light transparent alabaster. The surface is slightly rippled and was polished in such a way as to leave it slightly uneven; with its dull lustre and delicate curves it is in conformity with the cultivated style of life that prevailed during Dynasty XII.

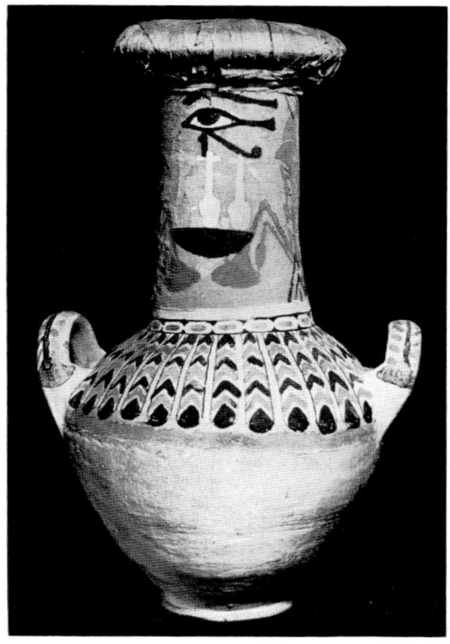

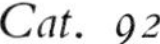

Cat. 92

Vase. Painted clay. From Kha's tomb at Deir el-Medina. Dynasty XVIII, *c.* 1420 B.C. Height 38 cm. Museo Egizio, Turin.

On the neck of the vessel between green papyrus plants is the hieroglyph *neb* ('all') in black, and above it, repeated three times, the sign *nefer* ('good,') that in the middle in white and those above and below in yellow: *i.e.*, 'all the best.' Over this is the eye, probably used here in a magical context. The handles and shoulder area of the vessel are painted cursorily in green, yellow and brown. The lid is affixed to the vessel by means of strips of linen.

Cat. 93

Alabaster lamp in the form of cups of flowers. From the tomb of Tutankhamun, Thebes. Dynasty XVIII, *c.* 1340 B.C. Height 27 cm. Cairo Museum.

The two outer cups are in the shape of the white lotus blossom; the middle one is in the shape of the blue lotus blossom; the curved stems and the horizontal leaves of the blue pond-lotus blossoms are rendered true to nature. The exuberant outline of this vase is characteristic of the graceful, occasionally playful, late Amarna style.

Cat. 94

Faience vase in the shape of a blue lotus blossom. Dynasty XVIII, *c.* 1400 B.C. Height 14 cm. Stiftung Preussischer Kulturbesitz, Staatliche Museen, Berlin.

The shape of the blue lotus blossom approximates to the curved bell of the papyrus cluster. The production and use of coloured glazes was known as early as the Archaic Period. From Amenophis III's reign onwards faience tiles were produced for use as a wall covering in palaces. Vessels of the most varied shapes and amulets were also made of faience.

Cat. 95

Cup with the throne-name of Thutmosis III. Light blue glass paste decorated with yellow and dark blue threads. Dynasty XVIII, *c.* 1450 B.C. Height 8.1 cm. Ägyptische Staatssammlung, Munich.

One of the few glass vessels that can be dated by the royal name, made when glass-working was in its infancy. The yellow and dark blue design is produced by 'combing' molten glass threads into the light blue glass past.

Cat. 96

Small amphora. Dark blue glass paste decorated with coloured threads. Dynasty XVIII, *c.* 1350 B.C. Height 8.8 cm. Ägyptische Staatssammlung, Munich.

The yellow and white glass threads 'combed in' form a festoon design around the body and neck. Around the lip are diagonal yellow stripes.

Cat. 97 a and b

Unguent bowl in the shape of an ape squatting on a globe or piece of fruit. Dark green slate. Dynasty XVIII, 14th cent. B.C. Height 12.8 cm. E. and M. Kofler-Truniger Collection, Lucerne.

Both sides of the unguent bowl are executed in relief. On one side the globe, not quite circular, upon which the ape is squatting is hollowed out to form a flat bowl with a level rim; on the other side, which is slightly curved, is the ape's tail. On figured cosmetic and unguent vessels from the New Kingdom the ape (long-tailed monkey) frequently appears. It is one of the animals most favoured by ladies.

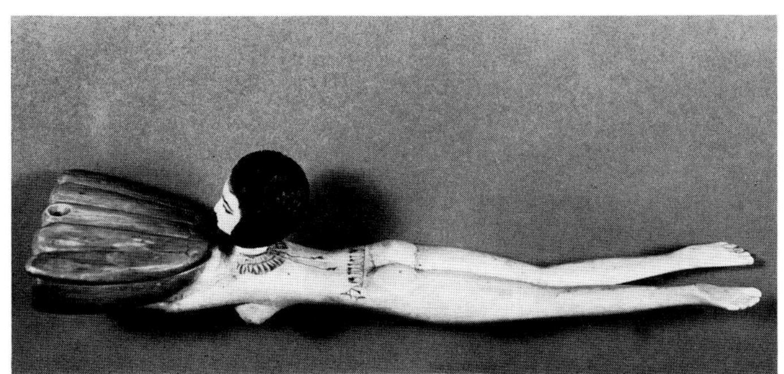

Cat. 98

Unguent spoon. Painted ivory and wood. Dynasty XVIII, 15th cent. B.C. Length 19.4 cm. Pushkin Museum, Moscow.

The girl swimming, with elongated body, is carrying in her outstretched arms a lidded vessel in the shape of a lotus blossom, used for cosmetic ointment.

Cat. 99

Unguent jar in the shape of a girl carrying a jug upon her shoulder. Wood. Dynasty XVIII, 14th cent. B.C. Length 31 cm. Musée du Louvre, Paris.

The girl, slightly stooping and clad only in a festal collar, is carrying upon her right shoulder, supported by her hand, a stand upon which rests the amphora-shaped unguent jar. In her left hand she is carrying a pouch.

Cat. 100

Head of a falcon. Gold. From Hierakonpolis. Dynasty VI, *c.* 2300 B.C. Height 10 cm. Cairo Museum.
The head, embossed in gold with inlaid eyes of obsidian, originally bore a royal diadem with two tall feathers and the erect uraeus snake. The body, of copper, was in a crouching posture upon the plinth. In front of the chest was a royal image, under the protection of the falcon.

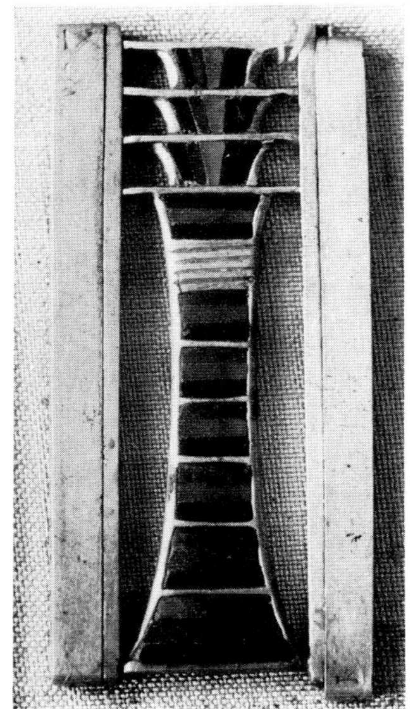

Cat. 101

Pendant with Djed pillar. Gold and semi-precious stones. From the tomb of Princess Sat-Hathor at Illahun. Dynasty XII, *c.* 1900 B.C. Height 6 cm. Cairo Museum.
The Djed pillar is the hieroglyph for 'permanence.' It is used symbolically or as an amulet.

Cat. 102

Pectoral bearing the name of Ramses II, from a mummy of the Apis bull. Gold with cornelian, turquoise and lapis lazuli. From the Serapeum at Saqqara. Dynasty XIX, *c.* 1260 B.C. Height 13 cm. Musée du Louvre, Paris.
Inserted in the rectangular frame of the pectoral, in the centre of the outspread wings, are the vulture and the cobra, the heraldic animals of Upper and Lower Egypt. Above them is the body of a bird with stylized bull's head, in its claws the hieroglyph for 'eternity' (a symbolic allusion to the Apis bull, for whom the pectoral was intended). Above, between the bird's wings, the throne name of Ramses II. In the lower corners is the hieroglyph for 'permanence,' the Djed pillar.

APPENDIX

TRANSLATOR'S NOTES

1. Pyramid Texts, § 275, in: *The Literature of the Ancient Egyptians* by Adolf Erman, translated by A. M. Blackman. London, 1927, pp. 4–5.
2. Erman, *op. cit.*, p. 5.
3. Erman, *op. cit.*, p. 43.
4. After *Altägyptische Liebeslieder* by S. Schott. Zurich, 1950, p. 131.
5. From the hymn placed before the harpist in the house of King Antef the Blessed. After Erman, *op. cit.*, pp. 132 f.
6. After Erman, *op. cit.*, pp. 30 f.
7. After Schott, *op. cit.*, p. 91.
8. After Erman, *op. cit.*, pp. 288 f.

BIBLIOGRAPHY

HISTORY

BREASTED, J. H., *A History of Egypt*. New York, 1905; reissue London-New York, 1950.

Cambridge Ancient History, revised ed. Chapters issued as separate fascicles.

DRIOTON, E., *L'Egypte pharaonique*. Paris, 1960.

DRIOTON, E. and VANDIER, J., *L'Egypte*. Les peuples de l'Orient méditerranéen, vol. II. Paris, 1962.

GARDINER, SIR ALAN H., *Egypt of the Pharaohs*. Oxford, 1961.

LANGUAGE, SCRIPT AND LITERATURE

BRUNNER, H., *Abriss der mittelägyptischen Grammatik*. Graz, 1961.

BUCK, A. DE, *Grammaire élémentaire du moyen égyptien*. Leyden, 1952.

EDEL, E., *Altägyptische Grammatik*, vol. I. Rome, 1955.

ERMAN, A., *The Literature of the Ancient Egyptians*. Translated by A. M. Blackman. London, 1927; New York, 1966.

GARDINER, SIR ALAN H., *Egyptian Grammar*. London, 1957.

LEFEBVRE, G., *Romans et contes égyptiens de l'époque pharaonique*. Paris, 1949.

RANKE, H., *Die ägyptischen Personennamen*. 2 vols. Glückstadt, 1935, 1952.

SCHOTT, S., *Altägyptische Liebeslieder*. Zurich, 1950.

SCHOTT, S., *Hieroglyphen: Untersuchungen zum Ursprung der Schrift*. Akademie der Wissenschaften und der Literatur. Abhandlungen der geistes- und sozialwissenschaftlichen Klasse, Year 1950, No. 24. Wiesbaden, 1951.

SPULER, B., *Handbuch der Orientalistik*, vol. I: *Ägyptologie*. Section 2: *Literatur*. Leyden, 1952.

RELIGION

BONNET, H., *Reallexikon der ägyptischen Religionsgeschichte*. Berlin, 1952.

BREASTED, J. H., *The Development of Religion and Thought in Ancient Egypt*. New York, 1912; reissue 1959.

BREASTED, J. H., *The Dawn of Conscience*. New York-London, 1933.

ČERNY, J., *Ancient Egyptian Religion*. London, 1952.

DONADONI, S., *La religione dell'antico Egitto*. Bari, 1959.

DRIOTON, E., 'Egyptian Religion,' in: *Religions of the Ancient East*, edited and translated by M. B. Loraine, part I. London, 1959.

ERMAN, A., *Die Religion der Ägypter*. Berlin, 1934.

FRANKFORT, H., *Ancient Egyptian Religion*. New York, 1948; reissue 1961.

FRANKFORT, H., *Kingship and Gods*. Chicago, 1948.

KEES, H., *Der Götterglaube im alten Ägypten*. 2nd ed. Berlin, 1956.

KEES, H., *Totenglauben und Jenseitsvorstellungen im alten Ägypten*. Berlin, 1956.

MORENZ, S., *Ägyptische Religion*. Stuttgart, 1960.

OTTO, E. AND HIRMER, H., *Osiris and Amun: Their Cult and Shrines*. London, 1967.

ROEDER, G., *Volksglaube im Pharaonenreich*. Stuttgart, 1952.

SAINTE-FARE-GARNOT, J., *La vie religieuse dans l'ancienne Egypte*. Paris, 1948.

VANDIER, J., *La religion égyptienne*. Paris, 1944.

HISTORY OF CIVILIZATION

ALDRED, C., *The Egyptians*. London, 1961.

ERMAN, A. AND RANKE, H., *Ägypten und ägyptisches Leben im Altertum*. Tübingen, 1923.

HAYES, W. C., *The Scepter of Egypt*. 2 vols. New York, 1953-60.

HELCK, H. W. AND OTTO, E., *Kleines Wörterbuch der Ägyptologie*. Wiesbaden, 1956.

KEES, H., *Ägypten*. Kulturgeschichte des Alten Orients, Sect. I. Handbuch der Altertumswissenschaft, Section 3, Part I, Vol. 3. Munich, 1932.

KEES, H., *Ancient Egypt: A Cultural Topography*. Edited by T. G. H. James. London, 1961.

MONTET, P., *Everyday Life in Egypt in the Days of Ramesses the Great*. Translated by A. R. Maxwell-Hyslop and M. S. Drower. London, 1958.

PIRENNE, J., *Histoire de la civilisation de l'Egypte ancienne*. 3 vols. Neuchâtel – Paris, 1961-3.

Posener, G., *A Dictionary of Egyptian Civilization.* Translated by A. MacFarlane. London, 1962.

Spiegel, J., *Das Werden der altägyptischen Hochkultur.* Heidelberg, 1953.

Wilson, J. A. and Jacobsen, Th., *The Intellectual Adventure of Ancient Man.* Chicago, 1946.

Wilson, J. A., *The Culture of Ancient Egypt.* Chicago, 1956.

ARCHAEOLOGY AND ART

GENERAL WORKS

Aldred, C., *The Development of Ancient Egyptian Art from 3200 to 1315 B.C.* London, 1952.

Bissing, F. W. Freiherr von, *Denkmäler ägyptischer Skulptur.* 3 vols. Munich, 1911-4.

Bissing, F. W. Freiherr von, *Ägyptische Kunstgeschichte von den ältesten Zeiten bis auf die Eroberung durch die Araber.* 3 vols. Berlin, 1934-5.

Capart, J., *Documents pour servir à l'étude de l'art égyptien.* 2 vols. Paris, 1927, 1931.

Davies, N. M., *Ancient Egyptian Paintings.* 3 vols. Chicago, 1936.

Fechheimer, H., *Die Plastik der Ägypter.* Die Kunst des Ostens, vol. 1. Berlin, 1920.

Fechheimer, H., *Kleinplastik der Ägypter.* Die Kunst des Ostens, vol. 3. Berlin, 1921.

Kayser, H., *Tausend Tore hatte Theben.* Hanover, 1965.

Komorzynski, A., *Das Erbe des Alten Ägypten.* Vienna, 1965.

Lange, K., *Ägyptische Kunst.* Zurich – Berlin, 1939.

Lange, C. and Hirmer, M., *Egypt: Architecture, Sculpture, Painting in Three Thousand Years.* Translated by R. H. Boothroyd. 3rd ed., revised. London, 1961.

Lucas, A., *Ancient Egyptian Materials and Industries.* 4th ed., revised and enlarged by J. R. Harris. London, 1962.

Mekhitarian, A., *Egyptian Painting.* Translated by S. Gilbert. Geneva, 1954.

Ranke, H., *Masterpieces of Egyptian Art.* London, 1951.

Schäfer, H., *Von ägyptischer Kunst.* 4th ed. Wiesbaden, 1963.

Smith, W. S., *The Art and Architecture of Ancient Egypt.* Harmondsworth, 1958; revised ed. 1966.

Steindorff, G., *Die Kunst der Ägypter: Bauten, Plastik, Kunstgewerbe.* Leipzig, 1928.

Vandier, J., *Manuel d'archéologie égyptienne.* 3 vols. Paris, 1952ff.

Woldering, I., *Egypt: the Art of the Pharaohs.* Translated by Ann E. Keep. London, 1963.

Wolf, W., *Die Kunst Ägyptens: Gestalt und Geschichte.* Stuttgart, 1957.

PREHISTORIC ERA

Baumgartel, E. J., *The Cultures of Prehistoric Egypt.* 2 parts. Oxford, 1960.

Massoulard, E., *Préhistoire et protohistoire d'Egypte.* Paris, 1949.

Otto, E., 'Ein Beitrag zur Deutung der ägyptischen Vor- und Frühgeschichte,' in: *Die Welt des Orients,* vol. I, pp. 431 ff. Göttingen, 1952.

Scharff, A., *Grundzüge der ägyptischen Vorgeschichte.* Morgenland, fasc. 12. Leipzig, 1927.

Scharff, A., *Die Altertümer der Vor- und Frühzeit Ägyptens.* Berlin, 1929-31.

Ucko, P., *Prehistoric Anthropomorphic Figurines from Predynastic Egypt and Neolithic Crete.* (In the press.)

Vandier, J., *Manuel d'archéologie égyptienne, I: Les époques de formation.* Paris, 1952.

ARCHAIC PERIOD

Anthes, R., 'Werkverfahren ägyptischer Bildhauer,' in: *Mitteilungen des Deutschen Archäologischen Instituts Kairo,* vol. 10, 1941, pp. 79 ff.

Beckerath, J. von, 'Der ägyptische Ursprung unseres Kalenders,' in: *Saeculum,* 4, 1953, pp. 1 ff.

Capart, J., *Primitive Art in Egypt.* Translated from the revised and augmented original ed. by A. S. Griffith. London, 1905.

Emery, W. B., *Archaic Egypt.* Harmondsworth, 1962.

Emery, W. B., *The Tomb of Hemaka.* Cairo, 1938.

Emery, W. B., *The Tomb of Hor-Aha.* Cairo, 1939.

Emery, W. B., *Great Tombs of the First Dynasty.* 3 vols. Cairo, 1949; London, 1954-8.

Kaplony, P., *Die Inschriften der ägyptischen Frühzeit.* 2 vols. Wiesbaden, 1963.

Parker, R. A., *The Calendars of Ancient Egypt.* Chicago, 1950.

Petrie, W. M. Flinders, *Royal Tombs of the First Dynasty*, I. London, 1900.
Petrie, W. M. Flinders, *Royal Tombs of the Earliest Dynasties*, II. London, 1901.
Petrie, W. M. Flinders, *Ceremonial Slate Palettes*. London, 1953 (1954).
Quibell, J. E., *Hierakonpolis*. 2 vols. London, 1900-2.
Saad, Zaki Yusuf, *Royal Excavations at Saqqara and Helwan* (1941-45, 1945-47). Cairo, 1947-51.
Scharff, A., *Das Grab als Wohnhaus in der ägyptischen Frühzeit*. Sitzungsberichte der Bayrischen Akademie der Wissenschaften, phil.-hist. Klasse, Year 1944/6, fasc. 6. Munich, 1947.
Schott, S., *Mythe und Mythenbildung im alten Ägypten*. Untersuchungen zur Geschichte und Altertumskunde Ägyptens, vol. 15. Leipzig, 1945.
Schott, S., 'Kulturprobleme der Frühzeit Ägyptens,' in: *Mitteilungen der Deutschen Orient-Gesellschaft*, no. 84, Dec. 1952.
Schweitzer, U., 'Das Wesen des Ka im Diesseits und Jenseits der alten Ägypter,' in: *Ägyptologische Forschungen*, 19, 1956.
Spiegel, J., *Das Werden der altägyptischen Hochkultur: ägyptische Geistesgeschichte im 3. Jahrtausend vor Chr.* Heidelberg, 1953.

OLD KINGDOM

Aldred, C., *Egypt to the End of the Old Kingdom*. London, 1965.
Aldred, C., *Old Kingdom Art in Ancient Egypt*. London, 1949.
Drioton, E. and Lauer, J. Ph., *Sakkarah: les monuments de Zoser*. Cairo, 1939; 2nd ed., 1951.
Edwards, I.E.S., *The Pyramids of Egypt*. Harmondsworth, 1947; revised ed. 1961.
Fakhry, A., *The Monuments of Snefru at Dahschur, I: The Bent Pyramid*. Cairo, 1959.
Goedicke, H., 'Das Verhältnis zwischen königlichen und privaten Darstellungen im Alten Reich,' in: *Mitteilungen des Deutschen Archäologischen Instituts Kairo*, 15, 1957.
Goedicke, H., 'Die Stellung des Königs im Alten Reich,' in: *Ägyptologische Abhandlungen*, vol. 2, Wiesbaden, 1960.
Goneim, Z., *Die verschollene Pyramide*. Wiesbaden, 1955.
Hasan, Selim, *Excavations at Giza*, vols. 1-8. Oxford – Cairo, 1932-53.
Iversen, E., *Canon and Proportions in Egyptian Art*. London, 1955.
Junker, H. (ed.), *Bericht über die . . . Grabungen auf dem Friedhof des Alten Reiches bei den Pyramiden von Gîza*, vols. 1-12. Vienna, 1929-55.
Klebs, L., *Die Reliefs des Alten Reiches (2980-2475 v. Chr.)*. Heidelberg, 1915.
Montet, P., *Les scènes de la vie privée dans les tombeaux égyptiens de l'ancien empire*. Strasbourg, 1925.
Reisner, G. A., *A History of the Giza Necropolis*, I. Cambridge, Mass., 1942.
Reisner, G. A., *A History of the Giza Necropolis*, II: the Tomb of Hetep-Heres, the Mother of Cheops. A Study of Egyptian Civilization in the Old Kingdom. Completed and revised by W. S. Smith. Cambridge, Mass. – London, 1955.
Ricke, H., *Bemerkungen zur Baukunst des Alten Reiches*. Beiträge zur ägyptischen Bauforschung und Altertumskunde, fascs. 4, 5. 2 vols. Zurich, 1944; Cairo, 1950.
Schoukry, A., *Die Privatgrabstatue im Alten Reich*. Cairo, 1951.
Smith, W. S., *A History of Egyptian Sculpture and Painting in the Old Kingdom*. 2nd ed. London, 1949 (1950).
Spiegel, J., 'Zur Kunstentwicklung der zweiten Hälfte des Alten Reiches,' in: *Mitteilungen des Deutschen Archäologischen Instituts Kairo*, 15, 1957, pp. 225 ff.

FIRST INTERMEDIATE PERIOD AND MIDDLE KINGDOM

Aldred, C., *Middle Kingdom Art in Ancient Egypt, 2300-1590 B.C.* London, 1950.
Badawy, A., *History of Egyptian Architecture*. Berkeley, 1967.
Evers, H. G., *Staat aus dem Stein*. 2 vols. Munich, 1929.
Hayes, W. C., 'The Middle Kingdom in Egypt: Internal History from the Rise of the Heracleopolitans to the Death of Ammenemes III,' in: *Cambridge Ancient History*, revised ed., vol. I, ch. 20. Cambridge, 1961.
Klebs, L., *Die Reliefs und Malereien des Mittleren Reiches*. Abhandlungen der Heidelberger Akademie der Wissenschaften, phil.-hist. Klasse, no. 6. Heidelberg, 1922.
Lange, K., *Sesostris: ein König in Mythos, Geschichte und Kunst*. Munich, 1954.
Lange, H. A. and Schäfer, H., *Grab- und Denksteine des Mittleren Reichs im Museum von Kairo*. 4 vols. Berlin, 1962.
Naville, E., *The XIth-Dynasty Temple at Deir el-Bahari*. 3 parts. London, 1907-13.
Stock, H., *Die erste Zwischenzeit Ägyptens: Untergang der*

Pyramidenzeit, Zwischenreiche von Abydos und Herakleopolis, Aufstieg Thebens. Studia Aegyptiaca, no. 2. Rome, 1949.

WINLOCK, H. E., *Excavations at Deir el-Bahari, 1911-1931.* New York, 1942.

WINLOCK, H. E., *The Rise and Fall of the Middle Kingdom in Thebes.* New York, 1947.

WINLOCK, H. E., *Models of Daily Life in Ancient Egypt.* Cambridge, Mass., 1955.

HYKSOS PERIOD AND NEW KINGDOM

ALDRED, C., *New Kingdom Art in Ancient Egypt during the XVIIIth Dynasty, 1590-1315 B.C.* London, 1951.

DESROCHES-NOBLECOURT, CH., *Tutankhamen.* London, 1963; Harmondsworth, 1965.

FECHT, G., 'Die Amarna-Probleme,' in: *Zeitschrift für ägyptische Sprache,* 85, 1960, pp. 83 ff.

GARDINER, SIR ALAN H., *The Temple of King Sethos I at Abydos.* Copied by A.M. Calverley, with the assistance of M.F. Broome and edited by A. H. Gardiner. 4 vols. London, 1933-58.

GARDINER, SIR ALAN H., 'The Memphite Tomb of General Haremhab,' in: *Journal of Egyptian Archaeology,* 39, 1953, pp. 3 ff.

HELCK, H., *Der Einfluss der Militärführer in der 18. ägyptischen Dynastie.* Untersuchungen zur Geschichte und Altertumskunde Ägyptens, vol. 14. Leipzig, 1939.

KLEBS, L., *Die Reliefs und Malereien des Neuen Reiches, XVIII.-XX. Dynastie, ca. 1580-1100 v. Chr.* Abhandlungen der Heidelberger Akademie der Wissenschaften, phil.-hist. Klasse, no. 9. Heidelberg, 1934.

LANGE, K., *König Echnaton und die Amarna-Zeit.* Munich, 1951.

LEEUWENBURG, L. G., *Echnaton.* The Hague, 1946.

LHOTE, A., *Les chefs-d'œuvre de la peinture égyptienne.* Paris, 1954.

MEKHITARIAN, A., *Egyptian Painting.* Translated by S. Gilbert. Geneva, 1954.

MERCER, S.A.B. (ed.), *The Tell-el-Amarna Tablets.* 2 vols. Toronto, 1939.

OTTO, E., 'Zur Bedeutung der ägyptischen Tempelstatue seit dem Neuen Reich,' in: *Orientalia,* 17, 1948, pp. 448 ff.

PEET, T. E., WOOLLEY, SIR L., FRANKFORT, H., AND PENDLEBURY J. D. S., *The City of Akhenaten.* 3 vols. London, 1923-51.

SÄVE-SÖDERBERGH, T., 'The Hyksos Rule in Egypt,' in: *Journal of Egyptian Archaeology,* 37, 1951.

SCHÄFER, H., *Amarna in Religion und Kunst.* Leipzig, 1931.

SCHARFF, A., *Ägyptische Sonnenlieder.* Berlin, 1922.

STEINDORFF, G., *Die Blütezeit des Pharaonenreiches.* 2nd ed. Bielefeld–Leipzig, 1926.

STEINDORFF, G. AND WOLF, W., *Die thebanische Gräberwelt.* Leipziger Ägyptologische Studien, fasc. 4. Glückstadt, 1936.

STEINDORFF, G. AND SEELE, K. C., *When Egypt ruled the East.* 2nd ed. Chicago, 1957.

VAN SETERS, J., *The Hyksos.* Newhaven, 1966.

LATE PERIOD AND ROMAN ERA

BOTHMER, B., *Egyptian Sculpture of the Late Period, 700 B.C.–A.D. 100.* Brooklyn Museum, N. Y., 1960.

BOSSE, K., *Die menschliche Figur in der Rundplastik der ägyptischen Spätzeit von der XXII. bis zur XXX. Dynastie.* Ägyptologische Forschungen, fasc. 1. Glückstadt, 1936.

DRERUP, H., 'Ägyptische Bildnisköpfe griechischer und römischer Zeit,' in: *Orbis antiquus,* fasc. 3, 1950.

LEFEBVRE, J., *Le tombeau de Petosiris.* 3 vols. Cairo, 1923.

PARLASCA, K., *Mumienporträts und verwandte Denkmäler.* Deutsches Archäologisches Institut, Wiesbaden, 1966.

ROEDER, G., *Ägyptische Bronzefiguren.* Mitteilungen aus der Ägyptischen Sammlung, VI. Berlin, 1956.

CHRONOLOGICAL TABLE

PREHISTORIC ERA		
5th millennium B.C.		Lower Egypt: cultures of Merimde, El-Omari, Faiyum Upper Egypt: Tasian culture
Early 4th millennium B.C.		Upper Egypt: Badarian culture
c. 3700 B.C.		Upper Egypt: Nagada I culture
c. 3200 B.C.		Nagada II culture
c. 3000 B.C. Before the foundation of the state		Kings: Scorpion, Narmer
ARCHAIC PERIOD		
c. 2900–*c.* 2780 B.C.	Dynasty I	Thinite kings: Horus-Aha/Menes, Djer (Zer), Djet (Zet) (Serpent), Udimu (Den)
c. 2780–*c.* 2660 B.C.	Dynasty II	Kings: Ninutjer, Peribsen, Khasekhemui
OLD KINGDOM		
c. 2660–*c.* 2600 B.C.	Dynasty III	Kings: Zoser, Sekhemkhet, Huni
c. 2600–*c.* 2480 B.C.	Dynasty IV	Kings: Snefru, Cheops, Dedefre, Chephren, Mycerinus
c. 2480–*c.* 2340 B.C.	Dynasty V	Kings: Userkaf, Sahura, Neferirkara, Niuserra, Isosi, Unas
c. 2340–*c.* 2170 B.C.	Dynasty VI	Kings: Teti, Pepi I, Pepi II, Merenra, Nitocris

FIRST INTERMEDIATE PERIOD		
c. 2170–*c.* 2134 B.C.	Dynasties VII, VIII	Dissolution of united state Numerous rulers North under descendants of Dynasty VI
c. 2134–2040 B.C.	Dynasties IX, X	Herakleopolitan dynasty rules Middle and Lower Egypt
	(Dynasty XI)	Theban princely family reigns over Upper Egypt (Antef I, II, III, Mentuhotep)
MIDDLE KINGDOM		
2040–1991 B.C.	Dynasty XI	Unification of state under Theban princely family Kings: Mentuhotep I, II, III
1991–1786 B.C.	Dynasty XII	Kings named Amenemhat and Sesostris Amenemhat I (1991-1962 B.C.) Sesostris I (first as co-regent) (1971-1928 B.C.) Sesostris III (1878-1843 B.C.) Amenemhat III (1842-1797 B.C.)
SECOND INTERMEDIATE PERIOD		
c. 1785–*c.* 1670 B.C.	Dynasties XIII, XIV	Numerous kings, some of whom ruled only over parts of the country; Dynasty XIV at Xois in the Delta
c. 1670–1552 B.C.	Dynasties XV, XVI	Alien rule by the Hyksos in Lower and Middle Egypt; residence at Avaris in the Delta; King Apophis
	Dynasty XVII	Theban princes in Upper Egypt: Antef, Taa I, Sekenenra-Taa II, Kamose

NEW KINGDOM		
1552–1306 B.C.	Dynasty XVIII	Kings: Ahmose (1552-1527 B.C.) Amenophis I (1527-1506 B.C.) Thutmosis I (1506-1494 B.C.) Thutmosis II (1494-1490 B.C.) Queen Hatshepsut (1490-1468 B.C.) Thutmosis III (1468-1436 B.C.) Amenophis II (1438-1412 B.C.) Thutmosis IV (1412-1402 B.C.) Amenophis III (1402-1364 B.C.) Amenophis IV/Akhnaton (1364-1347 B.C.) Semenkhara (first as co-regent) (1351-1347 B.C.) Tutankhamun (1347-1338 B.C.) Eye (1338-1334 B.C.) Horemheb (1334-1306 B.C.)
1306–1186 B.C.	Dynasty XIX	Kings: Ramses I (1306-1304 B.C.) Sethos (Seti) I (1304-1290 B.C.) Ramses II (1290-1224 B.C.) Merneptah (1224-1204 B.C.) Amenmesse, Sethos II, Queen Twosre and Siptah (1204-1186 B.C.)
1186–1070 B.C.	Dynasty XX	Kings: Setnakht (1186-1184 B.C.) Ramses III (1184-1153 B.C.) Ramses IV-XI (1153-1070 B.C.)
1090–950 B.C.	Dynasty XXI	Lower Egypt: Rulers of unknown origin; residence at Tanis in the Delta; King Smendes Upper Egypt: high priest Herihor in Thebes
950–730 B.C.	Dynasties XXII, XXIII	Libyan rule; Bubastite Dynasty: Sheshonk, Osorkon I, II, Petubastis
730–715 B.C.	Dynasty XXIV	Kings: Tefnakhte, Bocchoris; residence at Sais in the Delta Ethiopian kings Kashta and Piankhy in Upper Egypt

LATE PERIOD		
712–664 B.C.	Dynasty XXV	Ethiopian rule Kings: Shabaka, Taharka Assyrian invasion
663–525 B.C.	Dynasty XXVI	Saite Dynasty; residence at Sais in the Delta Kings: Psammetichus I (663-610 B.C.) Necho II (610-595 B.C.) Psammetichus II (595-589 B.C.) Apries (589-570 B.C.) Amasis (570-526 B.C.)
525–404 B.C.	Dynasty XXVII	Egypt becomes Persian satrapy. Achaemenid rulers
404–399 B.C.	Dynasty XXVIII	Amyrtaeus king of Sais in the Delta
399–380 B.C.	Dynasty XXIX	Kings of Mendes in the Delta: Nepherites I, Achoris
380–343 B.C.	Dynasty XXX	Kings of Sebennythos in the Delta: Nectanebo I, Takhos (Teos), Nectanebo II
343–332 B.C.		Egypt a Persian province
332–323 B.C.		Egypt conquered by Alexander the Great (332 B.C.)
323–304 B.C.		Struggle between the Diadochi for the succession to Alexander the Great
304–30 B.C.		Ptolemaic rule; Cleopatra last queen
30 B.C.		Egypt becomes a Roman province

Photographs by:

Ägyptische Staatssammlung (Anke Teichmann), Munich: Pl. XXIV; Pl. 61; Cat. 26, 37, 82, 85, 95, 96.

Ashmolean Museum, Oxford: Pl. XIX.

The Brooklyn Museum, Brooklyn, N.Y.: Pl. 2, 41, 49, 97, 104-106, 116; Cat. 35, 40, 65.

Ny Carlsberg Glyptotek, Copenhagen: Pl. V; Pl. 52, 94, 108; Cat. 9, 46, 83.

Maurice Chuzeville, Vanves (Seine): Cat. 19.

Giraudon, Paris: Pl. 7, 64; Cat. 18, 22, 36, 99, 102.

André Held, Ecublens/Lausanne: Pl. VIII, XI, XXI; Pl. 12, 13, 71, 81-83, 87, 92, 93, 111, 113; Cat. 6, 15, 25, 27, 29, 31, 32, 33, 59, 61, 62, 63, 74, 92.

Helga Photo Studio Inc., New York: Pl. X; Pl. 38, 47; Cat. 13, 14, 17.

Hermitage, Leningrad: Pl. 16, 46.

Foto-Hinz, SWB, Basel: Pl. I-IV, XII, XIV, XVI, XVIII, XX, XXIII; Pl. 1, 4, 8-11, 17, 25, 28, 29, 36, 37, 40, 48, 53-56, 59, 62, 63, 65, 69, 74-79, 84, 89, 90, 96, 98-103, 110, 115, 117; Cat. 4, 8, 16, 34, 43, 47, 49, 50, 51, 54, 60, 64, 66, 69, 73, 76, 77, 79, 80, 81, 84, 86, 87, 90, 97.

Hirmer-Fotoarchiv, Munich: Pl. IX, XV, XVII, XXII; Pl. 5, 15, 18, 19, 21, 30, 32, 33, 39, 42, 58, 60, 70, 73, 86, 88, 91, 95; Cat. 1, 2, 41, 45, 48, 72.

Kestner Museum, Hanover: Cat. 75, 78, 88, 89, 91.

Kunsthistorisches Museum, Vienna: Pl. 112; Cat. 7, 23, 28.

Paul F. Merckx, Publisher, Brussels: Pl. VII.

Metropolitan Museum of Art, New York: Pl. XIII; Pl. 44, 45, 50; Cat. 3, 20, 21, 39.

Musées Royaux d'Art et d'Histoire (A.C.L., C. Pyricht), Brussels: Pl. 3, 72.

Museum of Fine Arts, Boston: Pl. 22, 24, 26, 27, 114; Cat. 44.

Pushkin Museum, Moscow: Pl. 66, 67; Cat. 5, 98.

Editions d'Art Albert Skira, Geneva: Pl. VI.

Henri Stierlin, Geneva: Pl. 14, 20, 31, 34, 35, 43, 51, 57, 85, 107; Cat. 10.

Pierre Tétrel, Paris: Pl. 6; Cat. 67.

Uni-Dia-Verlag, Grosshesselohe and Stuttgart: Pl. 23, 68; Cat. 11, 24, 42, 55, 56, 57, 58, 93, 94.

University of Chicago, Oriental Institute, Chicago: Cat. 38.

The University Museum, Philadelphia: Cat. 68.

6 line-drawings after Bonnet: Bilderatlas zur Religionsgeschichte. Leipzig, 1924.

Pl. XVI and Cat. 51 are erroneously shown in reverse.

MAPS

EGYPT AND NEIGHBOURING COUNTRIES

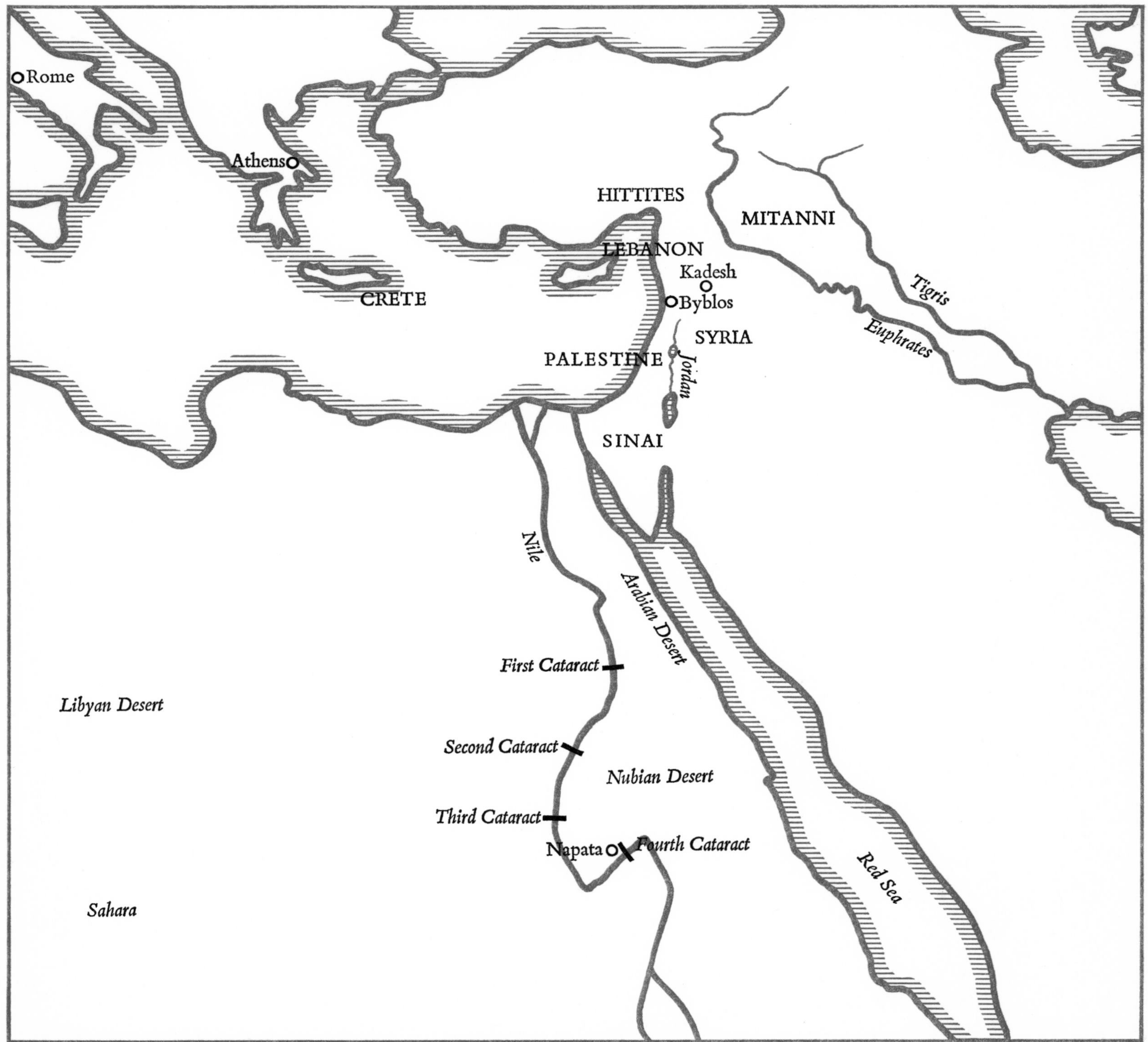
Rome
Athens
CRETE
HITTITES
LEBANON
Kadesh
Byblos
MITANNI
Tigris
Euphrates
SYRIA
PALESTINE
Jordan
SINAI
Nile
Arabian Desert
First Cataract
Libyan Desert
Second Cataract
Nubian Desert
Third Cataract
Napata
Fourth Cataract
Red Sea
Sahara

EGYPT — SITES AND CITIES

○ = cities
△ = sites

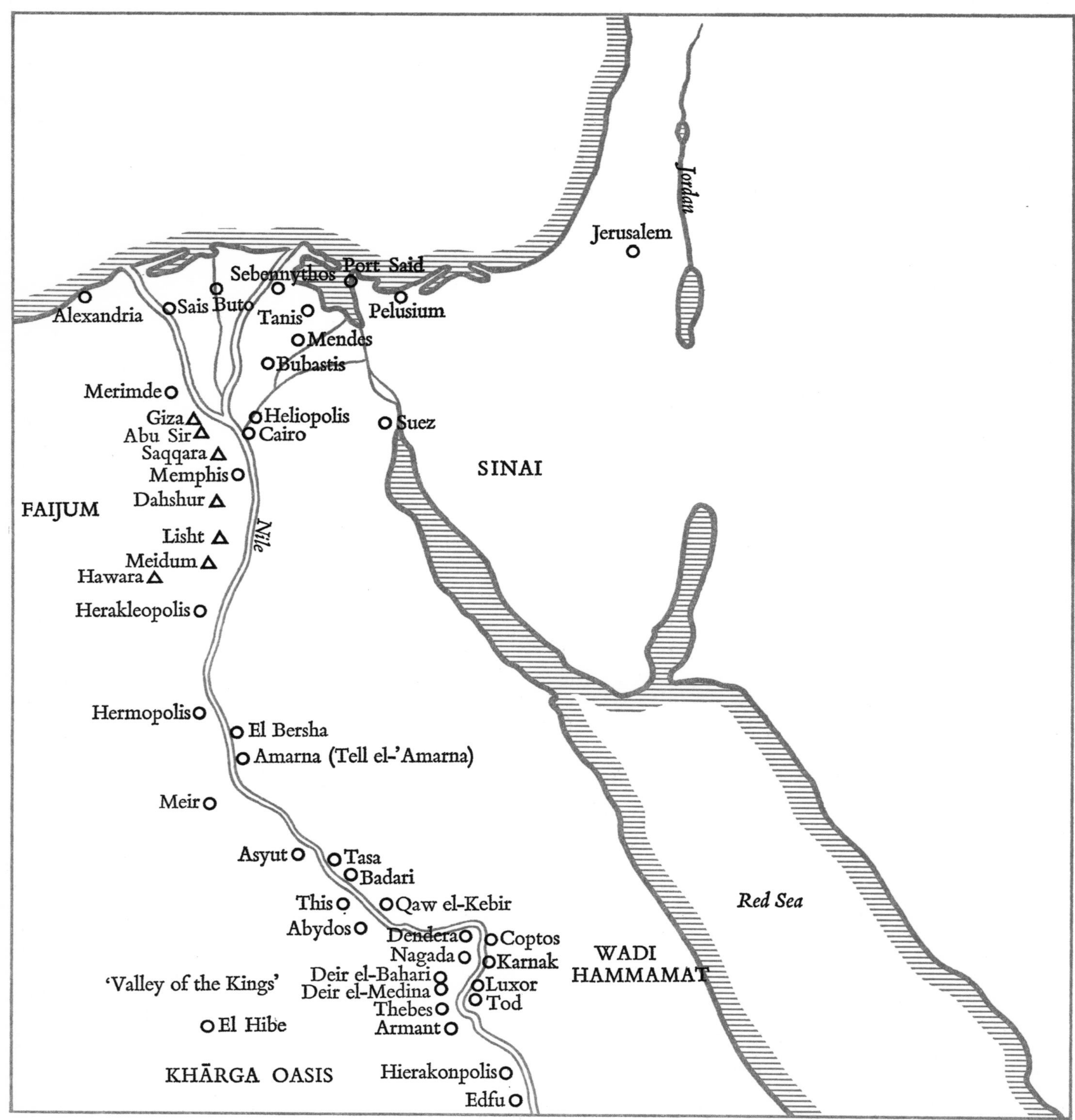
Jordan
Jerusalem
Port Said
Sebennythos
Alexandria
Sais
Buto
Tanis
Pelusium
Mendes
Bubastis
Merimde
Giza
Abu Sir
Heliopolis
Cairo
Suez
Saqqara
Memphis
SINAI
FAIJUM
Dahshur
Nile
Lisht
Meidum
Hawara
Herakleopolis
Hermopolis
El Bersha
Amarna (Tell el-'Amarna)
Meir
Asyut
Tasa
Badari
This
Qaw el-Kebir
Red Sea
Abydos
Dendera
Coptos
WADI
HAMMAMAT
Nagada
Karnak
'Valley of the Kings'
Deir el-Bahari
Deir el-Medina
Luxor
Tod
Thebes
El Hibe
Armant
KHĀRGA OASIS
Hierakonpolis
Edfu

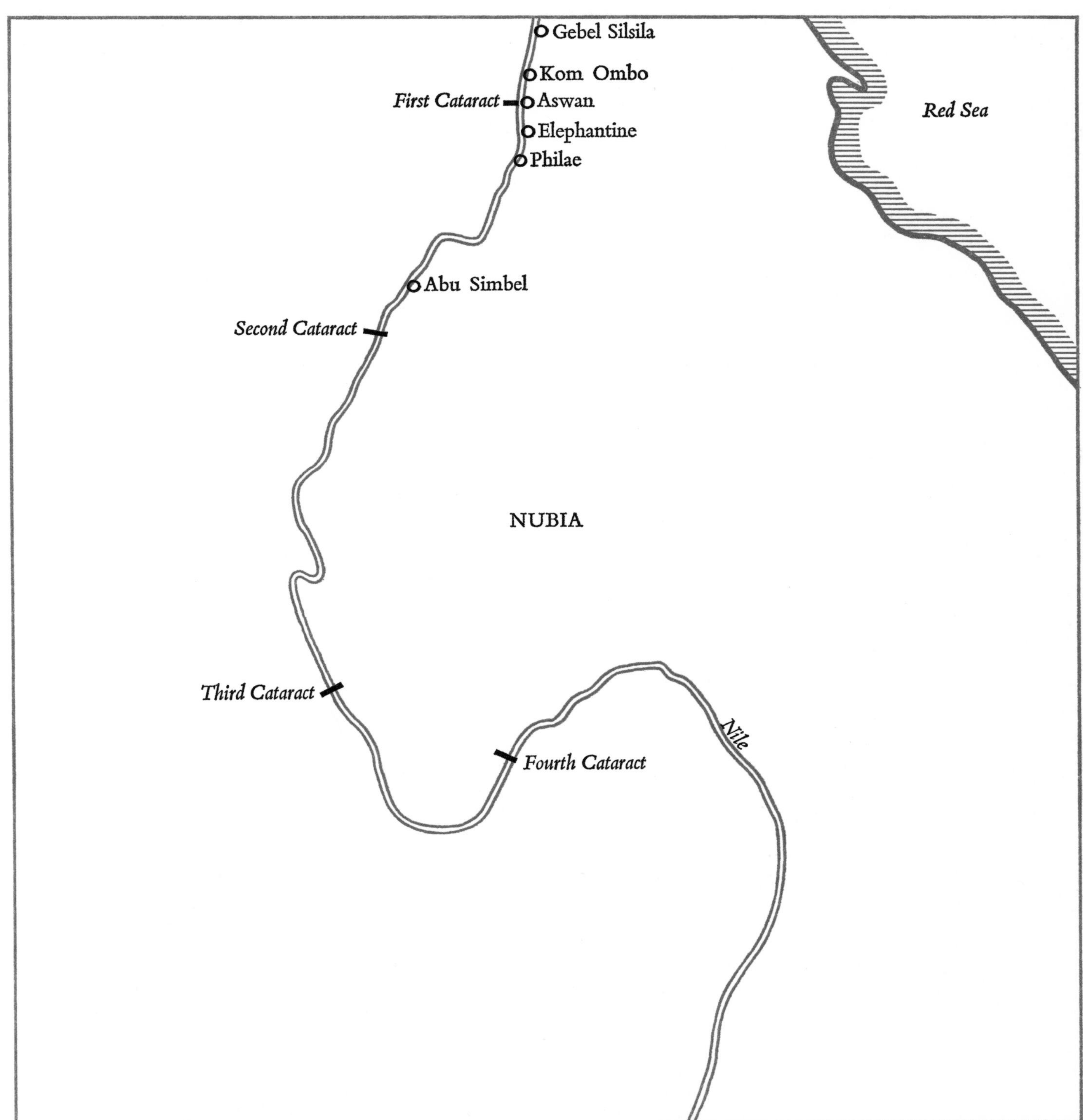
Gebel Silsila
Kom Ombo
First Cataract
Aswan
Elephantine
Philae
Red Sea
Abu Simbel
Second Cataract
NUBIA
Third Cataract
Nile
Fourth Cataract

INDEX

This book was printed in the workshops of Imprimerie Paul Attinger S.A., Neuchâtel. — The illustrations in four-colour offset were printed by Imprimerie Paul Attinger S.A., Neuchâtel, after photolithos by Process Engravers Schwitter Ltd., Zurich. — The heliogravure reproductions were executed by Braun & Cie S.A., Mulhouse-Dornach. — The half-tone blocks were made by Process Engravers Schwitter Ltd., Basel. — The binding is by E. Clerc & Cie S.A., Lausanne. — Lay-out by Irmgard Loeb, Basel, after a design by André Rosselet, Auvernier (Switzerland).

Printed in Switzerland